60—

Ethnic Chinese as Southeast Asians

The **Institute of Southeast Asian Studies (ISEAS)** was established as an autonomous organization in 1968. It is a regional research centre for scholars and other specialists concerned with modern Southeast Asia, particularly the many-faceted problems of stability and security, economic development, and political and social change.

The Institute's research programmes are the Regional Economic Studies Programme (RES) including ASEAN and APEC, Regional Strategic and Political Studies Programme (RSPS), Regional Social and Cultural Studies Programme (RSCS), and the Indochina Programme (ICP).

The Institute is governed by a twenty-two-member Board of Trustees comprising nominees from the Singapore Government, the National University of Singapore, the various Chambers of Commerce, and professional and civic organizations. A ten-man Executive Committee oversees day-to-day operations; it is chaired by the Director, the Institute's chief academic and administrative officer.

Ethnic Chinese as Southeast Asians

as

edited by
Leo Suryadinata

ISEAS

INSTITUTE OF SOUTHEAST ASIAN STUDIES

Singapore • London

Published by
Institute of Southeast Asian Studies
Heng Mui Keng Terrace
Pasir Panjang Road
Singapore 119596

Internet e-mail: publish@iseas.ac.sg
World Wide Web: http://www.iseas.ac.sg/pub.html

*The responsibility for facts and opinions expressed in this publication rests
exclusively with the authors and their interpretations do not necessarily reflect
the views or the policy of the Institute.*

Cataloguing in Publication Data

Ethnic Chinese as Southeast Asians/edited by
  Leo Suryadinata.
  1. China--Asia, Southeastern--Ethnic identity.
  I. Suryadinata, Leo, 1941-
DS523.4   C5 S721   1997

ISBN 981-3055-50-2 (softcover, ISEAS, Singapore)
ISBN 981-3055-58-8 (hardcover, ISEAS, Singapore)

For Australia and New Zealand, a softcover edition (ISBN 1-86448-463-2)
is published by Allen & Unwin, Australia.

For the USA and Canada, a hardcover edition (ISBN 0-312-17576-0) is
published by St Martin's Press, New York.

Typeset by International Typesetters Pte Ltd
Printed in Singapore by Saik Wah Press Pte Ltd

Contents

Preface   vii

Contributors   x

1. Ethnic Chinese in Southeast Asia: Overseas Chinese,
   Chinese Overseas or Southeast Asians?
   Leo Suryadinata   1
   Comments by *Tan Chee Beng*   25

2. The Ethnic Chinese in Indonesia: Issues of Identity
   Mely G. Tan   33
   Comments by *A. Dahana*   66

3. Malaysian Chinese: Seeking Identity in Wawasan 2020
   Lee Kam Hing   72
   Comments by *Ahmat Adam*   108

4. Ethnic Chinese in Myanmar and their Identity
   Mya Than   115
   Comments by *Khin Maung Kyi*   147

5. The Ethnic Chinese as Filipinos
    Teresita Ang See   158
    Comments by *Renato S. Velasco*   203

6. From Overseas Chinese to Chinese Singaporeans
    Chiew Seen Kong   211
    Comments by *A. Mani*   228

7. From Siamese-Chinese to Chinese-Thai:
    Political Conditions and Identity Shifts
    among the Chinese in Thailand
    Supang Chantavanich   232
    Comments by *Anusorn Limmanee*   260

8. Ethnic Chinese in Vietnam and their Identity
    Tran Khanh   267
    Comments by *Ta Huu Phuong*   293

Appendix
Women and Chinese Identity:
An Exchange at the Closing Session of the Workshop
*Mely Tan, Wang Gungwu, Leo Suryadinata and
Tan Chee Beng*   296

Index   301

Preface

Since the introduction of an open-door policy, many Chinese entrepreneurs outside China have begun to invest in mainland China. Attention has again turned to the Chinese in other parts of the world, including those in Southeast Asia, and writers, both in the West and Asia, have started to use the term "Overseas Chinese" and "Chinese overseas" to refer to these Chinese outside mainland China. This mainland China-centric view has confused the position and identity of the Chinese in Southeast Asia, with serious political implications as Southeast Asian Chinese are still considered to be "Chinese overseas" or "Overseas Chinese", not Southeast Asians.

In the light of this new development, a workshop was held on the theme of "Ethnic Chinese as Southeast Asians" to discuss the perception of the Southeast Asian Chinese in terms of their position in the respective Southeast Asian countries, their relationship with China, their self-identity, as well as the perception of "indigenous" Southeast Asians towards the ethnic Chinese in their countries.

At this workshop, only six ASEAN states and Myanmar were covered. Paperwriters were requested to include the following aspects with regard to their studies on their respective countries:

1. The indigenous and ethnic Chinese notion of a nation (nation-state) and the position of the ethnic Chinese in such a nation. Is the nation racially or culturally defined or both?
2. The relationship between China and the ethnic Chinese oversees — is this a problem for the integration of the ethnic Chinese (or for nation-building)?
3. Is culture and the economic position of the ethnic Chinese a problem for the integration of the ethnic Chinese in their country of domicile? With the rise of ethnic consciousness world-wide, is there national disintegration rather than national integration in Southeast Asia? Does this trend affect the Chinese communities?
4. Prospects of the ethnic Chinese in national integration — are ethnic Chinese "Southeast Asians" or "Overseas Chinese"?

Two groups of scholars from Southeast Asia were invited. One group consisted of ethnic Chinese (or of Chinese descent) and the other group comprised "indigenous" or non-Chinese scholars. The interaction of these two groups of scholars have provided a more comprehensive picture about the ethnic Chinese in Southeast Asia.

In the past, most of the works (for example, Suryadinata's work) were based mainly on one country. They were also not done in conjunction with both ethnic Chinese and indigenous scholars. Thus, this volume aims to be a major regional study incorporating a variety of regional perspectives on common themes relating to the question of the Chinese identity.

This volume consists of eight chapters. Each chapter is accompanied by a brief commentary by a discussant. The Appendix is based on the workshop discussion on the role of women in shaping ethnic Chinese identity. It is not a full-length paper but is included here with the hope that others may pursue this under-studied topic.

It should be noted here that the title of the workshop was "Ethnic Chinese as Southeast Asians". Southeast Asians here refer to people in the individual Southeast Asian states, and not a collective regional identity. The editor is fully aware that a regional identity has not yet emerged, but identification with an individual country has been in existence.

The editor would like to take this opportunity to thank all the workshop participants, especially the paperwriters and discussants, for their contributions and co-operation. Special thanks also go to Professor Chan Heng Chee, then Director of ISEAS, and Professor Wang Gungwu, Chairman of the Institute of East Asian Political Economy (IEAPE), for their kind support. We have all benefited tremendously from their full participation in the two-day workshop.

Leo Suryadinata

Contributors

Ahmat Adam, Ph.D., is Professor and Dean at the Centre for General Studies, Universiti Malaysia Sabah.

Anusorn Limmanee, Ph.D., is Associate Professor in the Department of Government at the Faculty of Political Science, Chulalongkorn University.

Supang Chantavanich, Ph.D., is Associate Professor and Head of the Asian Research Center for Migration, Institute of Asian Studies, Chulalongkorn University.

Chiew Seen Kong, Ph.D., is a Senior Lecturer in the Department of Sociology, National University of Singapore.

A. Dahana, Ph.D., is the Executive Director at the Fulbright Commission of Indonesia (American-Indonesian Exchange Foundation — AMINEF), Jakarta.

Khin Maung Kyi, Ph.D., is a Senior Fellow in the Department of Business Policy, National University of Singapore.

Lee Kam Hing, Ph.D., is a Professor in the Department of History, University of Malaya.

A. Mani, Ph.D., is a Senior Lecturer in the Department of Sociology, National University of Singapore.

Mya Than, Ph.D., is a Fellow at the Institute of Southeast Asian Studies, Singapore.

Teresita Ang See is the Executive Director at the Kaisa Para Sa Kaunlaran, Inc, Manila.

Leo Suryadinata, Ph.D., is a Visiting Fellow at the Institute of Southeast Asian Studies and Associate Professor in the Department of Political Science, National University of Singapore.

Ta Huu Phuong, Ph.D., is Associate Professor in the Department of Decision Sciences, National University of Singapore.

Tan Chee Beng, Ph.D., was an Associate Professor in the Department of Anthropology and Sociology, University of Malaya, and is now Professor in the Department of Anthropology, The Chinese University of Hong Kong.

Mely G. Tan, Ph.D., is a Senior Researcher at the Indonesian Institute of Sciences, Jakarta.

Tran Khanh, Ph.D., is Co-ordinator, Programme of Contemporary Issues in Southeast Asia, National Center for Social Sciences and Humanities of Vietnam, Institute for Southeast Asian Studies, Vietnam.

Renato S. Velasco, Ph.D., is Associate Professor in the Department of Political Science at the College of Social Sciences and Philosophy, University of the Philippines.

Wang Gungwu, Ph.D., Professor Emeritus, is Distinguished Senior Fellow at the Institute of Southeast Asian Studies and Chairman of the Institute of East Asian Political Economy, Singapore.

Chapter 1

Ethnic Chinese in Southeast Asia: Overseas Chinese, Chinese Overseas or Southeast Asians?

Leo Suryadinata

The Chinese in Southeast Asia have gained some measure of acceptance in the local scene. However, in recent years, with dramatic events such as the end of the Cold War, the globalization process, the opening up of the People's Republic of China (PRC) and ethnic Chinese investments in their ancestral land, people have begun to question the identity of the Chinese again. Old and outdated terms, such as "Overseas Chinese" and "Chinese overseas" have resurfaced and again become popular,[1] creating the impression that the Chinese are no longer part of Southeast Asia but China.

This chapter examines the current position of the ethnic Chinese in Southeast Asia. Do they perceive themselves as Chinese overseas or Southeast Asians?[2] What are the perceptions of the local population towards the Chinese? Are the Chinese accepted as members of Southeast Asian nations? What have been the respective state policies towards the Chinese? Have these policies achieved their objectives? What are the problems and prospects of the Chinese in this part of the world?

What is in a Name? Variety of Terms Used

There are many terms used to refer to the Chinese. During the colonial period, those Chinese who were born in Southeast Asia were often considered colonial subjects. However, Imperial China declared the Chinese as its subjects/citizens. Both the local born and new immigrants were then regarded as Chinese nationals overseas. It is true that many new immigrants who left China at the end of the nineteenth and early twentieth centuries often considered themselves as sojourners, and would eventually return to their ancestral land. In the eyes of the Chinese Government, these Chinese were in fact *Huaqiao* or Chinese nationals who resided overseas.[3]

Western writers consider the Chinese outside China as Overseas Chinese. In fact, the term "Overseas Chinese" became the English equivalent of *Huaqiao*. The English term was popularly used until the end of World War II. The situation began to change after the Southeast Asian countries gained independence and mainland China turned communist. The new migrants and their immediate descendants decided to remain in Southeast Asia and adopt local citizenship. In order to show their different national status and political loyalty, the Chinese began to coin other terms to refer to themselves. Those who were still well-versed in Chinese, especially in Malaya and Singapore, began to refer to themselves as *Huaren* (ethnic Chinese) or *Huayi* (Chinese descent). The term *Huaren* has been popularized to refer to the Chinese in Southeast Asia, who are mainly the citizens of their adopted land. However, those who are still Chinese nationals but Southeast Asian residents are often included in this category.

The English equivalent of *Huaren* is "ethnic Chinese". Local Chinese who were sensitive to Southeast Asian nationalism also began to use this term in place of "Overseas Chinese" or "Chinese overseas". However, some ethnic Chinese writers continue to use the terms "Overseas Chinese" and "ethnic Chinese" interchangeably. The same can be said about Western writers. In recent years, the term "Overseas Chinese" has gained new currency. Perhaps many still see the ethnic Chinese from mainland China's point of view, without realizing its implications. Others perhaps have done this on purpose to show that "once a Chinese, will always be a Chinese". They could never become Southeast Asians.

Many writers, both Asian and Western, often use the term "Overseas Chinese" to refer to the Chinese who live in Hong Kong, Macao and Taiwan.[4] This infers that they share a common identity with the Chinese in Southeast Asia. Strictly speaking, the former should not be called "Overseas Chinese" because the territories they reside in are politically and culturally part of China, quite different from the Southeast Asian countries. More importantly, the Chinese in Hong Kong, Macao and Taiwan regard themselves as Chinese or *Zhongguo ren* (the man from the central kingdom). In fact, these three areas form part of what is known as "Greater China".

Can the people in "Greater China" be considered ethnic Chinese or *Huaren*? The English term "ethnic Chinese" is commonly used to refer to the Chinese outside China. The Chinese term *Huaren* is also not used to refer to the Chinese in China. In general, the Chinese in China call themselves *Zhongguo ren*. But within the category of *Zhongguo ren*, there are various ethnic groups, namely Han, Man, Mong, Hui, Zang, and so forth. With regard to the Chinese in Hong Kong, Macao and Taiwan, the Chinese Government and scholars call them *Gang-Ao-Tai tongbao* (compatriots from Hong Kong, Macao and Taiwan). But the Chinese in these three areas call themselves simply Chinese, or Hong Kong Chinese, Macao Chinese or Taiwanese if they want to emphasize their local identity. Only when they are in Southeast Asia, do they refer to themselves as *Huaren* or ethnic Chinese, to differentiate themselves from the local Chinese.

The Chinese Government and scholars are aware of the connotation of the various terms. They have accepted the term *Huaren* and its English equivalent "ethnic Chinese". Nevertheless, they also use *Huaqiao* or "Overseas Chinese" when referring to a specific period (when all Chinese overseas were still regarded as Chinese nationals) or to those Chinese who are still citizens of China.

As a matter of fact, the picture of the ethnic Chinese is more complex than what has been presented. Apart from the problem of nationality, they have different degrees of Southeast Asianization, or acculturation. The *peranakan* Chinese in Java and in Peninsular Malaysia, the Sino-Thai in Thailand and the Chinese mestizo in the Philippines have been highly acculturated. Can these people still be called ethnic Chinese as, culturally, they have a high degree of mixture? If ethnicity is defined solely in terms of "common ancestry",[5] these people are "ethnic Chinese". However, ethnicity is often used to refer to ethnic culture as well.[6] The Sino-Thai and Chinese mestizo may therefore not be suitably classified as "ethnic Chinese" but "of Chinese descent" (or *Huayi*). If this is the case, should we include the latter in our discussion of the ethnic Chinese in Southeast Asia? I think it is important to include them if only for the purpose of showing that the "ethnic Chinese" are neither "unassimilable" nor constitute a homogeneous group. However, those of Chinese descent may have a different national identity compared to the newer migrants, or Chinese-speaking Chinese. This leads us to the question of the national identity of the Chinese in Southeast Asia.

Concepts of Nation in Southeast Asia

National identity is closely linked to the modern concept of nation. Nation is basically a Western concept which emerged in the last two centuries, first in Western Europe. In the past, the concepts of race, ethnic group and tribe were prevalent but the end of colonialism following World War II, saw the emergence of independent states in the Third World, when new "nations" came into being.

The term "nation" often means a political community, and is sometimes used interchangeably with "citizenship". However, "nation" is different from "citizenship" in the sense that "citizenship" is often used in a legal sense, while "nation" is both political and cultural. Some writers have even used the term "nation" in a psychological sense. However, for the purpose of our discussion, nation is used here to refer to a political and cultural entity which is larger than an ethnic group.

These so-called nations in Southeast Asia are in fact "nations-in-the-making". They are state-nations rather than nation-states. This means that there is no nation but an ex-colonial state. The state is created first and a new nation is built based on the state-boundary. Thailand is the only state in Southeast Asia which was never colonized. However, one can argue that the present concept of the Thai nation is still quite recent because the Thai state boundary was drawn in the twentieth century in accordance with Western definitions. Accordingly, all Southeast Asian countries are not "nation-states" but "multi-national states". For this chapter, I prefer to use "ethnic group" for a sub-national group within a state and reserve the term "nation" for a larger unit based on the state.

In other words, all Southeast Asian states are multi-ethnic states and their national identity is still weak and ethnic tension is often very high. Therefore, leaders of newly independent Southeast Asian countries make efforts to build a new nation based on colonial boundaries. It is generally believed that ethnic identity is a divisive force which may lead to political instability and eventually the disintegration of a state.

Nevertheless, the concept of "nation" or "state-nation" in Southeast Asia can be divided into at least two types: one is an immigrant state-nation and the other, an indigenous state-nation.

The immigrant nation does not have a fixed model. As the people of the state are made up of immigrants who are of different races, the components of the "nation" are those migrant races. It is true that there is an "indigenous" component (that is, the Malays) but the group is a minority and is weak in various aspects. The identity of this kind of "nation" is often not clear and it constantly looks for new balances in the international community. However, being in Southeast Asia, the identity needs to have some "neutral" (that is, Western) and local components (for example, Malay) in order to have racial harmony within the state and acceptance by the neighbouring states. There is only one such state in Southeast Asia: Singapore.

All other countries in Southeast Asia are indigenous state-nations. In other words, the nation is defined in indigenous group

terms. The indigenous population is used as the "model" of the
nation — including its national language, national symbols, national
education and national institutions.

In the indigenous states, there are two types of minorities —
the indigenous minority (or homeland minority) and the non-
indigenous minority (non-homeland or immigrant minority). The
indigenous minority, being a minority with a homeland in the
country, is in a stronger position than the non-indigenous minority.
The Chinese and Indians in Southeast Asia belong to the latter
category. The status of the indigenous and non-indigenous groups
differs. The indigenous group enjoys more rights compared to
the non-indigenous group. This is often reflected in government
policies and constitutions. When establishing a new national
culture, which is the essence of a nation, the cultures of indigenous
minorities are frequently taken into consideration but those of
non-indigenous minorities are often excluded.

The indigenous state-nations can be subdivided into those
which define a nation solely in cultural terms and those in both
cultural and racial terms. Thailand and the Philippines are the two
countries which define "nation" in cultural terms. An ethnic Chinese
will become a Thai or a Filipino/Filipina if the person has adopted
the local culture. However, in the case of Indonesia and Malaysia,
an ethnic Chinese is not *fully* accepted as a member of the nation.

However, all the indigenous nations use a dominant ethnic
group as the model or basis of the new nation. In Thailand, the
Thais are the basis of the nation, while in the Philippines, Tagalog-
speakers are often referred to as the model Filipinos. The Malays
in Malaysia form the essence of the Malaysian nation, while in
Indonesia the Javanese/Sumatrans are often used as the model of
the Indonesian nation. These nations are "ethno-nations" in the
making.

In the indigenous states which give priority to "indigenism",
citizenship is only one criterion used to differentiate a citizen
from a foreigner. However, among citizens there are also indigenous
and non-indigenous categories, with the former often having more
rights. For instance, both Indonesia and Malaysia have the concept
of *pribumi* (indigene) and *bumiputra* (native) which offers more
rights to the "native" population.[7] In Myanmar too, indigenous

Burmese are given privileges. In other words, there are unequal rights between two types of citizens.

It is obvious that citizenship is not nationhood. Citizenship connotes legal identity while nationhood (or nation) indicates politico-cultural identity within a state. Although both are not the same, citizenship can be used as a basis for building a nation. This is due to the fact that once a person is a citizen of a country, he/she will be subjected to the regulations and requirements of a state (in this case, Southeast Asian states). Gradually, many citizens of foreign descent come to share the "indigenous national culture", either partially or wholly. It is much more difficult for indigenous minorities to accept another culture which is imposed on them to be their "national culture".

Ethnic Chinese and Southeast Asian Citizenship
With the exception of Thailand, other Southeast Asian countries achieved their statehood only after the end of World War II. With statehood, citizenship was also introduced.

In the case of Thailand, in the nineteenth century there was already an institutional channel for ethnic Chinese to become Thais by cutting their queues and joining the Thai group.[8] In modern Thailand, a Chinese can be naturalized as a Thai citizen but he is still considered a Chinese up to the second generation. Nevertheless, a Thai Chinese of a third generation would be considered a Thai.

The majority of Sino-Thais are Thai citizens and have become Thai culturally. This is due partly to the *jus soli* principle adopted by the Thai government in its citizenship law. Although a Chinese born in Thailand has Thai citizenship, there are still 254,000 foreign-born Chinese who are foreigners,[9] most of them being more recent migrants.

In the Philippines, before Ferdinand Marcos promulgated martial law in 1972, citizenship was very difficult to obtain as the law relating to it was based on *jus sanguinis*, rather than *jus soli*. However, in the past there was a high degree of intermarriage between the Chinese and the indigenous people. The Chinese mestizos, who are the offsprings of such unions, have become Filipino/Filipina.

Nevertheless, there are migrant Chinese who are still regarded as Overseas Chinese by the local population. Some of them wanted to become Philippine citizens but this was very difficult until President Marcos issued Presidential Letters in the 1970s granting alien Chinese the right to apply for Philippine citizenship. Thus, a large number of Chinese were naturalized as Philippine citizens. However, there are approximately 40,000 Chinese in the Philippines who are still alien.[10]

When Indonesia declared its independence, it introduced a citizenship law based on *jus soli*. Any Chinese who was born in Indonesia was a citizen of the new Republic if he/she did not repudiate Indonesian citizenship. But in the 1950s Indonesia issued a new citizenship law based on *jus sanguinis*, which made it more difficult for foreign Chinese to obtain Indonesian citizenship. When President Soeharto came to power, there were still more than one million alien Chinese in Indonesia. A large number of them created security and political problems for the Soeharto government. Eventually in 1980 Suharto issued presidential decisions simplifying the procedure to become Indonesian citizens. Many alien Chinese applied for Indonesian citizenship and by the end of the 1980s the numbers of alien Chinese were reduced to only 288,000.[11]

In colonial Malaya, the Chinese were divided into British subjects and Chinese citizens. On achieving independence, the new Malayan government promulgated a citizenship law which granted citizenship to Malayan-born Chinese freely. As a result, many Chinese became citizens of Malaya. When Malaya became Malaysia, the *jus soli* principle continued to apply to the citizenship law.[12] Nevertheless, there are still some foreign-born Chinese who are unable to obtain Malaysian citizenship.[13]

Burma's citizenship law was based on *jus sanguinis*, making it difficult for many Chinese to obtain Burmese citizenship. After General Ne Win seized power in the military coup of 1962, however, the government switched to the *jus soli* principle in a move to resolve the alien Chinese problem. By the time Burma's new citizenship law was promulgated in 1984, many Chinese had become citizens of Burma (Myanmar, after June 1989). By 1994, there were approximately 460,000 ethnic Chinese in Myanmar, of which 58,000 are alien Chinese.[14] But acquisition of citizenship did not mean an end to discrimination. Myanmar divides its citizens into full citizens, associate citizens and naturalized citizens with different socio-political rights.[15]

Before the unification of North and South Vietnam, the Chinese in the south were declared citizens of South Vietnam while those in the north were free to choose their citizenship. However, after the communists unified the country in 1976, most Chinese were declared citizens of Vietnam. But the Sino-Vietnamese tension which developed into a war created serious problems for the Chinese in Vietnam. Ethnic Chinese became suspect and a large number of them fled the country. However, the approximately 962,000 ethnic Chinese[16] who still remain in Vietnam are mainly Vietnamese citizens. In fact, from the example of Vietnam, it appears that the China factor is important to the citizenship issue of the ethnic Chinese in Southeast Asia.

It can be seen therefore that the majority of the ethnic Chinese in Southeast Asia have become citizens of the country where they reside. However, the so-called Chinese problem in Southeast Asia has not been resolved completely. Many indigenous states in Southeast Asia still consider their Chinese citizens as "half" Southeast Asians.

The Ethnic Chinese Position in Southeast Asia
The dubious position of the ethnic Chinese in these new nations or "state-nations" is worth examining. It is probably due to a combination of factors: the history of Chinese migration in Southeast Asia, the self-perception of the Chinese, and ethnic Chinese relationships with the Southeast Asian states and China.

Initially, there was no mass migration of the Chinese from China and many of those who came to Southeast Asia and their descendants might have been integrated into the local societies. However, towards the end of the nineteenth century and the beginning of the twentieth, a new international situation contributed to the mass migration of the ethnic Chinese. While famine and political upheaval in China served as push factors, the economic needs of the European colonial powers in Southeast Asia served as pull factors. The colonialists badly needed cheap manpower to tap resource-rich Southeast Asia and Chinese labour served this purpose well. (The Chinese were prepared to slog under harsh conditions for meagre wages.) Those Chinese who came to Southeast Asia during this period were not really migrants. Many of them intended to return to China after they had made enough money in Nanyang. However, for various reasons many of them later decided to remain in Southeast Asia. And after the communists took over the mainland, more Chinese began to identify themselves with the countries in which they were residing. They were reluctant to return to a communist regime in China where they expected harsh living conditions.

As mentioned earlier, the Chinese in Southeast Asia are a heterogeneous group. In terms of citizenship, some are nationals of the PRC or Taiwan, but the majority are citizens of the Southeast Asian states. Politically, some look towards either Beijing or Taipei, but the majority are oriented towards their adopted land. Of course, there are those who are still culturally Chinese, but there are also many who are either acculturated or even assimilated into their host society, so much so that they have generally lost an active command of the Chinese language. The number of acculturated Chinese in some Southeast Asian states appears to be growing. Economically, there are rich and poor Chinese. It is true that the Chinese as a group has been economically influential and often form the middle class of the country in which they live. They are even considered by some to be the economic élite of Southeast Asia.[17]

Despite the heterogeneity of the Chinese, the perception of a homogeneous Chinese community persists. This is due partly to the relatively strong economic position of the Chinese as a group across Southeast Asia and the existence of a group of first-generation Chinese who refuse to identify themselves with the indigenous population. The perception is also often linked to the desire of the PRC government to utilize the ethnic Chinese to serve the interest of China. These factors have helped to perpetuate the prejudice against the Chinese population.

It is the desire of the governments in the region to integrate, if not to assimilate, their Chinese populations into the host societies. The indigenous (that is, non-Chinese) élite believe that by making the ethnic Chinese less "Chinese", the Southeast Asian states would enjoy better security as the PRC would have fewer opportunities to use the local Chinese community to its advantage. Although cultural and political loyalties may not always go hand in hand, the perception of the indigenous leadership is important as the government's policies are often influenced by these perceptions.

Government Policies towards the Ethnic Chinese

If the indigenous élite were eager to assimilate the Chinese, all Southeast Asian states (except Singapore) should have introduced an assimilationist policy. However, this has not been the case. The reasons probably lie in the different sizes of the Chinese communities in the region and the democratic or undemocratic nature of the political systems there.[18] If the size of the Chinese population is very small and the political system is authoritarian, the government is likely to adopt an assimilationist policy (or both assimilationist and expulsion policies), but if it is very small and the political system is democratic, the government is likely to adopt an accommodationist policy. However, if the Chinese population is large, regardless of the political system the government is likely to introduce an accommodationist policy as it would be unrealistic to pursue an assimilationist policy.[19]

Nevertheless, regardless of the population size and nature of the political system, the indigenous-dominated government will attempt to keep the number of Chinese small (by stopping new Chinese immigration into the country) or reduce the number of the Chinese (by increasing the indigenous population).[20]

Assimilationist Policy

Indonesia, Thailand and the Philippines have adopted assimilationist policies. Assimilation refers to "a blending process whereby two distinct groups form a homogeneous entity".[21] Donald Horowitz identifies two types of assimilation: one is "amalgamation", defined as "two or more groups united to form a larger group"; the other is "incorporation", defined as "one group assumes the identity of another".[22] In the case of Indonesia, "incorporation" has been used more than "amalgamation", while in the case of Thailand and the Philippines, "amalgamation" has been used more than "incorporation".

The above three countries have relatively small Chinese populations. The purpose of the assimilationist policy has been to reduce the ethnic characteristics of the minority, so that the Chinese can be absorbed into the "indigenous population". The ethnic Chinese in these countries are expected to "indigenize" their names, speak the national language of the country and eventually accept its national symbols. Of these three countries, the most radical has been Indonesia. In fact, Indonesia has eliminated three pillars which sustain Chinese society and identity, namely, Chinese schools, Chinese mass media (especially the press), and Chinese associations. In Thailand and the Philippines, although Chinese-language medium schools no longer exist, there are still Filipinized Chinese schools where the Chinese language is allowed to be taught. This is also the case in Thailand. Apart from the Chinese language, Chinese language newspapers and Chinese associations are also allowed.

It should be noted that the rate of Chinese assimilation in Thailand and the Philippines is the highest. This may be due to the prevalence of different concepts of nation. In both countries, nation has been defined more in cultural than racial terms. The components of the nation are the result of "amalgamation" rather than "incorporation", and therefore there are many elements which are also "Chinese". Moreover, the two countries are dominated by Buddhists and Christians. It appears that Buddhism and Christianity are more easily accepted by the Chinese, while Islam often emerges as an obstacle to the assimilation of the ethnic Chinese in the local communities. Nevertheless, if the three countries no longer accept massive Chinese migration, the local Chinese will be further indigenized.

Some writers in recent years have argued that the Chinese in Thailand are in fact not fully assimilated even after three generations. Many in fact hold dual identities. Indeed, there are still many Chinese in Thailand who are first-generation Chinese, and many of them are still foreigners. However, in the case of those who have already become Thai, their Thai identity is very strong, especially when it comes to the public display of such identity. Former Prime Ministers Chuan Leekpai and Banharn Silpa-archa are both of Chinese descent. Some observers have asserted that Banharn is still able to speak a Chinese dialect, and is therefore also a Chinese. According to this view, the Chinese in Thailand hold a double identity. They are Thai as well as Chinese. However, it has to be pointed out that these "Sino-Thai" (or Chinese-Thai) deliberately display their Thai-ness in public, speak "perfect" Thai and behave like indigenous Thais. Although they may have double identities (that is, Chinese ethnic and Thai national identities), their Thai national identity is stronger. It should also be pointed out that as some elements of Thai culture are similar to Chinese culture, a *certain degree* of Chineseness is not an issue in Thailand.

This is also the case in the Philippines.[23] Chinese mestizos such as former President Corazon Aquino (maiden name: Corazon Cojuangco) has acknowledged that she is of Chinese descent; Jaime Cardinal Sin has also paid a visit to his ancestral homeland in Fujian, China. However, their Chinese descent was and is not a problem for them to be accepted as Filipinos.

Accommodationist Policy

Malaysia and Brunei have adopted the accommodationist policy. The term "accommodation" means that "the groups develop working arrangements while maintaining their distinct identities".[24] However, I use this term in a liberal way and do not exclude some degree of common national identity. In Malaysia and Brunei, accommodation is often accompanied by "linguistic assimilation" through the national language policy.

Both Malaysia and Brunei have large Chinese populations and both are Muslim countries. Because of the large size of the Chinese community, Malaysia, and to a lesser extent, Brunei, allow the existence of Chinese culture, but require their citizens to learn Malay. It is also felt that the two governments want the Chinese to identify themselves with the Malay language policy.

However, Malaysia and Brunei have not adopted identical policies. Malaysia has been more liberal because of the presence of Chinese political and economic influence. The Malaysian constitution guarantees the cultural rights of the Chinese, and Chinese schools have so far been allowed to operate. Brunei, however, appears to be more restrictive. Chinese schools were converted to Malay schools in 1992.

   Strictly speaking, Brunei is a Malay Sultanate and an absolute
monarchy and there is no concept of "nation". Therefore, the
government has not embarked on a "nation-building" policy. But
in practice, Brunei is introducing this policy, which is not much
different from other Southeast Asian states.

Assimilationist and Accommodationist Policy
Countries may introduce different policies at different times. This
was the case in Vietnam. Before unification, north and south
Vietnam adopted the accommodationist policy. However, after
1976, an assimilationist and expulsion policy was introduced. But
since the *doi moi* (renovation) period, especially after the collapse
of communism in Eastern Europe and the Soviet Union, Hanoi
has readopted the accommodationist policy.

Pluralistic Policy/Cultural Pluralism
The term "cultural pluralism" is defined as the opposite of
assimilation and acculturation. It encourages the maintenance of
one's different cultural identity. This often creates an impression
that unity is not necessary. In practice, cultural pluralism also has
some common elements, and a common language is often an
essential component. In the case of the United States, the English
language has been used as the cornerstone of the "American
Nation". In fact, cultural pluralism in practice is similar to the
accommodationist policy.
   Singapore has since self-government in 1959 adopted cultural
pluralism because of its ethnic composition, special geographical
location and historical experience. Its language policy has developed
in accordance with the changing political situation; but English,
as the language of communication for various ethnic groups, has
been maintained. A bilingual policy has been emphasized in recent
years to enable various ethnic groups to retain their cultural
tradition. This allows the Chinese culture to continue to prevail.
   In the past, the government tended to stress on the Singaporean
identity. The goal was to create a melting pot in Singapore society
using English as the major language of communication among the
different races. "Mother tongue" was de-emphasized. However,
since the end of the 1980s, some leaders have felt that a

homogeneous nation in Singapore would be difficult to achieve and that ethnic cultures are needed for "national ethos". Thus, both ethnic and Singaporean identities have been equally stressed. The results of this recent shift is still too early to tell, but one thing is clear, the Chinese element in Singapore society will not disappear.

Are Ethnic Chinese Southeast Asians?

With the exception of Singapore, Southeast Asian governments have tried to reduce the Chineseness of their ethnic Chinese populations and to promote "indigenous" national identities. Some have been more extreme than others and many continue to discriminate against the Chinese by segregating their citizens into indigenous and non-indigenous groups. This is against the goal of "assimilation" or "integration". Because of political realities, however, all governments in Southeast Asia allow their Chinese communities to retain various degrees of religious freedom. Through religious identification, the Chinese are able to retain their ethnic identity. But, China's attitude towards the ethnic Chinese has often caused concern among some Southeast Asian governments and complicated the ethnic Chinese issue.

Let us examine briefly China's recent policy towards the ethnic Chinese.[25] China under Deng Xiaoping introduced the "Four Modernization Programmes". Needing both skills and capital to implement these programmes, Beijing urged the "Overseas Chinese" to assist mainland China. Initially, the response was poor as during the Cold War, both Southeast Asian governments and the West were suspicious of the PRC.

However, the collapse of the communist system which led to the end of the Cold War and the opening up of China provided a new opportunity for both China and the ethnic Chinese to interact more. Ideology (in the sense of communism) was no longer an issue. A number of ethnic Chinese capitalists from the region started to invest in the PRC.[26] This led some indigenous leaders to question the identity and political loyalty of the ethnic Chinese. Do the ethnic Chinese in Southeast Asia invest in China for ethnic ties or profits or both? There is no agreement on this issue. Some maintain that the ethnic Chinese are "patriotic" and "love their ancestral land", and their investments are to express their inner feelings and their strong sense of belonging to China. Others maintain that there are two types of ethnic Chinese: the Tan Kah Kee type who invested in China for patriotic reasons while the other, the Wing On/Sincere type, who invested in China merely for profits.

A brief survey of Southeast Asian Chinese capitalists who invested in mainland China reveals that they are mainly first-generation Chinese who are culturally Chinese. They are either able to speak Chinese dialects or Mandarin or both. A few are from the second generation but they too are still culturally Chinese. The *peranakan* Chinese or acculturated Chinese in Southeast Asia, having lost their command of Chinese, are unable to communicate with the mainland Chinese.

The Southeast Asian Chinese capitalists invested in China partly because of ethnic links. But they did not do so for ethnic reasons alone. In fact, a strong case can be made that they are primarily interested in economic profits. These Chinese did not move in to China when they felt that they would not be able to make money. The influx of investments by Southeast Asian Chinese capitalists only happened after they had made sober economic calculations.

It should be pointed out that the ethnic Chinese who have invested in China are ethnic Chinese capitalists. They are small in number and do not represent the average Chinese in Southeast Asia. In addition, these Chinese capitalists are multinationals who do not invest in China alone.

However, the reactions of the indigenous political public to ethnic Chinese investment in China vary. The indigenous Indonesians and Filipino élite have been rather critical, the Thais adamant, and the Malays divided.[27]

In fact, the impact of ethnic Chinese investment in China has been dampened in recent years owing to Beijing's improved relations with the Southeast Asian countries. Some argue that there has been a convergence of economic interest between the indigenous people and the ethnic Chinese élite, and hence the emotional reactions towards ethnic Chinese investments in China have been significantly reduced.

The behaviour of ethnic Chinese capitalists have often been

seen as the "typical" behaviour of the ethnic Chinese by many observers. Some have even confused Southeast Asian Chinese capitalists with their counterparts in Hong Kong and Taiwan. Their images of the Chinese in Hong Kong and Taiwan are transferred to those in Southeast Asia. Apart from ethnic Chinese investments in China, there have also been a general resurgence of ethnicity in the world. People have become more aware of their ethnic identity. There is no doubt that the resurgence of China has also contributed to the "resinification" of some Southeast Asian Chinese. These Chinese began to be attracted to the Chinese language and Chinese culture. However, the "resinification" of these Chinese will not be complete as long as they continue to live in Southeast Asia where indigenous nationalism is strong. In the last twenty or thirty years the ethnic Chinese as a group have also become stronger economically and hence have become more confident.

But are the ethnic Chinese really Southeast Asians? Is there any evidence to substantiate this? A few surveys conducted in Southeast Asia may give us some answers.

In Indonesia, for instance, prior to the normalization of relations between Beijing and Jakarta, *Editor* conducted a survey on the ethnic Chinese perception of Indonesia and China.[28] Among the 129 Chinese respondents,[29] only 14.72 per cent considered China (PRC) as their fatherland and wanted to visit China regularly and maintain Chinese customs. Another 41.86 per cent regarded China as their ancestral land but they did not feel the need to visit China, while 43.41 per cent regarded China as a foreign country. With regard to their attitude towards Indonesia, 93.79 per cent considered Indonesia as their "real fatherland", while 2.32 per cent said it was their second homeland, and 1.55 per cent regarded it as a place to trade and 2.32 per cent were ambiguous. When asked about their views on the normalization of Sino-Indonesian diplomatic ties, 44.96 per cent said that this would facilitate trade and business, 6.20 per cent said that this would facilitate visits to their relatives in China, while yet another 24.80 per cent considered this a good opportunity to study the ancestral culture, and 24.03 per cent felt it had no effect on their lives. It is interesting to note that of the respondents, only 5.42 per cent were still able to write and speak Chinese, 35.65 per cent understood some Chinese, while the rest did not understand Chinese at all.

In the Philippines, some scholars are of the view that there are major differences between the immigrant first-generation Chinese and those born in the Philippines. While the older migrant Chinese are still Chinese-speaking and China-oriented, the Philippine-born Chinese are generally Tagalog-speaking and local-oriented. Teresita Ang See conducted a survey of 381 Chinese students in 1989, and found that 10 per cent spoke only Chinese at home, 77 per cent spoke a mixture, and a high 38 per cent spoke only English and Tagalog.[30] Ang See also maintained that "even if the present local born can speak Chinese, it is an adulterated kind of Chinese mixed with Filipino prefixes and suffixes, which easily distinguishes them as Philippine-Chinese."[31] A survey was also conducted by a Research Centre on Philippine "Chinese school" students. When the students were asked which sporting teams they would support in a competition, those in favour of supporting the Philippine team were twice as many as those supporting the team from China and five times those choosing to support Taiwan.[32]

Even in pluralistic Singapore, two studies (conducted in 1969 and 1989) argue that "there is a large measure of social cohesion".[33] The surveys show that inter-ethnic friendships between Chinese and Malays, and Chinese and Indians, "have increased and are now at high levels". The 1989 survey discovered that 47 per cent of Chinese respondents were willing to marry Malays and 45 per cent were willing to marry Indians, while 62 per cent of the Malays and 58 per cent of the Indians were willing to marry Chinese. It is interesting to note that while the majority of the respondents (Chinese 58 per cent, Malay 70 per cent and Indian 63 per cent) agreed that "Singapore can be defended militarily", a significant number of respondents felt "politically alienated" (Chinese 41 per cent, Malay 57 per cent and Indian 52 per cent).

Many argue that indigenous leaders in Southeast Asia still doubt the loyalty of their Chinese population. And it is uncertain to what extent the Chinese have been accepted by the indigenous population. It is also questionable if the Chinese want to identify themselves with their adopted country.

In Malaysia, differences exist between the Chinese-educated and the non-Chinese-educated Chinese. It is obvious that the Chinese-educated Chinese are more concerned with the Chinese language but they too consider themselves Malaysians. They accept Malay as the national language although they want to retain their mother tongue. However, the English-educated Malaysian Chinese and *Baba*, in their language identification, lean more towards *bahasa Malaysia* (Malaysian language).

Although, some preliminary surveys on the identification of the ethnic Chinese with their adopted country have been conducted, it is clear that more systematic surveys and in-depth research are badly needed. From the sketchy findings presented above, however, one may draw the conclusion that the ethnic Chinese in Southeast Asia are a heterogenous group, and their identity varies from group to group and from country to country. Nevertheless, only a minority remain "Overseas Chinese" or "Chinese overseas". The majority are already Southeast Asians — or at least Southeast Asianized in terms of their language and culture. The indigenous population, however, are still suspicious of their ethnic Chinese community in general, although an increasing number of the indigenous population have accepted the ethnic Chinese as members of their "national family".

Conclusion
As the ethnic Chinese in Southeast Asia are not a homogeneous group, it is often difficult to make sweeping generalizations. Nevertheless, in terms of national identity, the following observations can be made.

Before World War II, the Southeast Asian states were largely colonies. Not surprisingly, the majority of the ethnic Chinese at that time were still Overseas Chinese (or Chinese overseas) in the sense that they were citizens of China and hence tended to be oriented towards their ancestral land, both politically and culturally. However, their identity underwent changes after the Southeast Asian countries attained national independence.

As the concept of nation is new in Southeast Asia, Chinese identification with the Southeast Asian nations is relatively recent. However, in some countries where the Chinese population is small and the concept of nation is more "inclusive", the Chinese can more easily identify themselves with a Southeast Asian "state-nation". However, when the Chinese population is large, and the concept of nation is more "restrictive", the local identity of the Chinese is more problematic.

The length of stay of the Chinese in the country is also a factor in their identification with the nation. Those who were born or whose families had lived in the country for many generations, generally tend to identify themselves with the country of domicile. Their "Southeast Asian" identity is strong. Nevertheless, some may have double or triple identities, but their national identity is often stronger than their ethnic identity.

For more recent migrants, however, their ethnic identity is stronger than their national identity. This is not a problem when China's relations with the local Southeast Asian state are cordial. But when Sino-Southeast Asian relations turn sour, those Chinese who maintain ethnic and economic links with China will become the focus of resentment from the indigenous people.

The resurgence of China can be a factor in the national identity of the ethnic Chinese in Southeast Asia. Some more recent migrants, for economic and cultural reasons, may identify themselves with China. This was especially the case when there were strong anti-Chinese feelings in the Southeast Asian countries where these Chinese reside. But the majority are likely to continue to be locally oriented, especially in countries where the ethnic Chinese are acculturated and accepted by the indigenous population.

It is safe to say that due to the complexity of the Southeast Asian situation and Sino-Southeast Asian relationship, in addition to the strong economic status of the ethnic Chinese population in this region, the issue of Chinese identity will resurface from time to time. In a country where the concept of "nation" is more liberal, it will be easier for the Chinese to adapt, while in a country where the concept of "nation" is rigid, this adaptation will be more difficult. However, the problem may not become serious if there is a higher degree of democratization in Southeast Asia and the economic condition of the local population improves.

TABLE 1

**Numbers and Percentage of Ethnic Chinese
in Southeast Asia (1990)***

	Total Population	Ethnic Chinese	% of Chinese in Total Population
Brunei	260,482	40,621	16
Burma (Myanmar)	33,300,000	466,000	1.4
Cambodia	5,100,000	50,000**	1.0
Indonesia	182,000,000	5,460,000	3.0
Laos	3,200,000	10,000	0.4
Malaysia	17,763,000	5,261,000	29.6
Philippines	67,000,000	850,000	1.3
Singapore	3,016,400	2,252,700	77.7
Thailand	55,888,050	4,813,000	8.6
Vietnam	64,412,000	962,000	1.5
Total	431,939,932	20,165,321	4.69

* Not all the figures on ethnic Chinese cited here are for 1990. Some are for 1985.
   With the exceptions of Brunei, Malaysia and Singapore, all figures are estimates.
** According to *Lianhe Zaobao* (1 July 1994, p. 30), Phnom Penh has a population
   of 800,000, of which one quarter are ethnic Chinese.

SOURCE: Cai Beihua, *Haiwai Huaqiao Huaren Fazhan Jianshi* (Shanghai: Social Sciences
   Institute, 1992) p. 170; Li Qing, "Jianlun Dongnanya Huaren yu Huaren
   Wenxue", *Wenxue Shijie*, no. 8 (1990), p. 13; Tran Khanh, *The Ethnic Chinese
   and Economic Development in Vietnam* (Singapore: ISEAS, 1993), pp. 26–27;
   Nirmal Ghosh, "Thugs will not stop Chinese-Filipino Activist", *Sunday Times*,
   10 July 1994; Jiang Baiqao, *Ershi shiji Taiguo Huaqiao Renkou Cutann* (Bangkok
   Bank, 30 April 1992), p. 20. *Singapore Census of Population 1990* (Singapore,
   1992), pp. 3–4; *Population Census of Malaysia 1990*, cited in Lee Kam Hing,
   "The Political Position of the Chinese in Post-Independence Malaysia" (Paper
   presented at the Luodi Shenggen Seminar, San Francisco, November 1991).

Notes

1. Most of the recently published books, if not all, use the term "Overseas Chinese". See David C.L. Ch'ng, *The Overseas Chinese Entrepreneurs in East Asia* (Melbourne: Committee for Economic Development of Southeast Asia, 1993); Sterling Seagrave, *Lords of the Rim: The Invisible Empire of the Overseas Chinese* (London & New York: Bantam Press, 1995); and *Overseas Chinese Business Networks in Asia* (Canberra: East Asia Analytical Unit, Department of Foreign Affairs and Trade, 1995).
2. Southeast Asia here refers to ten countries, namely, Brunei, Indonesia, Malaysia, Philippines, Singapore, Thailand, Vietnam, Laos, Cambodia and Myanmar. It does not mean that the ethnic Chinese in these countries have one regional identity already.
3. For a study of the term *Huaqiao*, see Wang Gungwu, "A Note on the Origins of 'Hua-Ch'iao'", in his *Community and Nation: Essays on Southeast Asia and the Chinese* (Kuala Lumpur: Heinemann, 1981), pp. 118–27.
4. A recent example is the book by S. Gordon Redding, *The Spirit of Chinese Capitalism* (Berlin and New York: Walter de Gruyter, 1993), pp. 17–24.
5. An ethnic group is defined as "those who conceive of themselves being alike by virtue of their common ancestry, real or fictitious, and who are so regarded by others". See Tamotsu Shibutani and Kian W. Kwan, *Ethnic Stratification: A Comparative Approach* (New York: Macmillan Co., 1965), p. 47. Cited in Richard M. Burkey, "The Basic Units: Ethnic Group, Race, Nationality and Society", in his *Ethnic and Racial Groups: The Dynamics of Dominance* (Menlo Park, California: Cummings Publishing Co., 1978), p. 1.
6. According to Richard Burkey, an ethnic group is "a community group based upon the ascribed status of a diffused ancestry that is maintained by similarities of culture, language and/or phenotype". Ibid., p. 8.
7. In my earlier study with Sharon Siddique, we examined the concept of indigenism with special reference to two ASEAN states. See Sharon Siddique and Leo Suryadinata, "Bumiputra and Pribumi: Economic Nationalaism (Indigenism) in Malaysia and Indonesia", *Pacific Affairs* 54, no. 4 (Winter 1981–82): 662–87.
8. William Skinner, "Change and Persistence in Chinese Culture Overseas: A Comparison of Thailand and Java", *Journal of South Seas Society* [Nanyang Xuebao] 16 (1960): 86–100.
9. This was the 1989 figure, cited in Bangkok Bank, *Ershi Shiji Taiguo Huaqiao Renkou Chutan*, 30 April 1992, p. 17.
10. The estimated number is between 40,000 and 200,000.
11. Xibo, "Xingshi Ruji he Sixiang Ruji", *Dipingxian*, no. 3 (1996), p. 23.
12. See Goh Cheng Teik, *Integration in a Plural Society: The Chinese in Malaysia* (Kuala Lumpur, 1978), p. 25.

13. By 1970, 176,799 (5.7 per cent) out of 3,117,896 Chinese residing in West Malaysia were still alien. See ibid. No recent figures are available.

14. The number of ethnic Chinese in Myanmar is merely an estimate. It ranges between 234,000 and 800,000. See Huo Shengda, ed., *Dangdai Miandian* [Contemporary Myanmar] (Chengdu: Sichuan Renmin Chubanshe, 1993), p. 350. See also the paper by Mya Than in this volume.

15. Ibid.

16. Cited in Tran Khanh, *The Ethnic Chinese and Economic Development in Vietnam* (Singapore: ISEAS, 1993), pp. 26–27. See also *Ethnic Minorities in Vietnam* (Hanoi: The Gioi, 1993), p. 233. (The figure cited in this book is 900,000.)

17. For a brief study of Chinese tycoons in Southeast Asia, see Yoshihara Kunio, *The Rise of Ersatz Capitalism in South-East Asia* (Kuala Lumpur: Oxford University Press, 1988), pp. 191–99; and *Shijie Huren Fuhao Bang*, a publication of Forbes Chinese edition of *Zibenjia* (Hong Kong, 1994).

18. An earlier version of my arguments can be found in my article, "Government Policies Towards the Ethnic Chinese in the ASEAN States: A Comparative Analysis", in *The Ethnic Chinese*, Proceedings of the International Conference on Changing Identities and Relations in Southeast Asia, edited by Teresita Ang See and Go Bon Juan (Manila: Kaisa Para Sa Kaunlaran, 1994), pp. 67–80.

19. For the size of the Chinese communities in Southeast Asia, see Table 1.

20. A good example is Mahathir's population policy which was intended to increase the Malaysian population to 70 million over an unspecified period. However, the policy has quietly been abandoned.

21. James G. Martin and Clyde W. Franklin, *Minority Group Relations* (Columbus, Ohio: Charles E. Merrill, 1973), p. 123.

22. Donald Horowitz, "Ethnic Identity", in *Ethnicity: Theory and Experience*, edited by Nathan Glazer and Daniel P. Moynihan (Cambridge, Mass.: Harvard University Press, 1975), pp. 111–40.

23. Many writers have maintained that the Philippine élites in fact consist of Spanish and Chinese mestizos.

24. Martin and Franklin, op. cit., p. 130.

25. For a brief analysis of the policy, see Leo Suryadinata, "China's Economic Modernization and the Ethnic Chinese in ASEAN: A Preliminary Study", in *Southeast Asian Chinese and China: The Politico-Economic Dimension*, edited by Leo Suryadinata (Singapore: Times Academic Press, 1995), pp. 193–215.

26. For a study of ethnic Chinese capitalists' investments in China, see ibid.

27. See the three articles by Leo Suryadinata, Teresa Chong Carino and Ho Khai Leong in ibid.

28. "Budaya, Bisnis dan Pengabdian", *Editor*, no. 48 (11 August 1990): 25–26.

29. The ages of the respondents were between 17 and 25. Ibid.

30. Teresita Ang See, "The Chinese in the Philippines: Continuity and Change", in *Southeast Asian Chinese: The Socio-Cultural Dimension*, edited by Leo Suryadinata (Singapore: Times Academic Press, 1995), pp. 29–30.

31. Ibid.

32. Ibid, pp. 31–32.

33. The 1969 survey was conducted by Chiew Seen Kong, while the 1989 survey was done by Chiew and Tan En Ser. See Chiew Seen Kong, "National Identity, Ethnicity and National Issues", in *In Search of Singapore's National Value*, edited by Jon S.T. Quah (Singapore: Times Academic Press, 1990), pp. 66–75.

Comments by
Tan Chee Beng on
"Ethnic Chinese in Southeast Asia: Overseas Chinese, Chinese Overseas or Southeast Asians?"
Presented by Leo Suryadinata

Leo Suryadinata's paper is quite comprehensive and appropriate as an introduction to this volume. The paper addresses the theme on whether the Chinese in Southeast Asia are Overseas Chinese, Chinese overseas or Southeast Asians? I agree with his emphasis that the Chinese in Southeast Asia are not a homogeneous group, and that the majority see themselves as Southeast Asians, although I would qualify the term "Southeast Asians".

Leo first discusses the terms used for the Chinese in Southeast Asia. This is a complex issue, which I cannot comment in just a few words. We agree with Leo that the Chinese in Southeast Asia do not like to be called "Overseas Chinese". When I say "we" I have in mind both the Chinese in Southeast Asia generally and those of us who have spoken out against various scholars who continue to use the term. At the 1991 Manila conference on the Chinese in Southeast Asia, for instance, there was a heated academic exchange on this issue between some of us and a few scholars from Taiwan (see Tan 1992, pp. 6–7). As proud citizens of our respective countries, we feel insulted to be called or even referred to as "Overseas Chinese". We are overseas in China but not when we are at home in Malaysia, Indonesia, the Philippines, and so forth.

Some scholars outside Southeast Asia do not understand our sensitivity; they cannot grasp the feeling of the Chinese in Southeast Asia. The pride of being local is not new nor merely political. It is a natural development of local consciousness. Even in the early period of Chinese settlement history, such as in Malaysia and Indonesia, the earlier and more settled Chinese had always been proud of their local status, and they looked down on later immigrants. The *Baba* in the Straits Settlements, for example, used their local status to claim a higher status over the *Sinkeh*, the new immigrants. In fact, the popularity of the label *Baba* had much to do with the contrast with *Sinkeh*. With the formation of the new states in Southeast Asia, most Chinese, not just the *Baba*, identified with the new states, and wanted to be a dignified part of the emerging new "state-nations", to use Leo's description. The point is that the rejection of the label "Overseas Chinese" is not merely for political reasons (for example, to ensure acceptance by the indigenous people), but it is very much the internal growth of local consciousness and genuine local identification.

There are a number of reasons and motives for the persistent use of the term "Overseas Chinese" in English. In the past there were Overseas Chinese but after independence, most Chinese in Southeast Asia ceased to see themselves as such, and the younger generations identify themselves as Malaysians, Indonesians, Singaporeans, and so on, of Chinese origin. Some writers have ignored this important aspect of historical development and have continued to treat the Chinese in Southeast Asia as Overseas Chinese. In Europe, America and Australasia, there has been a continuous influx of new immigrants from China, and this has complicated the use of a label for the Chinese there.

There are writers, including those of Chinese origin, who use the label "Overseas Chinese" out of convenience to refer to all the Chinese outside China. They are aware of the historical inaccuracy and the sensitivity of the local Chinese to the use of this term, but they ask what is the alternative label to cover all the Chinese referred to? To avoid this problem, in recent years some scholars, mainly those of Chinese origin, have used the label "Chinese overseas". I think this is translated from the Chinese *Haiwai huaren*. This term is more acceptable than "Overseas Chinese", but as expressed by Leo, some Chinese in Southeast Asia are still not comfortable with the presence of the word "overseas". Nevertheless, we should respect the good intention of writers who use the label "Chinese overseas". From the perspective of the writers from China, this is acceptable as it is a geographical term to refer to the Chinese outside their own country, that is, outside China. Of course, the label "Chinese overseas" includes both the local Chinese of different nationalities and the Overseas Chinese who are nationals of China.

There are, however, some writers from the West who are under a sort of "yellow peril" paradigm to intentionally portray an economically stronger China as a threat to world peace and security — actually meaning against Western interests. They group the Chinese from Hong Kong, Macau and Taiwan with the Chinese from Southeast Asia as "Overseas Chinese", who are portrayed as helping China to develop and dominate Asia. Leo correctly points out that it is misleading to consider the Chinese from Hong Kong, Macau and Taiwan as "Overseas Chinese". Furthermore, as many scholars have shown, the so-called overseas investment in China mostly come from Hong Kong, Macau and Taiwan, and not so much from Southeast Asia directly (cf. Li 1994). Leading Western newspapers and magazines, such as *The Economist*, have in recent years been consistent in portraying China as a threat to the rest of Asia and therefore argue for the need to contain China. In fact, the United States has been the dominating force in Asia and there is a fear in the West that a stronger China may threaten continuing Western domination. We have to speak out against this construction of the culture of domination by Western media and writers. We should be aware of the Western rhetoric on "Overseas Chinese" and China to justify containing China and perpetuating Western domination. Furthermore, this kind of rhetoric, if unchallenged, may cause the indigenous people and governments of Southeast Asia to distrust the local Chinese.

As pointed out by Leo and various other scholars, the investments in China by Southeast Asian Chinese capitalists have much to do with business opportunities and profit. Businessmen from all over the world have sought to invest in China, not just the people of Chinese descent. Although Chinese businessmen from Southeast Asia have the advantage of knowing the Chinese language (but not all Chinese in Southeast Asia can speak and read Chinese) and may have their social networks in China, this is a separate issue. What should be questioned is the misleading assumption that the people of Chinese descent, because of this fact, are always politically oriented towards China, and their investment in China is read from this perspective.

I should like to add that, in my opinion, the Chinese in different parts of the world do not form a single community. This is despite the increasing networking between Chinese businessmen, leaders and academicians world-wide. Nor is there a single Southeast Asian Chinese community; the Chinese in Southeast Asia identify with their respective countries and do not see themselves as belonging to a common wider Southeast Asian Chinese community. Leo and I may react to the use of the label "Overseas Chinese", but we do so out of our perception and experience of living in our respective Southeast Asian states.

It seems that we still lack a common term for the Chinese who have sunk their roots outside China. In recent years, some writers have talked of the Chinese diaspora, the term used to describe the Jewish people who are scattered all over the world. Perhaps because of our experience of having to deal with the local governments which treat the citizens of Chinese descent as still somewhat alien, and because of our strong local identification, we also find it difficult to accept the term "diaspora". We fear being perceived as scattered communities without a sense of belonging, whatever the good intentions of the term's users.

This leaves us with the term "ethnic Chinese" which appears to be the most acceptable one, at least in this region. By tradition of usage rather than its accuracy, the term has been used to refer to the Chinese in Southeast Asia who are citizens of their respective countries. In China, there are different Chinese ethnic groups but in Southeast Asia, the term "ethnic Chinese" is used in relation to other local ethnic groups. It is therefore local in orientation.

The term "people of Chinese descent" has also been used. I myself have used this label to refer to people (outside China) who identify themselves as Chinese irrespective of their nationality and level of acculturation. It is not without difficulty, especially if it is used loosely to include anyone who can trace some Chinese descent. Of course, the term is derived from the Chinese term *huayi*.

The Chinese in Southeast Asia generally refer to themselves as *Huaren*. The consistent use of this label instead of *Huaqiao* or "Overseas Chinese" after independence shows the shift in identity and the emphasis on the local orientation. *Zhongguo ren*, which means "people of China" or "Chinese", is avoided so as not to be confused with the citizens of China. *Huaren* also means "Chinese" but it is ethnic in reference; although it means Chinese in general, not just the Chinese in Southeast Asia. For the people in China the term *Zhongguo ren* is appropriate. The Chinese in Southeast Asia perceive the term *Huaren* as special to them and so have taken the term for granted. In the same way, in Southeast Asia, *Huayu* means the Mandarin language, although *Hua* actually means Chinese in general. For a person from China, *Huayu* can refer to any Chinese language, not just Mandarin. Thus, the Chinese magazine *Yazhou Zhoukan* usually provides *Putong Hua* in parentheses following the term *Huayu* to ensure that all readers know what it means.

Since the Chinese in Southeast Asia call themselves *Huaren* (that is "the Hua people") in Mandarin, it is reasonable to use the label "Hua people" as a general label. In fact, the Chinese in Vietnam have been called "Hoa". However, a label is also very much a matter of usage, and so far the term "ethnic Chinese" is more commonly used in English writings about the Chinese in Southeast Asia by those who wish to avoid the label "Overseas Chinese".

Overall, the Chinese in Southeast Asia should not be called "Overseas Chinese", a label which is appropriate only for citizens of China living overseas. Often, the context alone is sufficient to indicate the kind of Chinese referred to, such as the description "Chinese in Southeast Asia" or "Chinese worldwide". Where necessary, the terms "ethnic Chinese", "people of Chinese descent" or even "Hua people" may be used, as we have yet to find a commonly acceptable collective term for all Chinese living outside China and who are citizens of their respective countries.

Having dealt with the complex issue of labels, I need not say much about the concepts of nation, citizenship and government policies which Leo has discussed systematically. His distinction of state-nations and nation-states is useful for studying ethnicity and state in Southeast Asia. He points out clearly that "(T)he state is created first and a new nation is built on the state boundary". What is of interest is how the indigenous people and the Chinese view their new state-nations differently. Even within the Chinese community of each state, the nation is perceived differently by different sections of the Chinese population. In Malaysia, for example, a section of the Chinese-educated Chinese even think that the Chinese should have their own separate system of education, including a Chinese-medium university. Other Chinese Malaysians are more concerned with equal participation in nation-building and are not bothered very much about the medium of instruction at the secondary and tertiary levels.

The position of the ethnic Chinese is affected by government policies and citizenship laws. For example, indigenous economic nationalism when realized as government policies affect the interests of the Chinese. While the ethnic Chinese generally agree that poverty among the indigenous people has to be addressed and that the increased involvement of the indigenous people in business is important, they do worry about racial policies which discriminate against the Chinese. Overall, as is obvious in Leo's paper, it is the power relations between the indigenous people and the Chinese community concerned which determine the kind of policies towards the ethnic Chinese.

The position of the Chinese in Southeast Asia differs from state to state. Indonesia has adopted a rather assimilative policy but this is not possible in Malaysia which has a much higher proportion of Chinese who have some share of political power, albeit subordinated to that of the Malays. The "Chinese problem" in Indonesia is very much linked to the citizenship issue — in fact, the so-called Chinese problem is actually one of government attitudes and policies, and not a Chinese problem per se. The assimilative policy is misguided by the view that the loyalty of the Chinese can only be obtained by suppressing their ethnic distinctiveness. In fact, diversity is a fact of life, and unity in diversity can be achieved without trying to bring about uniformity, which is not realistic. Ultimately, it is subjective identification which counts, not cultural uniformity.

Lastly, I would like to deal with two issues which are relevant to the paper. On the question of ethnic identification, we should pay more attention to subjective identification by the people them-selves, irrespective of the level of change in their cultural identity. Are Melaka *Baba* Chinese, since their mother tongue is *Baba*

Malay rather than a Chinese language? Of course, they are Chinese as they perceive of themselves as such and are proud of being Chinese. We have to distinguish subjective identification and objective cultural manifestation, and it is misleading to use objective cultural criteria of Chineseness to determine whether the acculturated Chinese are Chinese or not. Surely if we study ethnic identity, the people's own ethnic perception must be our primary consideration, although we can study how acculturation has accounted for different ways of being Chinese. Thus, whether the more locally acculturated people of Chinese descent are Chinese or not is not so much a question of acculturation but a problem in our research ability to understand their perception.

In some cases, like the Chinese mestizo in the Philippines, outsiders may find it difficult to know whether they can be considered Chinese or not, or both Chinese and Filipino. A person can say that he or she is of Chinese descent, but if he identifies himself as a Filipino only and not Chinese, then he is Filipino and not ethnic Chinese, but if he also identifies himself as an ethnic Chinese, then he is one irrespective of the level of acculturation. President Corazon Aquino has acknowledged that she has Chinese ancestry and the Chinese press has written of her as if she is an ethnic Chinese. But how has she identified herself? Has she ever identified herself as an ethnic Chinese? As far as I know, she is just Filipino.

The phenomenon of double identity in Thailand is quite well known, as Leo Suryadinata has described. A person can be both ethnically Chinese and Thai, not just Thai by nationality. This should be distinguished from multiple levels of identities, as in the case of Chinese Malaysians who can be Hokkien at one level and ethnic Chinese in general in relation to the Malays, and Malaysian in national identity. The Chinese in Malaysia cannot be both Chinese and Malay at the same time, and so there is no double identity phenomenon. In my opinion, it is better to reserve the use of "double identity" to refer to the possession of two autonomous ethnic identities at the same time, not merely the possession of different levels of identities. In this respect, perhaps Leo can enlighten us whether the Chinese in Indonesia can have double identity, that is, being both *ethnically* Chinese and *ethnically* Indonesian at the same time.

Leo correctly concludes that the Chinese factor will always be important, but the Chinese in Southeast Asia will continue to be locally oriented. They are proud of their identities too. Of course, ethnic identities are not static, being constantly influenced by many factors such as government policies. Given the local orientation of the ethnic Chinese, a more liberal definition of nation will enhance their sense of participation, making meaningful integration possible. A policy of forced assimilation and discrimination will make them feel alienated. I fully agree with Leo that Chinese adjustment is not difficult if there is democratization and, more importantly, the economic condition of the local population improves.

References

Li, Guoliang. "Zhanhou Dongnanya Huaren Rentong Yanjiu de Gongshi yu Fengqi" [Studies on the Identity of Ethnic Chinese in Post-war Southeast Asia: Consensus and Dissension]. In *The Ethnic Chinese*, edited by Teresita Ang See and Go Bon Juan, pp. 243–49. Manila: Kaisa Para Sa Kaunlaran, Inc., 1994.

Tan Chee Beng. "Echos De La Recherche: International Conference on Changing Ethnic Identities and Relations in Southeast Asia: The Case of the Chinese Minority". *Archipel* 44 (1992): 3–13.

Chapter 2

The Ethnic Chinese in Indonesia: Issues of Identity

Mely G. Tan

Citizenship and Identity

It was thirty-four years ago that the ethnic Chinese in Indonesia had to make an active choice between Indonesian or Chinese (People's Republic of China) citizenship, based on the Sino-Indonesian Treaty on Dual Nationality, signed in Bandung on 22 April 1955. After due process, which took almost five years, during a two-year period from January 1960 to January 1962, those who were considered to have dual citizenship had to declare in a court of law that they rejected Chinese citizenship if they wanted to opt for Indonesian citizenship.[1] For virtually all of the ethnic Chinese qualified to take this action, this was the first time they had to face the reality of deciding who they were, where they were and how they saw their future — in other words, to determine their identity.

There were four categories of people who acted in different ways at the time: those who made up their mind that the only and best choice was to opt for Indonesian citizenship; those who agonized during the whole two-year option period and only decided to opt when the deadline drew near; those who decided not to do anything, thereby becoming aliens (*warganegara asing* or WNA); and those who were ignorant of the Treaty and the action they had to take, thereby losing the option to become Indonesian citizens.

At this point it is appropriate to ask whether by making an active choice of citizenship, the ethnic Chinese had a notion of a nation and being part of a nation. It is quite probable that most of them had not even thought about it, and had not considered it when making their choice. However, from the writings of those who had, it is clear that they adhered to the concept espoused by Soekarno, the first President of Indonesia. As shown in his speech "The Birth of Pancasila", delivered on 1 June 1945, Soekarno stated: "… What are the requirements of a nation? According to Renan, the requirements for a nation is the desire to be united. The people feel themselves to be united and want to be united. Ernest Renan said that the requirement for a nation is *le desir d'etre ensemble*, the desire to be united. According to Ernest Renan's definition, it follows that what becomes a nation is a group of people who want to be united, who feel themselves united". Then, he went on to quote Otto Bauer in his book *Die Nationalitaetenfrage*, "… *Was ist eine Nation?* and the answer is given: *Eine Nation ist eine aus Schicksalgemeinschaft erwachsene Charaktergemeinschaft* [A nation is a community of character which has grown out of a community of shared experience]".[2] Since then, this concept of nation espoused by Soekarno has been used by virtually everyone in defining the concept of a nation in Indonesia. Among them was the late Harsja W. Bachtiar, well-known Professor of Sociology at the University of Indonesia, in an article written in 1987 and reprinted in 1992.[3]

One of the ethnic Chinese who has been most articulate in propounding this concept is Harry Tjan Silalahi, a prominent politician, former member of Parliament and of the Supreme Consultative Council (Dewan Pertimbangan Agung) of Indonesia, and today a member of the board of directors of the Center for Strategic and International Studies (CSIS) in Jakarta. In a lecture to the participants of one of the regular courses of the National Resilience Institute (Lembaga Pertahanan Nasional) in April 1994, he stated that because of its pluralistic nature, the concept of nation in Indonesia has followed the definitions of Ernest Renan and Otto Bauer, quoting the same statements as those attributed to Soekarno, mentioned above. He further emphasized that the "Founding Fathers" reaffirmed that "... the Indonesian nation is not based on having the same mother tongue, or constituting one ethnic group, culture or religion. What unites the peoples of Indonesia is their shared history, shared suffering, shared oppression, the struggle for independence ... From this shared fate emerged the will to be together. This is the foundation of the unity of the Indonesian nation".[4] It is obvious that the ethnic Chinese who have become Indonesian citizens will adhere to this concept of the Indonesian nation as it is not based on race or ethnicity, and therefore constitutes the basis for and confirms their right to be part of this nation.

According to estimates, of the approximately 2.45 million ethnic Chinese in Indonesia during the option period, about one million could be considered to have dual nationality. Most of them registered their choice, and of these, according to official sources, about 65 per cent opted for Indonesian citizenship, while according to Chinese leaders the proportion was between 70 and 90 per cent (Mackie and Coppel in Mackie 1976, pp. 11 and 214). Thus, one could assume that the legal status of the ethnic Chinese was finally settled in 1962.

However, problems related to citizenship continued to emerge, and in 1969, the Indonesian Government unilaterally abrogated the Treaty. This meant, among other things, that whereas according to the Treaty the children of those who had an alien status could choose their citizenship within one year after coming of age (Article VI), now they could only become an Indonesian citizen through naturalization. Moreover, after the abortive coup of September 1965 (referred to with the acronym G-30-S for Gerakan 30 September), diplomatic relations between Indonesia and the PRC were frozen (starting in 1967), and only resumed twenty-three

years later in 1990. This event was marked by the signing of a
Memorandum of Understanding (MOU) by the foreign ministers
of both countries on 8 August 1990 in Jakarta, witnessed by
President Soeharto for Indonesia and Prime Minister Li Peng for
the PRC. This document consists of only four paragraphs, and
two of them deal with dual nationality (referring to Indonesian
citizens of Chinese origin), and non-interference in each other's
domestic affairs. It is interesting to note that a figure of 300,000
was mentioned as the number of people whose citizenship status
needed to be resolved (Tan 1991, p. 115).

As a follow-up to the signing of the MOU, a series of meetings
on a bilateral basis ensued both in Jakarta and in Beijing. Most of
these meetings occurred in 1992. On 14–16 April 1992, a Senior
Officials Meeting (SOM) was held in Jakarta with delegations from
both countries. This was in preparation for the signing of the
MOU by the Indonesian Minister of Justice Ismael Saleh and the
Minister of Justice of the PRC Cai Ceng, in Beijing on 4 May
1992. The deliberations dealt with the determination of the status
of the approximately 300,000 (the figure mentioned was 299,224)
persons considered to be aliens, but who had settled in Indonesia
for decades. The PRC Government stated that it was prepared to
provide them with PRC passports. There were also those catego-
rized as illegal immigrants. These included about 3,058 persons
who had left Indonesia with the status "exit permit only", as a
result of the disturbances related to the implementation of regulation PP10/1959 (*Kompas*, 1 April 1992). Included in this category
were also those who had entered Indonesia with a false/forged
passport.

Then there were those who were already in possession of an
"exit permit only" document but who did not leave Indonesia
because the transportation provided by China was not sufficient
to take them. Figures mentioned that of the approximately 140,000
who had registered, only about 40,000 were able to leave, and
about 100,000 remained in Indonesia. Apparently, over the years
their numbers were reduced as a result of Keputusan Presiden
or Keppres (Presidential Decision) No. 13, 1980, which provided
for a less complicated, faster and cheaper naturalization process.
Besides, it appears that many of the women married Indonesian

citizens, and, of course, there were also those who had passed away (*Suara Karya*, 18 September 1992).

Furthermore, on 17 September 1992, both ministers met in Jakarta and signed a "Record of Discussion", where it was agreed that the process of dealing with illegal immigrants was to be extended to 3 January 1993. On the same day, the Minister of Justice, Ismael Saleh, told the press that those considered citizens of the PRC, but who had lived in Indonesia for decades, number-ing about 230,000, could become Indonesian citizens through naturalization (*Kompas*, 18 September 1992).

What was the reaction of those affected by these agreements between the governments of Indonesia and the PRC? If the report from the situation in Central Java is any indication, the reaction was positive. According to the head of the regional office of the Department of Justice of Central Java, there were 17,000 requests for Indonesian citizenship. However, he stated that none had been granted yet because this depended on the decisions made at the national level (*Kompas*, 7 October 1992). At the same time, there were also reports that in Pangkalpinang, for example, 3,827 aliens of Chinese descent, might lose the opportunity to become Indo-nesian citizens because they did not have enough funds to acquire their citizenship papers (*Media Indonesia*, 11 December 1992). In West Kalimantan province, with an ethnic Chinese population of 406,182 (one of the largest numbers of ethnic Chinese in Indo-nesia), by 30 June 1990, 155,512 had received the Surat Bukti Kewarganegaraan Republik Indonesia (SBKRI or the Certificate of Indonesian citizenship) document (*Bisnis Indonesia*, 11 December 1992).

These agreements and the follow-up actions were designed to resolve the problem of the citizenship status of those ethnic Chinese who did not possess the appropriate documents. If the figures mentioned are accurate or approximately accurate, this would involve about 300,000 people.

What about those who have become Indonesian citizens since the option period 1960–62, and through further regulations, such as Instruksi Presiden or Inpres (Presidential Instruction) Republik Indonesia No. 2, 1980, issued on 31 January 1980, which was meant to provide those who were considered de facto citizens, but who lacked the documents to prove this, with a Surat Bukti Kewarganegaraan Republik Indonesia and the Keputusan Presiden or Keppres No. 13, 1980, issued on February 1980, mentioned earlier. These regulations, especially the SBKRI, most probably influenced the outcome of the 1980 census, which was taken in October 1980, about two months after the expiration of the implementation of this regulation. This census registered the number of alien Chinese as 462,314, which was a drastic drop from the 1,028,935 in the 1971 census (Tan 1987, p. 65). This figure was probably used as the basis for determining the number of 300,000 mentioned in the MOU of 1990.

A further development was the confirmation that children of Indonesian citizens of foreign descent need not have the SBKRI. This was stated by the Minister of Justice Ismael Saleh on 27 March 1992, at a ceremony to present the SBKRI symbolically to a number of youths in Pontianak, West Kalimantan. He confirmed that those children need not possess the document themselves (*Kompas*, 30 March 1992). This regulation became formal by the Decision of the Minister of Justice, signed on 10 July 1992. It was stipulated that the status of children of parents who have an SBKRI can be ascertained from their birth certificate and Kartu Tanda Penduduk (KTP) or identification card (*Business News*, 6 November 1992).

If we keep to the figure of 3 per cent as the proportion of ethnic Chinese in the Indonesian population, now estimated at about 195 million, this would mean an absolute number of around 5,850,000. This is the number of ethnic Chinese we are concerned with in this chapter.

There is today an upsurge of interest in the ethnic Chinese, especially in Southeast Asia. The popularity of books such as John Naisbitts' *Megatrends Asia* and Sterling Seagrave's *Lords of the Rim* (both published in 1995) attest to this. The thrust of these recent writings is that the ethnic Chinese in Southeast Asia, in particular the business people, have kept their identity as Chinese, which is sustained by the network that has developed among them. This chapter will discuss how the ethnic Chinese in Indonesia identify themselves today and perceive their prospects for the future.

Issues of Identity

Conceptually, the most comprehensive analysis of the identity of the Southeast Asian Chinese to date is probably still Wang Gungwu's "The study of Chinese identities in Southeast Asia" (in Cushman and Wang 1988, pp. 1–23; also reproduced in Wang 1991, ch. 11). He notes a very important development among this group of people: that during the past decades, contrary to the stereotype "once a Chinese, always a Chinese", the ethnic Chinese in Southeast Asia have changed and they are capable of undergoing further change.

A number of studies have indicated that there are people of Chinese descent who have become citizens of the country they settled in and who do not consider themselves Chinese. Then there are those who had lost almost all their affinity with their Chinese origin, but who have rediscovered their Chineseness and who are trying to be resinicized. There is yet another category of ethnic Chinese who have what Wang calls a "double identity". These people are citizens of, and identify with, their country of adoption, yet remain conscious of being Chinese.

Based on these observations Wang identifies the following types of ethnic Chinese identity in Southeast Asia:

1. a historical identity, which is a pre-World War II phenomenon, and is now encapsulated in the concept of cultural identity;
2. a Chinese nationalist identity, which is also a pre-World War II phenomenon and today practically non-existent;
3. a communal identity, which is a characteristic of the Malaysian situation and which may change to ethnic identity;
4. a national or local identity, which is now found among most Southeast Asian Chinese who have become citizens of their country of residence;
5. a cultural identity, a concept that has absorbed the traditional historical identity;
6. an ethnic identity, which corrects the cultural identity on the point of racial origins;
7. and a class identity, which depends on crossing ethnic boundaries.

Wang points out that in reality some of these identities overlap, and it is therefore more appropriate to approach this topic through the notion of multiple identities. In other words, the ethnic Chinese in Southeast Asia usually have more than one identity at the same time.

How these identities are determined, Wang suggests, is through the concept of norms. He identifies four types of norms that exist in any society: physical norms, political norms, economic norms and cultural norms. By combining four of the now still existing common identities, that is, national, cultural, ethnic and class, with the four types of norms, he shows that, depending on the pressures put on the ethnic Chinese in terms of the norms, they will lean towards any one of the four types of identity or a combination of them.

Using this model, Wang has come up with some interesting observations about the type of identity existing in a number of Southeast Asian countries. In this chapter, we will only discuss his observations on the situation in Indonesia.

He notes that: "Indonesia provides the most complex, and even contradictory picture. On the one hand, political norms weigh so strongly on people of Chinese descent that there are few options open to them. Access to Chinese cultural norms is kept to a minimum and the normative national identity is the primary standard for all. On the other hand, up to half the Chinese population are aliens and are unable to obtain Indonesian citizenship. For them, the cultural identity route to survival and success remains their only option" (Wang 1988, p. 16).

Wang's paper was presented and discussed at a symposium in Canberra in June 1985, about eleven years ago. Nonetheless, the model is still useful in analysing the situation in Indonesia today, although some of the facts and the relationship between Indonesia and the PRC have changed significantly.

No doubt, the position of the ethnic Chinese in Indonesia is still complex and much attention has been and is still being paid by the media[5] to the relationship between the two countries, especially the question of citizenship of those whose status was declared unclear. As mentioned earlier, the number of those considered aliens at the time of the signing of the MOU to resume diplomatic relations in 1990 was about 300,000. This is contrary to the observation of Wang that in the 1980s half the ethnic Chinese in Indonesia were aliens.

Nevertheless, an indication of the complexity of the position of the ethnic Chinese is the fact that although the MOU on the resolution of citizenship was signed by the ministers of justice of the two countries in 1992, the status of about 208,000 ethnic Chinese is still being processed.[6]

Apparently, President Soeharto himself was made aware of the slowness of this process and on 14 August 1995 he signed a Presidential Decision (Keppres No. 57, 1995) on the procedure to resolve requests for naturalization, followed by a Presidential Instruction (Inpres No. 6, 1995), signed on 10 November 1995. The intent of both documents was to speed up the process to acquire naturalization. The deadline was mentioned as 31 March 1996. The issuing of these documents indicates that Indonesia is prepared to grant citizenship to these people, although they still have the option to be nationals of the PRC.

As it was generally known that the delay was at the implementation stage, after the two regulations were issued, the office of the Cabinet Secretariat called a meeting in Jakarta on 27 November 1995. It was attended by the highest officials in the government agencies involved in the implementation of the two documents.

This development indicates that at the top level of government there is agreement about resolving the citizenship status of the ethnic Chinese involved. It is at the level of implementation that the problems arise. Considering the history of the process since 1990, it remains to be seen whether by the end of March 1996 the naturalization process will indeed be concluded.[7]

What are the issues involved in determining the identity of the ethnic Chinese in Indonesia? How true is the observation of Wang that the pressure of political norms on the ethnic Chinese is so strong that they have no choice but to lean towards a normative national identity? These questions will apply to virtually all the ethnic Chinese, as those considered aliens have been reduced to about 200,000 and if the naturalization process is resolved as scheduled, almost none will be left. Thus, in discussing the issues of identity, we will deal with all ethnic Chinese who are Indonesian citizens.

Although the majority of Indonesians tend to group all ethnic Chinese together as one entity, there are clear differences among them and this has implications for the determination of their identity. An important distinction is by cultural orientation, which is the result of their educational experience, the number of generations their family has settled in Indonesia, and whether they are of mixed descent. This has led to the distinction between the *totok* and *peranakan*.[8]

The *totok* are those who are usually not of mixed descent, whose families have been in Indonesia for two or three genera-tions, have had a Chinese language education and a Chinese cultural orientation, primarily indicated by the fact that they speak Mandarin or one of the Chinese dialects at home — at least, the older generation. By occupation, most of these *totok* are in business and trade.

The *peranakan* are those who are of mixed descent, whose families have settled in Indonesia for at least three generations, who may have had some Chinese language school education but do not speak Chinese as the home language, and whose cultural orientation is more towards the culture of the area in which they have settled. By occupation, many of them have had a university education and are in the free professions (physicians, dentists, engineers, lawyers, accountants), but a sizeable number are also in business and trade.

Today, the validity of this distinction into *totok* and *peranakan* is being questioned, especially the distinction into *totok*. This is no doubt largely due to the fact that since 1966 Chinese language schools have been closed down, and in 1967 the government issued a regulation prohibiting the use of Chinese characters in public places, and the expression of cultural elements construed to be of Chinese origin, such as the Chinese lunar new year, outside the home environment. This is part of the assimilation policy, consistently, albeit with some lapses, followed by the government.[9] Whenever it is felt that this regulation has been transgressed, it is put into effect again.

This happened with the 1996 lunar new year (the Year of the Rat) which fell on 19 February, one day before the end of the Moslem fasting month of Ramadhan, referred to as Idul Fitri, when there is a two-day national holiday. As had been the case for the past several years, in the week before new year's day, especially on the eve before the event, the Chinese temples in Jakarta were crowded with people who burned candles, incense sticks and took out joss sticks to ascertain their future.

The Governor of Jakarta apparently felt that these festivities needed to be curbed. On 14 February, in a letter (No. 4, 1996, dated 14 February 1996) (*Suara Pembaruan*, 15 February 1996) concerning the celebration of the lunar new year (referred to as Tahun Baru Imlek), he noted that in the past few years, the festivities had been contrary to the regulations in force. According to the governor, these activities would hinder the process of assimilation and threaten the unity of the nation. He therefore exhorted that the lunar new year be celebrated in accordance with Inpres No. 14, 1967, on Chinese religion, beliefs and tradition, the Joint Decision of the Minister of Religious Affairs No. 67, 1980, the Decision of the Minister of Home Affairs No. 224, 1980 and of the Attorney General No. KEP-III/J.A/ 10/1980 on Instruction for the Implementation of Inpres No.14, 1967.

He further reiterated that the celebration of Imlek be within the family circle, or within the premises of the temple. Imlek, he noted, was not part of the Buddhist religion but a tradition in Chinese culture, and therefore should not be celebrated in the temple. He also appealed to the people not to put up decorations, banners, printed material or symbols that were manifestations of Chinese culture. They should also not have in public places festivities, theatre performances, dances, and other expressions of culture that are based on Chinese stories or pictures.

As a result of these policies, especially the closing down of Chinese language schools, the ethnic Chinese in Indonesia have refrained from speaking Chinese in public, and from expressing their cultural traditions, or at least have kept them to a minimum and within the family circle. This situation is of course not conducive to maintaining and observing traditional customs.

Nonetheless, visiting older relatives as an expression of paying respect to parents, grandparents and relatives of the older generation is still being practised on the occasion of the lunar new year. The custom of presenting children and younger relatives with a "red packet" (referred to as *ang pao* in Hokkien) is still maintained. This, of course, forms an added incentive for the young to visit the old. This tradition of paying respect to parents and other older relatives has great potential for survival, as it is one of the strongest values inculcated among the young.

There are other ways of distinguishing among the ethnic Chinese. It can be by area of settlement, where their cultural life and values are strongly influenced by the culture of the dominant ethnic group of the area. This form of acculturation is expressed in the use of the local language or a mixture of the local language and Indonesian at home, as, for instance, Javanese in Central and East Java, Sundanese in West Java, Minangkabau in West Sumatra, Menadonese in North Sulawesi, Ambonese in the Moluccas, and Balinese in Bali.

Another distinction is by generation: the older generation (50 years and over) who still speak their local language, and Dutch or Chinese, depending on their educational experience;[10] and the younger generation (in particular those under 35, who were born a few years before or after the upheaval of 1965), who speak mostly Indonesian and, among those who have studied abroad, the language of the country they studied in, usually English. The distinction by generation also means a difference in historical experience. The older generation had experienced the colonial period under the Dutch, when the population was systematically divided by race (Dutch, foreign orientals including Chinese, Arabs and Indians, and indigenous people); the Japanese occupation when all Chinese (*totok* and *peranakan*) were lumped together in one category; and the revolutionary period, when at one point the Chinese were accused of collaborating with the Dutch. The younger generation has had no such experience. What some of them may have experienced is the role of ethnic Chinese university students in the turbulent period after 1965, when some of them became well-known members of the "1966 generation" — the young people, mostly university students who were instrumental in the overthrow of the "Old Order" government under President Soekarno (Tan 1991, pp. 123, 124).

The understanding of these distinctions is important in discussing the issues of identity. As shown above, language used at home is a crucial indicator; so are educational experience, occupation and residence.

Some Empirical Studies

So far, very few substantive empirical studies exist that describe and analyse the changes in the social structure and cultural outlook of the ethnic Chinese since the beginning of the New Order. One of the few, though limited in scope, is Stuart Greif's *Indonesians of Chinese Origin. Assimilation and Goal of "One Nation-One People"*. Greif did the study in 1985, when he interviewed ethnic Chinese on their views of their position in Indonesia, how they identified themselves, their reasons for the riots in Solo and Semarang which occurred five years before (1980), the naturalization of alien Chinese, and on the possibility of the resumption of diplomatic relations between Indonesia and the PRC.[11] The study involved interviews with 25 (17 men and 8 women) ethnic Chinese, presumably selected at random. They were from Jakarta (10), Semarang (4), Yogya (4), Bali (3), and Solo and Bogor (2 each). Distinguishing them by age, there were nine in the younger (30 years and less) group, and sixteen in the older (31 years and older). Two of them were aliens (*warga negara asing* or WNA) and another two naturalized citizens. This was a qualitative study and the report was presented in the form of case studies based on the questions and answers from the interviews. For our purpose here, we will focus on the question on identity.

The answers to this question varied greatly, but all (except for the two who were WNA) stated that they were Indonesians or WNI (*warganegara Indonesia*), but always with some qualification, indicating that they felt "different". A sample of the most interesting responses follow.

A thirty-one-year-old *peranakan* woman from Denpasar, Bali, who, together with her husband (*peranakan* of mixed Chinese and Balinese origin) is in the tourism business, and running a guest house and a handicrafts shop, said: "We are Indonesians of

Chinese origin, but we also know we are not Balinese.... We are different from the Balinese, but then we are not real Chinese either" (pp. 32, 33).

A thirty-one-year-old man from Semarang, who is an accountant in his father's hardware shop said that his family was WNI by birth, but his in-laws had become citizens by naturalization some ten years before. "We are of mixed racial background, but consider ourselves Indonesians of Chinese origin. I cannot speak Chinese. My father knows a little, but never uses it" (p. 21).

A forty-year-old man from Bali, born in Surabaya and owns a restaurant, and whose father was a Hakka WNA until his death while his mother was Javanese, had assumed his mother's nationality, that is, WNI. His wife was a Protestant Torajanese, and he had become a Protestant. He said, "[I regard myself] as an Indonesian of Chinese origin. The traditional way of looking at things in Indonesia stipulates that you are what your father is. Thus, my children are Chinese, but should my daughter marry a *pribumi*, her children will be *pribumi*. It is very arbitrary" (p. 26).

A forty-six-year-old man from Bogor, a *peranakan* born in Bandung, but who moved to Bogor after the 1963 riots when his family lost everything, said "We are Indonesians first ... the trend in the cities, especially in Java, is toward loss of Chinese identity" (p. 45).

A thirty-three-year-old *peranakan* man from Yogyakarta, born in Semarang, who was in the family transport, food distribution, and bus service business, spoke both Javanese and Indonesian and said that his family continued to practise the Chinese religion, and for the Chinese lunar new year they would go to Semarang to pray at the Sam Poo Kong temple, though some members of the family had become Catholic: "We are all Indonesians" (pp. 61, 62).

A fifty-eight-year-old woman from Jakarta, with *peranakan* ancestors who had lived in Jakarta for an unknown number of generations and whose family and husband's family were involved in the wholesale foodstuff and transport business, said: "We are Batavian Chinese. ... We have a firm place in Indonesian history and society and are proud of our heritage. Some of us do not even look Chinese, but we call ourselves Chinese because of our distinct class in colonial days. We do not speak Chinese and are very Indonesianized, but we still prefer to remain a separate group. Our loyalty is to Indonesia, not to China. But we are neither *totok* nor *pribumi*. ... We marry amongst ourselves. ... At one time we were the most Indonesianized of the Chinese, but now we are among the most determined to hold onto our identity" (pp. 40, 41).

A forty-five-year-old man from Jakarta, born in Central Java, who owned a clothing factory, said: "My outlook is Indonesian .... Our children do not even look Chinese. I have seen tremendous changes taking place in Indonesia, and I am confident of the future. The Chinese are changing along with everyone else, especially here in Jakarta" (p. 58). He was of *peranakan* stock and his wife was Sudanese.

A thirty-four-year-old woman from Jakarta, who is a secretary in a law office and whose parents and husband were from a *peranakan* background, said she had many *pribumi* friends: "The social structure of Jakarta, at the higher levels anyway, is not racial, but based upon professional standard and income. Race relations are good on every level, especially at the top. There is plenty of room for peaceful competition. People have no doubt where we stand as far as nationality is concerned. We are accepted as 100 per cent Indonesian" (p. 63).

The above examples were responses of those in the older age group (31 years and over). We will now look at the views expressed by six in the younger age group (30 years and less). (Of the nine cases, two were WNA and one was a naturalized citizen.)

A twenty-eight-year-old man from Yogyakarta, who was born there, as were his parents and grandparents, said: "We are half Javanese, and I do not know our exact Chinese origins. Culturally, we are Javanese, and we speak Javanese more often than Indonesian. ... we are Indonesians in every way ...." On how far the assimilation process should go, he said, "As far as individuals want to take it. There should be no regulation of human behaviour. If people want to intermarry that is their business. If they want to remain distinct, that is their right, too, just as long as they are loyal Indonesians" (pp. 51, 52).

A twenty-eight-year-old man, a university graduate from Jakarta and born there, whose *totok* parents came from Padang, said: "[Parents] still keep many Chinese customs and are disappointed that their children have no real interest. We can speak Hakka but we rarely do so. Our wives and husbands either have left their *totok* ways or are *peranakan*. … I am a university graduate, as is one of my brothers, and this further removes us from the Chinese past. We use Indonesian almost all of the time and our thinking is Indonesian …. Pancasila guarantees us freedom of religion" (p. 65).

A twenty-eight-year-old man from Jakarta, and born there, whose parents were from East Java, and grandparents from Fukien, spoke Chinese but could not read or write it, while his *peranakan* wife did not know Chinese. He said, "As a result of a silly decision on the part of my parents before I was born, I was obliged to spend a lot of time and money getting naturalized. … to enhance my position in business I legally changed my name as well." On whether naturalization and his name change were both sincere acts, he replied, "Certainly, the naturalization was. After all this is my home and country. I think of myself as an Indonesian with every right to be here. The name change I am not sure about. In time, I suppose, I shall conceive of myself by that name, but my children will never have such doubts" (p. 30).

A twenty-nine-year-old man from Semarang, born there and a Hakka WNA, and married to a Hakka, claimed that his family history in Indonesia went back a hundred years. He ran an electrical goods shop, but still helped in his family's furniture business. He said, "I can speak Chinese, but prefer to use Indonesian only with my wife and children, since I do not want my children to be disadvantaged in school. We are WNA, but I shall want to do something about this so that my children can have a higher education if they choose to." On being aware of difficulties in getting naturalized, he said, "Very much so. It will take time and money, but in my case, it will be worth it. … I am paying the price for my parents' mistakes …." On the manifestation of Chinese culture in his family, he said, "In every way, from business ethics to relationships, to cultural and religious outlook, cooking, etc." (pp. 33, 34).

A twenty-nine-year-old woman from Semarang, and born there, whose grandparents were from Canton, and whose family was *totok*, as was her husband, said that they usually spoke Cantonese at home. "We are not Indonesian citizens, but Indonesia is still our home. We live fairly contented lives here and look forward to the future." On why not become naturalized, she replied, "It is very expensive and time consuming. ... It is better to put the time and money into the business. We lose little by our WNA status, although being WNI means greater security." On WNA status, she said, "We are paying the price for a decision made by our parents before we were even born" (pp. 47, 48).

A twenty-six-year-old woman from Jakarta, born in Medan but who had come to Jakarta with her parents when she was eight years old, and whose parents were full-blooded Chinese, and husband *peranakan*, worked as secretary in her husband's legal firm. She said, "A lot of our work [in husband's legal firm] is with Chinese, but the bulk is with *pribumi* or foreign companies .... through education and experience I am Jakartan. I can speak Chinese, but I cannot read or write. ... Through education I have become an Indonesian .... There are no real ways of keeping a separate Chinese identity" (pp. 35, 36).

These case studies provide a number of interesting observations:

1. Although Greif's study was done eleven years ago and limited to people in a few big cities in Java and Bali, the findings can be seen as indicative of the situation at the time, and is probably to a great extent still valid for the situation today;

2. He interviewed only twenty-five people, thus obviating any claim to be representative of the ethnic Chinese as a whole, yet they do show the great variety of this group and represent a group of people that form the majority of the ethnic Chinese, that is, people who are self-employed or work in a medium-size family enterprise. As such, they can be put in the category of medium or small businessmen and can be considered part of the so-called "lower middle class", a group that has not been studied much (Gondomono 1990);

3. The findings show that there is not much difference in identity between those in the older and the younger age group and by gender: except for the two who were WNA, all identified themselves as Indonesians, but recognized the fact that they

were of Chinese origin, and therefore different from the majority ethnic Indonesians. Those who considered themselves *peranakan* emphasized that they were neither ethnic Indonesian (in most cases Javanese, and in some Balinese), nor *totok*;

4. Most of them were of the opinion that the government policy of assimilation had worked to a large extent, as indicated by the fact that most of them did not speak Chinese at all, and the few who did, could only speak, but not read or write it;

5. Almost all of them accepted the regulation of 1967 on restricting expressions of Chinese culture within the family environment or temple grounds. As one respondent stated: "… it may be a price that must be paid. … My parents have paid a far greater price, but still they stayed and never thought of leaving" (p. 54).

It is interesting to note the conclusions Greif made on the basis of his findings. He observes that although the assimilation process has been painful, it is succeeding. He appears confident that what he found in 1985 has made all previous studies in the English language outdated: "In five years' time, this present study will be a source material for a history of the Chinese here, since it, too, will be already outdated. Terms such as *totok*, *peranakan*, Indonesian Chinese or Chinese-Indonesians are virtually meaningless. Rather, at least in Java and Bali, we have Indonesians of Chinese or mixed Chinese origin" (p. 69).

Greif himself admits that his study was mostly concentrated on WNI Chinese who have been successful and have benefited from the government policy of assimilation. In his observation, younger Chinese have no resentment against the assimilation process, as it is their parents who have had to pay the initial price. He notes that there is widespread support of the government in general, and that there is a general feeling that the government is, in fact, pro-Chinese.

Recent Developments

In the light of recent developments, these observations seem overly optimistic and too sweeping, especially considering the fact that the findings are based on the views of a limited number of people, whose selection, as admitted by the author himself, was biased towards those who had benefited from the government's assimilation policy.

A major development that needs to be examined carefully is the process of globalization, which is expressed predominantly in the economy and in informatics, in particular the mass media. The impact of this process is seen especially in the cities, and in Indonesia, in Jakarta. In the economy, it is manifest in the influx of foreign investment, in particular from other Asian countries, and the increase of expatriate workers.

There is the observation that there is a specific "Jakarta culture" that affects everybody. This has led to a form of "internationalization", adopting a specific lifestyle, seen in big cities all over Asia, and affecting especially the younger generation. This "international culture" has elements of Western culture and contemporary Asian culture, with a dominance of Chinese and Japanese culture. This is expressed, among others, in the popularity of martial arts (*kung fu*) movies from Hong Kong and Taiwan, and the proliferation of karaoke joints in many hotels, restaurants, and other entertainment places in the business and shopping areas all over Jakarta and other big cities.

As a result, there is a move away from traditional culture, be it Chinese or Javanese, towards a contemporary culture, which has a streak of hedonism and individualism. In the view of a businessman informant,[12] it used to be that people with education were respected; today, it is people with money. He stated that he felt not entirely accepted by the ethnic Indonesians, and that one always had to be on the alert. When there was social unrest, one could easily become a victim. However, he added that when he visited China he also did not feel comfortable among the Chinese there.

In terms of identity, in the view of a *peranakan* high functionary of a state enterprise, the ethnic Chinese are confused, especially among the younger generation in the business community. Although they see themselves as Indonesian rather than Chinese, they recognize their Chinese origin, albeit knowing very little of Chinese culture and tradition.

The younger generation feels much more Indonesian than their elders but they also say that one has to be on the alert. On a person-to-person basis relations are good, but it is different at the group level. A young *peranakan* man, who is branch manager of a big private bank, and who belongs to the fourth generation in Indonesia, stated that he felt comfortable with other *peranakan* Chinese, which was not a feeling he shared with ethnic Indonesians. When they went out for meals, for example, it was almost always taken for granted by the ethnic Indonesians that the ethnic Chinese would pay.

Among the well-to-do families, many of the younger generation have studied abroad (to get an MBA is very popular), in the United States, Australia, Singapore. There is also a trend to send their children to primary schools in Singapore, where they are considered to get a good "modern" education, plus an opportunity to learn Mandarin. This is seen as a good preparation for them to move into Asian business circles later on. Thus, according to a businessman informant, to give children this kind of education is motivated by purely practical considerations for the future.

This kind of reasoning and explanation is questioned by ethnic Indonesians and rekindles suspicions of a return to "Chineseness", that is, the phenomenon of the "China factor". This is the view of the potential influence of China on the ethnic Chinese, through culture and the economy, which is considered to be especially plausible since the resumption of diplomatic relations in 1990. This view is reinforced by the investments in China of some of the prominent Chinese-Indonesian big businessmen, referred to as "conglomerates", which continue to receive extensive coverage in the Indonesian press.[13]

Meanwhile, according to one of the very few *peranakan* politicians, there is among the ethnic Chinese, especially among the big businessmen, a growing feeling of impatience that they are still treated differently, and that they are basically being used, because of the continuous requests for large funds. For instance, at the meeting at the Tapos ranch of President Soeharto in March 1990, twenty-nine out of the thirty-one big businessmen invited were ethnic Chinese. The gist of the President's speech at the time was to request big business to set aside a certain percentage of their profits to help the development of co-operatives. Apparently, this plan did not really get off the ground.[14]

More recently, there was a meeting of ninety-six ethnic Chinese and ethnic Indonesian big businessmen at Jimbaran, Bali, from 25–27 August 1995. At the end of the meeting, which was meant to inculcate the ideas of Pancasila (the Penataran Pedoman Penghayatan Pancasila or P4 course) to these businessmen, a declaration, referred to as the Deklarasi Jimbaran, was issued. The declaration consisted of seven points, the gist of which was that they were prepared to assist in the development of medium and small enterprises. This was planned to be realized in 1996, starting with the assistance of 2,500 small enterprises.[15]

This declaration was followed by Presidential Decision (Keppres) No. 90, 1995, issued towards the end of the year. It required companies (apparently including the foreign ones) to set aside 2 per cent of the net profit after tax which exceeds Rp.100 million, to help families in the category of *pra-sejahtera* (pre-welfare) and *sejahtera I* (welfare I). This was a programme initiated by the Minister of Population and Coordination of Family Planning, and supported by President Soeharto (*Media Indonesia Minggu*, 14 January 1996).

The most recent development in which ethnic Chinese big businessmen were involved was the establishment of P.T. Dua Satu Tiga Puluh on 16 February 1996. This company was set up to secure funds needed for the development of the jet plane N-2130 (hence the name of the company), to be produced by P.T. Industri Pesawat Terbang Nusantara (IPTN) headed by J.B. Habibie. At the initial stage, the funds needed would be four trillion rupiah, and the source for these funds would be the *konglomerat*. The signing of the memorandum of understanding (MOU) between the two companies (by Saadilah Mursjid as Direktur Utama of PT 2130 and J.B. Habibie as Direktur Utama of PT IPTN) was witnessed by President Soeharto and about fifty *konglomerat* of the Jimbaran group. Seen standing next to the President in the picture accompanying the article were Mohamad (Bob) Hasan, Eka Tjipta Wijaya, Prayogo Pangestu, Henry Pribadi (all ethnic Chinese) and Sudwikat-mono (prominent ethnic Indonesian businessman) (*Sinar*, 2 March 1996, p. 76).

This feeling of being treated differently from the majority ethnic Indonesians also exists among the younger generation. Although there is a directive by the Minister of Justice indicating that the offspring of WNI of foreign descent do not need an SBKRI (certificate of citizenship), and that an identification card is sufficient, in reality children of WNI still need a document declaring that they are WNI when, for example, they enrol in a school, make a passport, or make an identification card and each time they have to renew it. According to the politician respondent, as a result, there is a tendency among the younger generation to be more conscious of their ethnicity. This was also indicated in a study of ethnic Chinese high school students in the town of Sukabumi in West Java, where one of the major findings was that the younger generation tended to withdraw within their own group, and to be more aware of their ethnic Chinese identity — which may not mean that they emphasize their Chineseness, but at the least that they see themselves as different from the ethnic Indonesians.[16]

The politician respondent stated that it annoyed him that as a Member of Parliament he still had to show documents proving that he was a WNI whenever he had to renew his identification card or his passport. Or when he felt compelled to assist his children in getting their Indonesian citizenship documents, while in fact legally this was not necessary. It is this inconsistency and arbitrariness in the implementation of existing regulations, and having to face a bureaucracy that can find ways to circumvent them, as these informants indicated, that frustrates most of the ethnic Chinese who identify themselves as Indonesians but are constantly reminded that they are of Chinese origin, and therefore different.

Prospects for the Future

After fifty years of independence, the last thirty years under the New Order government, how do the ethnic Chinese identify themselves today and what are their prospects for the future? As conversations with a number of ethnic Chinese in business, state enterprises, politics, in the Bakom-PKB, and in research work indicate, the trend is definitely towards integration and identification as Indonesians, albeit still recognizing their Chinese origin. This form of identity, as hyphenated Indonesians, will probably continue through the present younger generation. In Wang Gungwu's model, this type of identity is a combination of national and ethnic (cultural) identity.

However, we should note that whereas national identity is clearly based on citizenship, there is variation in the degree of cultural identity, constituting a continuum ranging from those who completely identify as Indonesian to those who are still Chinese-oriented in that their language at home and at work is Mandarin or one of the dialects, and that they observe rituals and tradition recognized as elements of Chinese religion and culture. With the eventual acceptance of virtually all ethnic Chinese, including those whose citizenship status was unclear, as Indonesian citizens, this variation in cultural identity is inevitable.

At one end of this continuum are the ethnic Chinese who have become completely absorbed into the local community and the culture of the area they have settled, as, for instance, becoming completely Javanized. An outstanding example of a Javanized ethnic Chinese was the late Professor Tjan Tjoe Siem, an internationally known Javanologist, who was married to a Javanese woman. He and his late brother, the internationally known sinologist Professor Tjan Tjoe Som, came from Surakarta, where they belonged to a well-known family who have been Moslems for generations.

Today, one of the best-known, both nationally and internationally, Javanologist is Kanjeng Raden Hario Tumenggung (KRHT, a title of nobility conferred on him by the Sunan of Surakarta) Hardjonagoro. He was born in Surakarta in 1931 with the name Go Tik Swan, and is a descendant of the Luitenant der Chinezen (the head of the Chinese community during the Dutch colonial period). Known as Hardjono Gotikswan, he is an expert in all aspects of Javanese culture, including batik, keris (Javanese dagger), literature, gamelan, Javanese dances and wayang (shadow play) (*Kompas*, 11 February 1996).

At this same end of the continuum are also those who have converted to Islam. One of the best known figures is Junus Jahja, a Rotterdam-trained economist, who became a Moslem in 1979, and married a Sundanese woman some years later. He is convinced that the best road to assimilation is by becoming a Moslem, the religion of some 87 per cent of ethnic Indonesians. Another figure was the late Masagung (Tjio Wie Thay), owner of one of the first and biggest book stores in Indonesia, and founder of the Islamic Center built at the cost of Rp 1.5 billion. Other businessmen include Jos Sutomo and Jusuf Hamka (foster son of the late Moslem leader Buya Hamka) (*Media Indonesia Minggu*, 18 February 1996). Among the academics, there is Professor Muhammad Budiyatna, dean of the Faculty of Social Sciences and Politics at the University of Indonesia, and Professor Haji Muhammad Hembing Wijayakusuma, an expert in alternative medicine, who has a weekly programme on this topic on one of the private TV stations.

Still in this category of Moslem converts are a number of *da'i*, or preachers, who not only preach among converts but are also popular among the Moslem population in general. During the month of Ramadhan in 1996, a number of them appeared regularly in the Ramadhan programme on TV stations. Among this group is Alifuddin El Islami (Sim Song Thian), who was born in 1951 in Deli Serdang, North Sumatra. Other TV figures are Anton Medan (Tan Hok Liang), born in Medan, and Muhamad Syafi'i Antonio, born Nio Cwang Chung in Sukabumi in 1967. This information on *da'i* of Chinese descent appeared in a series of articles on this topic in the news magazine *Gatra* of 17 February 1996. In the article on these *da'i*, there was a listing of eight of the most popular, among whom were two women: Putri Wong Kam Fu, whose name at birth was Pak Kiem Lioe and whose Moslem name is Leoni Fatimah, a professional astrologer and granddaughter of the well-known astrologer Wong Kam Fu; and Qomariah Baladraf, born in Gorontalo, North Sulawesi, with the name Tan Giok Sien.

Among those who identify themselves as Indonesian, without any qualification, are also those who fully believe in assimilation, in the sense of being absorbed into the local community of residence. These include people like K. Sindhunata, who until this year was the chairperson of Bakom-PKB from its inception (in the present board of officers, he is a member of the Dewan Penyantun or Advisory Council), Harry Tjan Silalahi (also a member of the Dewan Penyantun), Indradi (secretary-general of Bakom-PKB), and many younger people who have become Catholic or Protestant.

At the other end of the continuum are those who are culturally still Chinese-oriented, have had a Chinese language education, and many of whom have become citizens through naturalization. Among them are some of the big businessmen, like Sudono Salim, who speaks sub-standard Indonesian with a Chinese accent, Mochtar Ryadi, and others, still referred to as *totok*. Their offspring, however, belong to the category that has been internationalized, having studied abroad and belonging to a network of business people involved in international or at least regional trade.

In this category are also those who can be considered to belong to the "lower middle class", who are self-employed, have a small family business, or a shop. Examples are the four families mentioned in Gondomono's study[17] of the Chinese community in Jakarta: the older generation still speaks Mandarin, Hakka or Hokkien, and some of their children also do. However, because of marriage to *peranakan*, who do not speak Chinese, and in one family there is intermarriage with ethnic Indonesians, the language used at home is mixed. All the families also practise some form of the Chinese religion.

In between these two ends is the majority of ethnic Chinese, mostly *peranakan*, who are culturally more Indonesia-oriented, speak Indonesian or the local language at home, do not speak Chinese at all, and are minimally knowledgeable about Chinese religion and tradition. They earn enough to live comfortably, but the number of those who have difficulty in making ends meet, or who are actually poor, is usually underestimated. In Jakarta, these people can be found in the back streets, behind the glittering shopping malls in the downtown area that is still considered the Chinatown of Jakarta. In fact, they can be found in all big cities in Indonesia where there is a sizeable ethnic Chinese population. They have no doubts about being Indonesian citizens, but they still recognize their Chinese origin.

How they determine their identity and their children's identity depends very much on their assessment of the way the government and the majority of ethnic Indonesians perceive them. From the case studies by Greif, the conversations referred to above, and other writings, there is the perception that there is still an ambiguous attitude in accepting the ethnic Chinese fully as fellow citizens. There is also the feeling of insecurity, that during an outbreak of social unrest, they will always be a target in one way or another. In October and November 1995, for instance, there were incidents in Purwakarta (West Java) and Pekalongan (Central Java) that turned into actions against property (mainly shops and vehicles) owned by ethnic Chinese (*Suara Pembauran*, 11 January 1996).

Nonetheless, there are indications that the government recognizes the importance of social and political stability, especially in the face of the implementation of agreements on the liberalization of trade and investment of the Asia Pacific Economic Cooperation (APEC), and in general, fulfilling the requirements for the acceptance of a market economy as the prevailing economic system. Hence, in the recent outbreaks of unrest, incidents were kept localized owing to the speedy intervention of the security forces.

In the view of the respondent from a state enterprise, the acceptance of the market system has created a real dilemma for the government and ethnic Indonesians: the more open the economy, the more the ethnic Chinese can take advantage of it, thereby enriching them even more; the more closed the economy, the more the ethnic Indonesians, as the majority population, will suffer.

Another interesting development is the composition of the board of officers of the Bakom-PKB. This new board was installed by the Minister of Home Affairs on 12 December 1995 for the period 1995–2000. K. Sindhunata, a Catholic *peranakan* lawyer and former officer of the Indonesian Navy, who had been the General Chairperson (Ketua Umum) since its inception, was replaced by Juwono Sudarsono, a professor of political science and former dean of the Faculty of Social Sciences and Politics at the University of Indonesia, and presently the Deputy Governor of the National Resilience Institute (*Media Indonesia*, 13 December 1995).

In an interview in *Media Indonesia Minggu* (14 January 1996), Sudarsono stated that the programme for the next five years will focus not on the problem of the "non-pri" ("non-pribumi", meaning non-indigenous, a term used to denote ethnic Chinese) and "pri" ("pribumi", meaning indigenous, a term used to denote ethnic

Indonesians), but on the problem of nation building, which includes inter-religious and inter-ethnic relations. He put his views as follows: "I would like to ask the 'pribumi' to be more honest, to restrain themselves, and to recognize the fact the 'non-pri' should really be viewed as an asset. ... We should be more open, see the future more clearly. First, this is a long-term program of at least 15 years. Second, we cannot satisfy everybody. Third, there will continue to be friction between 'pri' and 'non-pri'. The 'non-pri' will always be at fault, while in fact the fault also lies with the 'pribumi'. These are the ideas I want to develop". Furthermore, he stated that ethnic or racial origin should not be an issue. "We should respect people's origin. ... If someone declares himself an Indonesian, we should consider him [her] an Indonesian. Where is our maturity after 50 years of independence, that we should still make an issue of a person's physical features, skin colour or shape of the eyes?".

For the first time, the nucleus of the board of officers of the Bakom-PKB consists of mostly ethnic Indonesians. Besides Juwono Sudarsono as General Chairperson (Ketua Umum), the other chairpersons are Rosita Noer (a Minangkabau woman physician), Dr Bachtiar Ali (from the University of Indonesia), Dr Dillon Singh (an agriculturist from the Department of Agriculture, who is of Indian descent), Natalia Subagio (a Javanese businesswoman, with a degree in Sinology), Usman Atmadjaja, and M. Indradi Kusumah, a *peranakan* lawyer, as the Secretary General. The former members of the board, who are mostly *peranakan* Chinese, are now members of the Council of Advisors, including K. Sindhunata, Jusuf Wanandi, Sudono Salim (Liem Sioe Liong), William Soerjadjaja, Harry Tjan Silalahi, and Soekamdani Sahid Gitosardjono (an ethnic Indonesian).[18]

As the Bakom-PKB is under the aegis of the Department of Home Affairs, the composition of the board and the programme and approach, as outlined by Juwono Sudarsono, must have had the approval of the government. This can be seen as an indication that there are influential people who are willing to try to resolve the problem of the ethnic Chinese in a comprehensive manner, as part of the overall process of nation building.

Although it still remains to be seen how the work of the Bakom-PKB will evolve, for the ethnic Chinese this is an indication that they are viewed as part of a national problem that needs to be resolved nationally, rather than as an isolated problem that needs a special solution. For the ethnic Chinese who have struggled for decades to resolve the so-called "Chinese problem", this must be an encouraging development, which will boost their efforts to continue seeking for the solution most acceptable to all parties concerned, thereby ensuring better relations between all ethnic groups in general and between the ethnic Chinese and ethnic Indonesians in particular.[19]

Notes

1. For the full text of the Sino-Indonesian Treaty on Dual Nationality, signed in Bandung on 22 April 1955, by Chou Enlai, Minister of Foreign Affairs of the People's Republic of China and Sunarjo, Minister of Foreign Affairs of the Republic of Indonesia, see Leo Suryadinata, *China and the Asean States: The Ethnic Chinese Dimension* (Singapore: Singapore University Press, 1985), pp. 166–72. See also Mary Somers-Heidhues, "Citizenship and Identity: Ethnic Chinese and the Indonesian Revolution", in *Changing Identities of the Southeast Asian Chinese since World War II*, edited by Jennifer Cushman and Wang Gungwu (Hong Kong: Hong Kong University Press, 1988).

2. Sukarno, "The Pantja Sila (1945)", in *Indonesian Political Thinking 1945–1965*, edited by Herbert Feith and Lance Castles (Ithaca and London: Cornell University Press, 1970), pp. 40, 41. This important sourcebook includes the writings and speeches of Soekarno from 1930 ("The Promise of a Brightly Beckoning Future") to 1965 ("Storming the Last Bulwarks of Imperialism").

3. Harsja W. Bachtiar (who passed away in December 1995) was a professor of sociology at the University of Indonesia, with a Ph.D. from Harvard University (1973). He has written extensively on national integration. He was a member of the board of the Bakom-PKB from 1990–95. His ideas on nation, nation-building and national integration in Indonesia, are expounded in an article entitled "Integrasi Nasional Indonesia" in *Wawasan Kebangsaan Indonesia. Gagasan dan Pemikiran Badan Komunikasi Penghayatan Kesatuan Bangsa*, revised edition (Bakom-PKB Pusat, 1987 and 1992), pp. 7–56. On the concept of nation, he espoused the ideas adhered to by Soekarno, adding the information that Ernest Renan presented his concept of a nation in a public lecture entitled "Qu'est-ce qu'un nation?" at the Sorbonne, Paris, in 1882.

4. The paper presented by Harry Tjan Silalahi to the participants of the short regular course at the National Resilience Institute (Lemhannas) on 13 April 1994, was entitled "Cina dan Permasalahannya". For his biography, see Leo Suryadinata, *Prominent Indonesian Chinese: Biographical Sketches* (Singapore: Institute of Southeast Asian Studies, 1995), pp. 149–51.

5. The interest in matters related to the ethnic Chinese in Indonesia and in Southeast Asia in general is continuing. This can be seen in the coverage by the printed media, which has been compiled by, among others, the Center for Strategic and International Studies (CSIS) in Jakarta. On the topic of the Surat Bukti Kewarganegaraan Republik Indonesia (SBKRI), there were 53 pages of clippings, covering the period from September 1991–December 1992. There were 68 pages of various writings on or related to ethnic Chinese covering the period from October 1991 to October 1993. These were clippings from the major Jakarta newspapers, including *Kompas, Suara Pembaruan, Republika, Media Indonesia, Merdeka, Pelita, Suara Karya, Angkatan Bersenjata, Jakarta Post*, and the news magazine *Tempo*. In February 1996, due to the coincidence of the lunar new year on 19 February and the Idul Fitri (end of Ramadhan) on 20 and 21 February, *Media Indonesia Minggu* (18 February 1996) appeared with a lead article and various other articles on the Moslem Chinese in Indonesia and on the celebration of the lunar new year among the ethnic Chinese, while the news magazine *Gatra* (17 February 1996) had a special coverage on ethnic Chinese *da'i*, or Moslem preachers.

6. The information on the most recent developments in resolving the citizenship status of the about 300,000 ethnic Chinese, was received from a key functionary in the Bakom-PKB, who has been assisting in the implementation of the policies concerning citizenship of the ethnic Chinese in Indonesia. He has an extensive knowledge of the history of this issue, the way the policies have been implemented and the figures involved. He is one of those deeply concerned about the problems of the implementation of the regulations, as, for example, the fact that children of WNI parents are still asked to show their citizen papers, while this is no longer legally necessary.

7. According to a news item in the *Suara Pembaruan* of 13 June 1996, the date has been extended to 30 June 1996.

8. On *totok* and *peranakan*, see Leo Suryadinata, op. cit., pp. 3, 11. See also Mely G. Tan. "The Role of Ethnic Chinese Minority in Development: The Indonesian Case", in *Southeast Asian Studies* 25, no. 3 (December 1987): 64, 65.

9. For the full text of the Instruction of the Cabinet Presidium No. 37/ U/IN/6/1967, concerning the Basic Policy for the Solution of the Chinese

Problem, see Leo Suryadinata, op. cit., pp. 173–77. This policy concerns the alien Chinese. On the policies concerning Indonesian citizens of Chinese origin, that is, Presidential Instruction No.14/1967 and Presidential Decision No. 240/1967, see Mely G. Tan, "The Social and Cultural Dimensions of the Role of Ethnic Chinese in Indonesian Society", in *Indonesia, 1991* (Proceedings of the symposium held at Cornell University, July 1990), pp. 114–25.

10. For the languages spoken by the various types of ethnic Chinese, see Dede Oetomo, "The Chinese of Pasuruan: A Study of Language and Identity in a Minority Community in Transition" (Ph.D. thesis, Cornell University, 1984); and Dede Oetomo "Multilingualism and Chinese Identities in Indonesia", in *Changing Identities of the Southeast Asian Chinese since World War II*, edited by Jennifer Cushman and Wang Gungwu (Hong Kong: Hong Kong University Press, 1988).

11. Stuart William Greif, *Indonesians of Chinese Origin. Assimilation and Goal of "One Nation-One People"* (New York: Professors of World Peace Academy, 1988). At the time of the study he held a position in political science at the University of Otago in New Zealand. He had then written two books and several articles on the "Overseas Chinese" in New Zealand and in Fiji. He first visited Indonesia in 1980 and made two more trips. In 1985 he started on the study of the ethnic Chinese in Java and Bali. He worked on this project because he felt that in most studies on the Indonesian Chinese in the English language, "the human aspect was missing".

12. The information in this section was the result of interviews in an informal manner, more like conversations, with an older generation businessman, who still speaks Chinese, but whose sons and daughters (except one working with him) do not speak any Chinese; a *peranakan* Jakartan (wife Javanese), who has a high position in a state enterprise; a *peranakan* key functionary of the Bakom-PKB; a *peranakan* politician and Member of Parliament (from Golkar, the government-backed party); a young, *peranakan* branch manager of one of the big private banks; a *peranakan* economist working in a government research institute, and a *peranakan* woman sociologist.

13. The investment in China by a number of prominent ethnic Chinese "conglomerates" in Indonesia, and especially the Second World Chinese Entrepreneurs' Convention held in Hong Kong in November 1993, which was meant to be a meeting to promote investment in China, received wide coverage, mostly in a negative vein, from the press in Indonesia. See Mely G. Tan, "The Ethnic Chinese in Indonesia: Issues and Implications", in *Southeast Asian Chinese: The Socio-cultural Dimension*, edited by Leo Suryadinata (Singapore: Times Academic Press, 1995), pp. 20, 21.

14. For an elaboration of the Tapos meeting in March 1990, see Mely G. Tan, "The Social and Cultural Dimensions of the Role of the Ethnic Chinese in Indonesian Society", in *Indonesia (1991)*.

15. Suyono A.G., "Deklarasi Jimbaran, semoga tidak sekedar janji", in *Rekaman Peristiwa 1995* (Jakarta: Pustaka Sinar Harapan, 1996). (This is an annual publication comprising a selection of what the publishers consider the most prominent news items that appeared in the daily *Suara Pembaruan* in the past year.) The article questions to what extent this Declaration will be realized, considering previous efforts along this line that have not materialized. Among the 96 big businessmen who participated in the P-4 and subsequently were signatory to the Jimbaran Declaration, were such media figures as Liem Sioe Liong (Sudono Salim), his son Anthony Salim, Eka Tjipta Widjaja, Sofjan Wanandi, Prajogo Pangestu, William Suryajaya, Ciputra, Harry Darmawan (all ethnic Chinese), while among the ethnic Indonesians were noted Bambang Trihatmodjo and Sigit Hardjojudanto (second and first son of President Soeharto), and Aburizal Bakrie.

16. Stephen Suleeman, "Persepsi golongan keturunan Tionghoa Indonesia terhadap golongan bumi putera". *Skripsi Sarjana Ilmu Komunikasi*, (Universitas Indonesia, 1986), as quoted in Tan, "The Social and Cultural Dimensions", pp. 123, 124.

17. Gondomono, "The Chinese Community in Jakarta: A Study of Chinese Familism in an Indonesian Urban Environment" (Ph.D. dissertation in Anthropology at the University of California, Berkeley, 1990). This is one of the very few studies on the type of ethnic Chinese in Indonesia, who can be considered to belong to the so-called "lower middle class". This kind of study indicates that there are "other ethnic Chinese"; that only a small minority of ethnic Chinese fit the stereotype of being wealthy big businessmen.

18. This information was received from a key functionary of the Bakom-PKB.

19. On 13 May 1996, the Bakom-PKB under the new leadership organized a one-day seminar, in co-operation with the Lemhannas (the National Resilience Institute), with the Institute as the venue. As noted earlier, the General Chairperson (Ketua Umum) of the Bakom-PKB is also the Deputy Governor of the Lemhannas, and a professor of political science at the University of Indonesia. The theme of the seminar was "Negara Bangsa dalam Era Globalisasi" (The nation-state in the era of globalization). This theme and the presenters as well as the substance of the papers reflect the new approach as expounded by the chairperson. The keynote speech was given by the Minister of Defence, General (ret.) Edi Sudrajat. In his paper, he also referred to Indonesia as a nation that is not based on race, ethnicity or religion, but on shared intent, and the spirit to live as a nation (*bangsa*) within the same state,

disregarding differences in ethnicity, race, religion or group. The paper presenters included only one ethnic Chinese, the historian Onghokham. Another ethnic Chinese, James Riady (son of Mochtar Riady of the Lippo Group) was mentioned in the programme as "still to be confirmed", but he did not show up. All the others were ethnic Indonesian (except one of Indian descent) academics, mostly historians. There were also a playwright (the former chief editor of the banned tabloid *Detik*), a politician and member of the Indonesian Human Rights Commission, and a businessman.

References

Bachtiar, Harsja W. "Integrasi Nasional Indonesia". In *Wawasan Kebangsaan Indonesia. Gagasan dan Pemikiran Badan Komunikasi Penghayatan Kesatuan Bangsa*. Jakarta: Bakom-PKB Pusat, 1992.

Coppel, Charles A. *Indonesian Chinese in Crisis*. Kuala Lumpur: Oxford University Press, 1983.

Cushman, Jennifer and Wang Gungwu, eds., *Changing Identities of the Southeast Asian Chinese since World War II*. Hong Kong: Hong Kong University Press, 1988.

Gondomono. "The Chinese Community in Jakarta: A Study of Chinese Familism in an Indonesian Urban Environment". Ph.D. dissertation in Anthropology at the University of California, Berkeley, 1990.

Greif, Stuart William. *Indonesians of Chinese Origin. Assimilation and the Goal of "One Nation- One People"*. New York: Professors World Peace Academy, 1988.

Jahja, Junus, ed. *Non-pri di Mata Pribumi*. Jakarta: Yayasan Tunas Bangsa, 1991.

Mackie, J.A.C. and Charles A. Coppel. "A Preliminary Survey". In *The Chinese in Indonesia: Five Essays*, edited by J.A.C. Mackie, pp. 1–19. Sydney: Thomas Nelson (Australia) Ltd., 1976.

Naisbitt, John. *Megatrends Asia. The Eight Asian Megatrends that are Changing the World*. London: Nicholas Brealey, 1995.

Oetomo, Dede. "The Chinese of Pasuruan: A Study of Language and Identity in a Minority Community in Transition". Ph.D. thesis, Cornell University, 1984.

————. "Multilingualism and Chinese Identities in Indonesia". In *Changing Identities of the Southeast Asian Chinese since World War II*, edited by Jennifer Cushman and Wang Gungwu. Hong Kong: Hong Kong University Press, 1988.

Seagrave, Sterling. *Lords of the Rim*. London: Bantam Press, 1995.

Sidharta, Priguna. *Seorang Dokter dari Losarang. Sebuah Otobiografi*. Jakarta: P.T. Temprint, 1993.

Somers Heidhues, Mary F. "Peranakan Chinese Politics in Indonesia". Ph.D. thesis, Cornell University, 1965.

Somers Heidhues, Mary F. "Citizenship and Identity: Ethnic Chinese and the Indonesian Revolution". In Wang, ed., pp. 115–39.

Suleeman, Stephen. "Persepsi golongan keturunan Tionghoa Indonesia terhadap golongan Bumiputera". *Skripsi Sarjana Ilmu Komunikasi.* FISIP, Universitas Indonesia, 1986.

Suryadinata, Leo. *China and the ASEAN States: The Ethnic Chinese Dimension.* Singapore: Singapore University Press, 1985.

Tan, Mely G. "The Role of Ethnic Chinese Minority in Development: The Indonesian Case". *Southeast Asian Studies* (Centre for Southeast Asian Studies, Kyoto University, Kyoto, Japan) 25, no. 3 (December 1987): 63–82.

―――. "The Social and Cultural Dimensions of the Role of Ethnic Chinese in Indonesian Society". *Indonesia (1991)*, pp. 113–27.

―――. "The Ethnic Chinese in Indonesia: Issues and Implications". In *Southeast Asian Chinese. The Socio-cultural Dimension*, edited by Leo Suryadinata, pp. 13–28. Singapore: Times Academic Press, 1995.

Toer, Pramoedya Ananta and Stanley Adi Prasetyo, eds. *Memoar Oei Tjoe Tat. Pembantu Presiden.* Jakarta: Hasta Mitra, 1995.

Wang Gungwu. *China and the Chinese Overseas.* Singapore: Times Academic Press, 1991.

―――. "The Study of Chinese Identities in Southeast Asia". In Cushman and Wang, eds., op. cit., pp. 1–23.

Newspapers and Magazines:

Kompas, Suara Pembaruan, Media Indonesia, Media Indonesia Minggu, Suara Karya, Business News, Tempo, Gatra, Sinar.

Comments by

A. Dahana on

"The Ethnic Chinese in Indonesia: Issues of Identity"

Presented by Mely G. Tan

Before I begin, please allow me to say three things as an opening to my remarks. First, I would like to say thank you to the organizers of this conference for inviting me to participate. This is my first return to the Institute since 1982 when I was a research associate collecting data for my dissertation. Secondly, although my field of research is China, my main interest is Chinese affairs on mainland China. I am not an expert on ethnic Chinese in this region, although I always follow current developments in this area. Therefore, please regard my comments on Dr Tan's paper as additional information, rather than a discussion, coming from a layman based on observation and not as a critic from an academician. Thirdly, any discussion on the issues related to the ethnic Chinese in Indonesia will always involve controversy. Such old themes as whether or not they have been fully assimilated into Indonesian society and other related issues are still relevant for many people in Indonesia. The "Chinese problem" or *masalah Cina* is still in the minds of many people from various walks of life. Based on the fact that controversies still exist, I would like to present a different conclusion from that of Dr Tan.

To start with, I basically agree with all the data, information and arguments presented by Dr Tan. But let me begin my discussion by repeating the question she raised: "... it remains to be seen whether by the end of March 1996 the naturalization process will indeed be concluded". It is now April, and do we see the results? I am sorry to say that to my knowledge we are still waiting for something important.

My first impressions on the development of *pribumi–non-pribumi* relationship during the last thirty years is that it is no better nor worse than during the 1950s and 1960s. During the Soekarno era there were several ministers with ethnic Chinese background. Now we do not have even one. Perhaps if we were still under Soekarno, people such as Jusuf Wanandi and Harry Tjan — two of several prominent ethnic Chinese leaders mentioned by Dr Tan — would have been ministers or at least be in high positions in the bureaucracy or Golkar, the ruling party.

Although there is a clear distinction between the *peranakan* and the *totok* in the area of cultural orientation, the government's policy still treats and the Indonesian public still regards the Indonesian ethnic Chinese as a single entity. Although they are not barred from economic activities, their political participation and rights are to some extent still limited. Consequently, although I agree with Dr Tan that most of the Indonesian ethnic Chinese have fully identified themselves as Indonesians, there seems to be two tendencies which are not beneficial to the full assimilation of the ethnic Chinese into Indonesian society. On the one hand, most ethnic Chinese, both *totok* and *peranakan*, are active in business and trade, but on the other, there is a corps of bureaucrats dominated by the *pribumi*. This situation is more or less similar to the situation in Malaysia prior to the New Economic Policy (NEP). Consequently, there is still traditional mistrust and stereotyping of *pribumi* towards the non-*pribumi* and vice-versa. The ethnic Chinese are still identified with such attributes as: they are rich, economic animals, an exclusive group, unpatriotic, oriented towards China, having double loyalty, and so forth. The term *hoakiau* or *Cina perantauan* or "Overseas Chinese" is still widely used despite the fact that it is dated.

Secondly, as a consequence of the first factor, and in contrast to Dr Tan's argument that there is no such tendency among the ethnic Chinese to become more culturally Chinese and to search for a Chinese identity, there is concern and fear within the government and some segments of the Indonesian public that there is a "*totok*ization" process of the *peranakan* in the making. Take, for example, the popularity of learning Mandarin among young people of Chinese origin. Dr Tan has argued that learning Mandarin does not mean a return to being culturally Chinese or a search for a Chinese identity, but rather an act of survival in an era of globalization when the Asia-Pacific will play a greater role in world economic development as we enter the twenty-first century.

The Indonesian Government sees it differently. The interest in learning Mandarin is regarded as detrimental to the objective of the full assimilation of the Chinese. There is therefore a strict regulation regarding the teaching and learning of Mandarin.

The government's policy to eliminate any remnant of Chinese identity, like confining the Imlek celebrations to temples, homes and family circles, and the ban on Chinese characters from public display, is based on the consideration that it is for the purpose of national unity and for the complete assimilation of the Chinese into Indonesian society. However, the result is contrary to the objective as it makes most Chinese feel alienated. This tendency is clearly illustrated in Greif's study, that is, although they identify themselves as Indonesians, they are still different from the *pribumi*.

How does this feeling of being Indonesians but of Chinese origin fit into the assimilation process of the Chinese into Indonesian society? It is not enough to view this solely from the ethnic Chinese angle. Assimilation or integration is a two-way process, and it is therefore important to know how the *pribumi* identify the non-*pribumi*. This is a challenge for sociologists to do research on this issue. Most works we have today deal with the question of how the Chinese identify themselves within the changing Indonesian society. We have still to see works on how the *pribumi* see the Chinese. My observation is that the government's policy and the view of the Indonesian public towards the Indonesian ethnic Chinese have not changed. Therefore, I fully agree with Dr Tan's notion that "how [the Chinese] determine their identity ... depends very much on their assessment of the way the government and the majority of ethnic Indonesians perceive them". (p. 15)

I wish I could share Dr Tan's optimistic conclusion which she presented in the section "Prospects for the future" (pp. 13–16), in which she mentions that the tendency is towards "integration and identification as Indonesian, albeit still recognizing their Chinese origins". Again, based on my observations, the process of integration of the Indonesian Chinese has still a long way to go. For this I would like to discuss some examples she presents in the last part of her paper.

First, take the dramatic fate of two brothers, the late Professors Tjan Tjoe Som and Tjan Tjoe Siem. The two prominent academicians were Moslems and had become culturally Javanese. However, because of their participation in the left-leaning academic organization, both were dismissed from their professorships at the University of Indonesia following the political upheaval of 30 September 1965. It is because of the 1965 affair that most Indonesian Chinese, with the exception of a few, are now reluctant to participate in any political activity.

The short cut towards assimilation by converts into Islam, exemplified by Drs Junus Jahja and his group, is a new phenomenon and indeed very interesting to note. The group feels that the only way towards total assimilation is through abandoning their Chinese identity and conversion into the mainstream, that is, by becoming followers of Islam. The group is currently very active under the umbrella of Yayasan Abdul Karim Oei (Abdul Karim Oei Foundation) in efforts to spread the teachings of Islam among the Indonesian Chinese. With due respect to their efforts, however, it is unclear whether this strategy is popular among the ethnic Chinese and whether it can stand firm during times of crisis.

What about the role of the BAKOM-PKB? The government's hand in regulating the assimilation of the Chinese is sometimes regarded as too bureaucratic. People have no doubt about the good intentions of the officials and prominent people who sit on the central board of the organization. But some segments of the ethnic Chinese community feel that the assimilation process should be natural without too much interference from the authorities. Furthermore, most of my Chinese friends whom I spoke with said that the local boards of the organization at the provincial levels usually act only as a tool for soliciting financial contributions from the local Chinese communities for national and local celebrations.

As a final note, and this is again based on my observations, I see at least three factors which could be considered detrimental to the objectives of assimilation. The first factor is in the area of education. It is said that there is an unwritten regulation limiting the number of ethnic Chinese high school graduates entering state universities. This policy is based on three assumptions. First, since state universities have limited seats for new students, priority should be given to *pribumi* children. Secondly, since non-*pribumi* are economically better off than the *pribumi*, they would be able to send their children to expensive private universities or even to study abroad. Thirdly, if the number of ethnic Chinese children entering state universities is not limited, they will come to dominate the population in the universities. Again, this is an assumption, as Chinese children are usually graduates of private schools with academically high standards and would likely be more successful in the tight competition to enter state universities. Knowing that their chances are limited, many high school graduates of Chinese origin simply do not bother to participate in the examinations to enter state universities.

As a result, we see a trend which is not beneficial to the objective of integration of the ethnic Chinese into Indonesian society. The majority of the Chinese students are concentrated in certain private universities, or they study abroad. Studying abroad is currently popular among Indonesian high school graduates whose parents can afford it. My observation is that the majority of those who study abroad are students of Chinese origin.

The second factor is job distribution which I have mentioned earlier. Most Chinese are concentrated in trade and business activities, while native Indonesians mostly go into government service. Related to this, there is a strong belief among the public that collusion between Chinese businessmen and the Indonesian bureaucracy is rampant. This belief is fuelled by a strong suspicion that at high levels, there is collusion between élite members of the bureaucracy and the Chinese *cukong* (*taipans* or big business-men). This is further exacerbated by the existence of a economic gap between the poor and the rich and consequently, because the Chinese are always identified with the rich, any grudge or dis-satisfaction towards the government is always attributed to the Chinese. They have become scapegoats, since they are weak victims.

Lastly, the booming real estate business since the mid-1980s and early 1990s has created "new Chinatowns" in the big cities.

Take Jakarta as an example. Most occupants of new neighbour-hoods, especially in West and North Jakarta, are ethnic Chinese. The Indonesian capital city is unconsciously practising segregation between *pribumi* and non-*pribumi* in the way housing is arranged. The objective of national unity can only be achieved when all sections of the community can live together, understand each other, and be tolerant to differences.

Chapter 3
Malaysian Chinese:
Seeking Identity in Wawasan 2020

Lee Kam Hing

Introduction

The rise of China as a major regional power and the maintenance of a vibrant business network among the so-called "Overseas" Chinese have led some observers to look once again at the integration process of the ethnic Chinese within Southeast Asia. Some scholars and political leaders argue that the emerging international stature of China could conceivably encourage a cultural re-sinification of the Southeast Asian Chinese. This new concern comes at a time when increasing evidence suggest that the ethnic Chinese are integrating into the local Southeast Asian societies. In some countries, the Chinese have even progressed some way towards assimilation.

Within these new discussions, the question of the loyalty of the ethnic Chinese to the countries of domicile is sometimes raised and there is rekindled the previous suspicion of the Chinese in

Southeast Asia as potential fifth columnist. In the years after the communist take-over in 1949, China was seen by the West and in some Southeast Asian countries as an expansionist power and therefore a threat to the region's security. China was said to have supported armed insurgences in the region. Consequently, over the years the various Southeast Asian countries have engaged China differently. Where China is strongly perceived as a threat, the Chinese in those countries are liable to experience a stricter test of loyalty. There are now suggestions that the Chinese are using their networking to serve the economic interests of China. Reports of such economic linkages conjure up images of a broad Chinese economic sphere where the labour of mainland China combines with the marketing skills, technology, and capital of the overseas Chinese. Given this new economic and political stature of China, its supposed links with and influence on ethnic Chinese in Southeast Asia naturally arouse some unease. Observers have attributed China's impressive economic development to the inflow of large foreign investments, and some analysts estimate that nearly 80 per cent of these funds come from the "Overseas" Chinese who have invested largely in the southeastern part of China from where the ancestors of most of them had emigrated.[1] These journal reports, by highlighting the success of the Chinese overseas and their role not only in the economic emergence of China but also in the countries they presently reside, could cause hostile reactions against the Chinese especially in Southeast Asia, however unintended these may be.

Linking the Overseas Chinese and the rise of China sustains a persistent presumption that Beijing continues to command the affection of these local Chinese. Such a perception is not helpful to the integration process of the Southeast Asian Chinese. Indeed, it could be argued to the contrary that as the ethnic Chinese become more integrated, China would be less of a sentimental attraction. When this happens, there ought to be less doubts about the loyalty of the local Chinese, and governments will be more prepared for new economic and political engagements with China that are beneficial to all sides.

But the China factor counts as only one element in this integration process, and this is increasingly becoming of less importance. New social and cultural forces are emerging to reshape the national identity. Of these, renewed ethnic sentiments and religious resurgence are the two most powerful. They sometimes set new parameters for integration and inter-ethnic harmony. The dynamics of inter-ethnic relations are taking place within a context of regionalism and growing economic interdependence and these could determine how indigenous Southeast Asians view themselves, and in turn affect the way ethnic Chinese view themselves in the evolving society.

The situation of the Chinese in Malaysia differs significantly in some respects from that in other Southeast Asian countries. For a start, the community is, with the exception of Singapore, the largest in percentage terms. The Chinese form about 30 per cent of the population and they are able therefore to play some effective role within the Malaysian political system and to have their concerns seriously noted.[2] However, they are not large enough to ensure that all of their most crucial demands are met. There is also a very large Indian population of about 10 per cent as well as several indigenous minority groups. Many of the political and economic concerns affecting the Chinese are shared by the Indians, and therefore unlike elsewhere, the issues are not just Chinese but broad non-Malay ones. The Malaysian Indian Congress is able sometimes to win significant concessions because in representing a much smaller community it is seen as non-threatening, and in the process this has helped the Chinese. Not surprisingly therefore, some of the most articulate in representing Chinese issues in education and language are of Indian origin, such as the Seenivasagam brothers and presently, Karpal Singh.

Nearly half the Chinese in Malaysia live in the rural or semi-rural areas where they are by occupation farmers, fishermen, miners, and labourers. In 1980, 39 per cent of economically active Chinese were in production, transport and other worker category, 19 per cent were in agriculture and 9 per cent in the services. The Chinese are represented in the public service, and a much smaller number in the armed forces and the police. There are poor Chinese and of these many live in villages with inadequate resources. Represented in almost all spectrum and levels of economic life, it is difficult to generalize the Chinese in Malaysia as urban merchants, as might be the case in other countries. Some scholars suggested that many issues currently presented as ethnic issues may be appropriately looked at in class terms.

Nevertheless, the evolving inter-ethnic political balance is still essential to explain the nature of Malaysia's relations with China. Until Malay political power was assured, the government was wary of opening up ties with China. Malay sensitivity had to be considered especially at a time when there was still apprehension that too much political concessions had been given to the Chinese and to open up ties with China at that stage might not be acceptable to most Malays. It was also not wise to risk exposing the Chinese to possible competing loyalties at a time when many had just become citizens, and within the country adjustments were still being made to the new inter-ethnic co-operation.

Indeed, until the end of World War II, many Chinese saw themselves as transient, and the term "Overseas" Chinese or *Huaqiao* would be quite appropriate in referring to them. China was the sentimental homeland and the visits of political activists seeking moral and financial support sustained this attachment towards China. During that period too, successful Chinese from Southeast Asia invested in China. Linked together through trade in Southeast Asia these businessmen combined to open up enterprises in Fujian and Guangdong. Although they were essentially business ventures there was nevertheless also a sense of mission to help China modernize. The imperial Chinese Government sought out the expertise and investments of these Southeast Asian Chinese, and in recognition of their contribution conferred awards and appointed some as honorary Chinese consuls.[3]

Large-scale Chinese immigration into Malaya and their continued political attachment to China were noted by Malay nationalists. Then in June 1948 Malay unease with the local Chinese sharply increased when the mainly Chinese-backed Malayan Communist Party (MCP) launched a rebellion against the British. Founded in the 1920s, the MCP sought independence through revolutionary means. It claimed to be non-racial but its support came largely from young Chinese, who were mostly Chinese-educated and who felt that colonial policies had long discriminated against them in higher education or job opportunities. The MCP's links with the Chinese Communist Party also appealed to their feelings of Chineseness. Earlier, the Malayan People's Anti-Japanese Army (MPAJA), the precursor of the MCP and which had led a resistant movement during World War II, had exacted retribution on Malays whom they accused of collaborating with the Japanese. The Malays fought back and the violence assumed a racial dimension. The "Emergency" took on a further ethnic character when Malay troops joined in operations against the largely Chinese guerrillas.

In the early years of Malaysia's independence, Kuala Lumpur had no diplomatic relations with China. Malaysians were also not allowed to visit China. This was despite a growing trade between the two countries, particularly in rubber. In explaining its non-recognition of China, Kuala Lumpur contended that Beijing was supporting the MCP in the jungle war. The pro-West Tengku Abdul Rahman also saw China as a threat to regional security and, during the Sino-India border conflict, launched a "Save Democracy" fund in support of India in 1962. The Tengku's assessment seemed confirmed when in the 1963–65 period, Beijing aligned itself with Indonesia's confrontation against Malaysia.

For the older generation of Chinese, the government's China policy cut off all social visits. Given the political atmosphere of the Emergency, it was not possible to argue against this policy. The Tengku developed links with Taiwan instead. The Malaysian Government allowed travel to Taiwan for business and education. Several hundred Malaysian students, mainly from Chinese schools, enrolled each year in Taiwanese universities.[4] A trade mission was sent to Taiwan in November 1965.

It was under the premiership of Tun Abdul Razak that Malaysia opened up relations with China. Tun Razak wanted to shift away from the country's largely pro-West foreign policy. By then too, the MCP as a serious military threat was destroyed and remnant units were confined largely to the Thai-Malaysian border. In 1974 Tun Razak made an official visit to Beijing. With a reputation as a Malay nationalist, Razak's China initiatives were generally trusted by the Malays.

Despite the opening of ties, domestic concern continued to shape the nature of the relations. There was still the links between the Chinese Communist Party (CCP) and the MCP that bothered Malaysia. Secondly, despite Beijing's rejection of dual nationality during the 1974 discussions, Kuala Lumpur believed that China was still treating returning Malaysian Chinese as Overseas Chinese. It noted that the Office for Overseas Chinese was restored in 1978. The newly-opened relations with China was consequently placed on a government to government basis.[5] Travel to China by Malaysians was still banned but this was eventually relaxed to allow social visits for those over the age of sixty. Private traders could buy from Chinese corporations or through agents in Hong Kong or Singapore. But Pernas, the national trading company, was granted supervisory power and the responsibility to encourage Malay participation in the China trade. However, in the 1974–84 period, while the volume of Malaysia-China trade grew, its percentage in overall Malaysian trade declined from 3.5 to 1.5 per cent.

Developing New Malaysia-China Relations

Under Prime Minister Dato Seri Dr Mahathir Mohamad, Malaysia enhanced ties with China. This was part of Dr Mahathir's shift towards an emphasis on East Asia. Described as "controlled relationship", the government allowed businessmen to visit China. Travel to China was subsequently opened to all Malaysians. In 1985, there were about 250 Malaysian companies trading there. In November that year, Dr Mahathir led a large trade and investment delegation of about 130 businessmen on an official visit to China. Four major trade agreements were signed during the visit. Since then, relations between Malaysia and China have continued to improve with the exchange of official visits. Dr Mahathir has made three more officials visits to China, the most recent being in August 1996. The growing congruence in interest of the two countries was highlighted during the first Malaysia-China Forum held in Kuala Lumpur in January 1995. Dr Mahathir, in his keynote address, indicated that Malaysia does not regard China as a military or political threat, noting that China's military spending is less than that of Japan, Korea, and the United States. In turn, President Jiang Zemin declared China's support of the EAEC (East Asian Economic Caucus) proposal by Malaysia during his official visit to Kuala Lumpur in November 1995.[6]

In 1993, bilateral trade between Malaysia and China was worth over RM6 billion. This was an almost seventeenfold increase, compared to trade figures of twenty years earlier. By 1994, it had reached RM8.5 billion.[7] Over the years, China had been among the largest buyers of Malaysian rubber and since 1994 it had also become the biggest importer of Malaysian palm oil. The sharp growth in trade between Malaysia and China in the last few years has been due, in part, to the recession during the mid-1980s as well as the liberalization in trade ties between the two countries. During the recession, a number of Malaysian Chinese companies ventured overseas, including China, in search of investment opportunities.

In 1994, it was reported that thirty-six large corporations listed on the Kuala Lumpur Stock Exchange had signed Memoranda of Understanding (MOU) or joint-venture agreements with China, with an estimated value of RM8 billion. These agreements included highway and power plant construction, financial services, manufacturing, and retail. Many of these contracts were entered into by corporations such as Petronas, Renong, UMW (United Motor Works), Hicom, and Eon which have predominant Malay or government equity. Other Malay groups have since joined in. In October 1994, Bornian Corporation reportedly joined a consortium of contractors from China and Malaysia to construct the RM700 million hydroelectric power plant in Liwagu. The consortium was also to build twenty 50-megawatt power stations at the Dalian Economic Zone.[8] Sateras, another *bumiputra* (indigenous) company, is moving into the car assembly business in China.

A number are joint Sino-Malay ventures. In June 1993 during Dr Mahathir's visit to China, Bridgecon Engineering Sendirian Berhad, headed by Datuk Wan Adli Wan Ibrahim, joined a consortium of Malaysian companies that included the Berjaya Group (Cayman) and Country Heights Construction in an agreement to construct the Second Nanjing Yangtze River Bridge. Kuala Lumpur Industries, under its chairman Tan Sri Wan Sidek Hj Wan Abdul Rahim, signed an MOU with Ping An Insurance Company of China to set up a representative office of its subsidiary company, People's Insurance Company (M) Sdn. And Tengku Ahmad

Rithauddeen, formerly the foreign minister and now chairman of Road Builder announced plans to diversify into China.

The two Malaysian companies usually cited as most successful in China are Kanzen and Lion Corporation. Though largely Chinese, both Kanzen and Lion Corporation have significant Malay equity.[9] In 1986, Lim Kim Hong who started Dreamland Corporation, which later became Kanzen, signed an agreement with Dreamland Tianjin Pte Ltd to produce and market mattresses. Dreamland Malaysia held 40 per cent of the equity. By 1990 Dreamland had established eight factories in different parts of China. The Lion Corporation is presently engaged in various development projects in China but its most successful is the retail business where it has opened a chain of Parkson stores. The success of Kanzen and Lion are looked upon as examples in which Chinese business skills and networking have worked to the advantage of Malaysian business in China.

Some Malaysian Chinese groups certainly hope to benefit from such cultural affinity and networking to enhance business opportunities in China. In May 1995, it was reported that the Federation of Hokkien Associations of Malaysia proposed to set up an industrial park in Fujian province. A mission led by its president, Datuk Lim Gaik Tong, surveyed the area of Xiamen, Chuan Chou and Fu Zhu to look for a 2,000 hectare site. It also planned to set up a one-stop agency to assist Malaysians investing in Fujian. The delegation also visited China to promote the second World Fujian Clan Conference to be held in Kuala Lumpur in August 1996.[10]

While numerous MOUs and contracts have been signed, the number that have actually been carried out is relatively low. Many companies have merely joined in as part of the present rush to China, attracted by the prospects but finding projects difficult to take off. Various companies have prematurely made announcements of obtaining gaming concessions from different provincial governments. There is also the suspicion that these company statements were intended to interest investors, especially in the stock market. Furthermore, Malaysia's investments in China make up only a fraction of total foreign funds.

Mahathir's New Society

Malaysia's growing trade links with China should be seen in the context of Dr Mahathir's effort to take the country to a developed status by the year 2020. This aim of achieving developed status, now popularly referred to as Wawasan 2020, was first outlined in a speech he made to the inaugural meeting of the Malaysian Business Council in 1991. To achieve this goal, there is to be liberalization in trade and investments. New infrastructure are being built and a multi-media super corridor planned to ensure that Malaysia would be a developed nation by the year 2020. The recent expansion of private tertiary education and the use of English are to open up educational opportunities and to turn the country into a regional learning centre. Through these, Dr Mahathir wants Malaysia to play a more influential role in international trade and diplomacy.

In the speech in 1991, Dr Mahathir also gave his vision of a new and united society by the year 2020 and expressed the hope that a people who would be entirely Malaysian in perspective, that is, a truly *bangsa Malaysia*, would emerge. This *bangsa* would help the nation to be confident, democratic, liberal, tolerant, caring, and instilled with strong moral and ethical values. He spoke of the economy being competitive, dynamic, robust and resilient and its wealth justly and equitably distributed to create a progressive and prosperous population. The idea of a *bangsa Malaysia* continues to appear in Dr Mahathir's statements.

The new policies are significant to inter-ethnic relations and they certainly reflect a very confident Malay leadership. Dr Mahathir's policies suggest that he sees the struggle of Malay nationalism as broadening towards a more international framework. Success for Malaysia in international economics would be an achievement for Malay nationalism. Assured of political dominance and growing influence in the economy, the leadership is willing to adopt policies beneficial to the country even if these at first appear to initially favour the non-Malays. Seeking greater regional and international economic participation would undoubtedly benefit the Chinese. But already, major corporate changes have created Malay conglomerates such as Renong, MCRB, Sapura, and Arab-Malaysian Finance, which are equally capable of entering into ambitious ventures overseas. Malaysia's multi-ethnic character can be turned into a strength. Its standing as a Muslim-majority country helps Malaysia in dealing with the Middle East and Muslim Central Asia, while its businessmen of Indian and Chinese origin are competing strongly in South and East Asia respectively.

Although not defined, non-Malays reacted very favourably to the idea of a *bangsa Malaysia*. The term conveys the notion of a *bangsa Malaysia* that is still evolving and not one where an existing *bangsa* is to be imposed on the rest. Recent loosening of government regulations have given non-Malays grounds to be optimistic about the commitment of senior Malay leaders towards such a goal. More recently, Dr Mahathir in declaring open the second World Hokkien Conference said that Malaysia accepts multi-culturalism and that while "the Malay language is the national and official language, the languages and cultures of the other races will be preserved."[11] Opening a world Hokkien conference was already a significant gesture, but even more important was his statement that the different roots of the people should not affect their loyalty to the nation.

Equally significant was the launching in August 1996 of a three billion ringgit investment fund to be managed by the government, which would be open to all Malaysians between the ages of 12 and 20. In the past, all government-managed investment funds such as the Amanah Saham Nasional, which have yielded very attractive dividends and bonuses, had been reserved for Malays. If any one institution symbolized the affirmative action of the government to help the Malays, it surely must be the Amanah Saham Nasional. This had resulted in considerable resentment from the other races. This time round, 49 per cent of the issues will be for non-Malays. Launched by Dr Mahathir, the new Amanah Saham Wawasan 2020 is an affirmation that young Malaysians of all races have a stake in the future of the country.[12]

The idea of *bangsa Malaysia* outlined by Dr Mahathir is an ideal sought by leaders of all the major communities. Gaining broad acceptance will be challenging and by presenting this idea Dr Mahathir affirms a confidence that the country has achieved a degree of consensus among the various communities to begin putting it into place. If indeed *bangsa Malaysia* is interpreted as replacing the different existing *bangsa*, or at the least that all *bangsa* are subsumed under *bangsa Malaysia*, this would represent major progress in the thinking of all sides. Certainly, for a long time there had been reservations towards such an idea.

For the Malays, the struggle had always been for a *bangsa Melayu* (Malay nation). The Malays had earlier seen an independent Malaya more as a restoration of the old Malay sultanates. Malaya was a Malay country with fully developed indigenous political institutions and cultural symbols. The period of British rule was merely an interruption, and independence in 1957 was a return to the original course of Malay history and identity. In emphasizing a historical continuity of Malay identity and with Islam defining that identity, *bangsa Melayu* strictly would exclude all non-Malays. For some early Malay nationalists, this indeed was the goal of the struggle. When it became clear that the political realities required accommodating the non-Malays, the term *bangsa Melayu* was still insisted on for the new nationality. Granting citizenship to large numbers of immigrants was a major concession to be reciprocated by the new citizens acknowledging Malay rights and the continuity of a Malay character in the new nation. But since a central feature in the original *bangsa Melayu* is Islam, the application of this term broadly to include non-Muslims raised difficulties and consequently found little support among both Malays and non-Malays.

Early Inter-ethnic Co-operation
The willingness of the Malaysian Government to move towards what the Chinese regard as a more liberal and tolerant approach, both in domestic politics and in dealing with China, stems from a decisive power shift favouring the Malays. Until then, the inter-ethnic political equilibrium appeared more evenly balanced. The early inter-ethnic balance was created immediately after the war and was maintained on the basis of trust among the major races. It took considerable bargaining to fashion out a basis of inter-ethnic co-operation within which the interests of the Chinese, the Malays, and other races were accommodated, but this coalition always came under pressure from the communal demands of all sides. The inter-ethnic understanding could be forged at a crucial moment in the country's history because of expected political

change and because there was sufficient shift in the political orientation of the Chinese.

It was only towards World War II that some Chinese realized the need to work for a political future of the community in Malaya. They were beginning to be aware of impending political changes as nationalist stirrings in Asia were already having an impact on Malaya. Malay political consciousness was in evidence especially in the growth of radical and religious organizations. Gradually, therefore, the political orientation of some Chinese turned to issues affecting them in Malaya. They began to talk about independence, of a new Malayan society, and the role of the Malayan Chinese in this change.

It was this new consciousness that began to provide some common direction to what was then a very disparate group of Chinese. The Chinese were divided along dialect and district lines. There was the division between those born in China and those born locally. Among the local born there were those who had incorporated elements of Malay culture. Even among this group, referred to as *peranakan* but more popularly as Baba, there developed differences between those in Penang and Malacca, and those Chinese long domiciled in Kelantan who manifest a variant of the Baba culture. But the major cleavage within the Chinese community was that between the Chinese- and the English-educated. Representing the diverse background as well as occupational and economic interests of the different Chinese groups in the country were a host of associations and organizations. These included chambers of commerce, clan and guild associations as well as organizations of the Chinese educationists.

One of the first groups to assume a leadership role of the Chinese was the English-educated. Many were Straits-born and a number came from families which had been in Malaya for several generations. The Straits Chinese, such as Tan Cheng Lock, enjoyed some early links with British and Malay political leaders. Tan Cheng Lock and his associates had long developed business connections with British firms.[13] They had served in representative bodies such as the Chinese Advisory Boards, the Legislative Council, and the state councils. There was early contact with Malay radicals but eventually it was with Dato Onn Jaafar and

UMNO (United Malays National Organization) that the MCA (Malaysian Chinese Association) leaders evolved a sustained political relationship. UMNO was formed in 1946 to mobilize Malay opinion against the Malayan Union, a constitutional change which threatened the special status of the Malays.

There were also the Chinese-educated who had for long played an important social and political leadership role within the Chinese community. They commanded more influence, and represented a much broader spectrum of social, cultural, and economic interests of the Chinese than the English-educated. While some had involved themselves in the politics of China, others were just as concerned with the future of the local Chinese and in particular the status of Chinese education and culture. There was a re-orientation away from China and many of them believed strongly that the Chinese as citizens in a new Malayan nation should be given the right to maintain their identity, and that this could only be possible through preserving the use of the Chinese language in the country. Through the school boards, the Chinese-educated merchants were brought into contact with the influential Chinese educationist groups.[14]

The Chinese-educated and the English-educated got together just after the start of the "Emergency" to form an expressly Chinese party, the Malayan Chinese Association. The leaders of both groups were mainly businessmen involved in tin, rubber, and trade, and they had much to lose should the communists win the jungle war. The British believed that it was from these two groups that an alternative leadership of the Chinese should be encouraged if the communists were to be defeated. The "Emergency" continued to be difficult despite British deployment of some 40,000 regular and 70,000 auxiliary troops, and the support of the Chinese was therefore essential.[15] A credible Chinese leadership was needed because this was also a period when constitutional changes were being negotiated and the large Chinese community could not be entirely ignored.

Thus, at the most crucial juncture in the political history of Malaysia, the MCA was formed to provide a leadership acceptable to the British and the Malays as well as to a fair section of the Chinese population. The Western-educated within the party were able to convince the British and the Malays that the Chinese were loyal and committed to political goals similar to theirs. The Chinese-educated leadership won some significant support of the Chinese community and thereby demonstrated to the British and the Malays that the MCA was a credible Chinese party. The Chinese-educated leadership achieved this because of their commitment to Chinese education and Chinese culture, being aware that these must be prominent in the agenda of the party if it was to gain the support of the community. In this, they were backed by the Western-educated who agreed that Chinese language and education were essential to preserving the identity of the community.

The MCA continued to play a key part in ensuring some political role for the Chinese in Malaysia at this crucial juncture. It helped thousands of Chinese to register as citizens and thereby to be eligible in the political process. The MCA also raised money to assist nearly half a million Chinese who had been resettled in 550 new villages across the country. The party provided representation to many Chinese suspected of communist links and threatened with deportation to China. The MCA leaders were alarmed that the British were arbitrary in the arrest of mostly Chinese. Such actions reflected the prevailing assumption held by the British and to some extent the Malays, of guilt of the entire Chinese community. Certainly, this was not helped by the fact that hundreds of Chinese youth returned to China rather than be called up in the general mobilization against the communists. But against this, several hundred MCA members were assassinated in the course of the "New Village" work by the MCP. Home guards in Perak formed by the Chinese protected tin-mines and fought the communists. The MCA thus provided a leadership for those Chinese not implicated in the rebellion.

In 1952 and 1955, the MCA combined successfully with UMNO and the Malayan Indian Congress (MIC) to win newly-introduced local elections. The MCA leaders, realizing how damaging the "Emergency" had been on the political position of the Chinese, decided that it was through working with the Malays that they could rebuild a credible role. The leadership of UMNO accepted the MCA, recognizing that unless there was some demonstration of multi-racial co-operation, significant constitutional concessions could not be obtained. To expedite progress towards independence, the leaders of the major communities agreed to some accommodation on various contentious issues. The Alliance memorandum to the Reid Constitution Commission was a compromise against a background of competing demands from the different communities.

Overall, the constitution favoured the Malays. This was because the thrust of nationalism had come from the Malays and because some colonial administrators believed that the British, having signed the earlier treaties in 1874 with the Sultans allowing for intervention, had an obligation to protect the interests of the indigenous communities. Furthermore, during the communist insurrection, the Malays had proved politically reliable. The constitution recognized the special status of the Malay language, Islam, and the Malay sultanates, and it provided for special privileges to assist the Malays, the majority of whom then were rural and poor.[16] But important concessions were also made to the non-Malays. The most important of these was that citizenship conditions for non-Malays were liberalized. Equally important was that the non-Malays were allowed to use their languages and to practise their cultures, including the freedom of religion.

The constitution and inter-ethnic co-operation were possible because of an unwritten understanding arrived at between the MCA and UMNO leaders. Under this, the Malays would have political power while the Chinese would retain economic influence. Neither side realized at that time the full implications of the bargain nor did the leaders articulate clearly what they expected from it. The Chinese thought that what they then conceded was political pre-eminence rather than dominance. The MCA leaders generally conceived of Malaya as a new nation whose cultural identity was to be created, and within this evolving entity Chinese culture and language would be granted equal status. This assumption was argued on the principle that equality of status is the entitlement of all citizens. Sometimes, the more chauvinistic would contend that equality has been earned through the contribution of non-Malay immigrant labour in building modern Malaya.

Tension in Inter-ethnic Coalition

However, once the expediency and urgency of decolonization were
no more, stresses in inter-ethnic relations emerged. All sides had
not been entirely happy with the different provisions in the constitution. In the years after independence, many Chinese complained that the constitutional bargain had seriously weakened the
position of the community. This was reflected in the composition
of the government and in Parliament. Although forming nearly 38
per cent of the population, Chinese-majority seats in parliament
was slightly less than a third. This discrepancy was due to weightage
favouring the rural areas which were predominantly Malay. But it
was the Chinese-educated who felt most aggrieved, pointing out
that Chinese education and language were not accorded the recognition as had been expected. Chinese was not recognized as an
official language and Chinese-language secondary education was
not part of the national school system. They feared that Chinese
features were being peripheralized in the course of developing a
national culture. There was also the grievance that few Chinese
were given scholarships and their quota for public service appointment was very low. Many Chinese felt that the newly gained
citizenship had not offered equal rights and entitlements.

Even as the Chinese began to regard Malaya as their new
home, a persistent demand from the Malays was that acceptance
of them rested on the demonstration of new loyalties. This new
loyalty was more than just abandoning political attachments to
the old homeland. It was required that symbols of the new state
be embraced. But there was disagreement regarding the range of
such symbols and how much of the Chinese distinctives could be
included, and over the years these have become a source of tension
in inter-ethnic relations. Consensus has not been easy because of
the significant size of the community, the economic role it plays,
and its immigrant background. Given the community's size, it
will take a longer time for integration, and this leads to the
accusation of its unwillingness to be an indistinguishable part of
a larger society. Its immigrant background has been convenient to
the more communal elements who, by pointing to the past when
the Chinese in Malaysia had sought inspiration from political

developments in China, question the commitment and loyalty of the Chinese.

As in the MCA, the moderate Malay leadership itself faced pressure from Malay frustration. Despite various programmes, the economic position of the Malays was still depressed. Malays continued to have a lower per capita income and a higher unemployment rate than the Chinese. For the cultural nationalists, there was disappointment that English and not Malay was widely used for official purposes. For the religious groups, there was unhappiness that Islamic laws were not introduced. Thus, for many Malays, what had been promised in the independence struggle had not been fulfilled.

So long as this political unhappiness of the various communities was contained within the coalition through regular consultation, inter-ethnic relations were kept at a manageable level. However, as these issues came to be taken up by the opposition, the attacks began to erode the coalition's electoral standing. The MCA, in particular, lost in local elections in Penang and in Seremban to the Labour Party and in Ipoh to the People's Progressive Party. In such circumstances, the mechanism of accommodation within the coalition came under stress. This happened when members from the ruling coalition publicly took up opposition issues and the solidarity within the coalition came to be severely tested. There had been expectations that the leaders of the different communities would be loyal to the mechanism of inter-ethnic political consultation and committed to the terms of the political understanding. But the ruling élites had increasingly to contend with strong pressure from their communities.

Just two years after independence, the difficulties faced by inter-ethnic coalition came out into the open. The MCA, under pressure through electoral losses, was anxious that there should not be any changes made to the federal constitution which could be disadvantageous to the Chinese. It therefore asked for a third of the seats to be contested in the impending elections. More importantly, the party wanted a review of the Education Act, especially the position of Chinese-language education. This demand was a response to the Chinese educationists and the traditional guilds and associations which were then strong within the party.

The growing electoral strength of Parti Islam, which prompted the MCA's two demands, was seen by UMNO as an even more serious threat to it, and the Prime Minister then, Tengku Abdul Rahman, certainly felt unable to make the concessions asked by the MCA without incurring a serious Malay backlash. The Tengku turned down the MCA's demands, and the party's leadership eventually resigned.[17] The 1959 crisis led to a withdrawal of support from the MCA by the influential Chinese educationists.

The position of the MCA was further eroded when the People's Action Party (PAP) entered Malaysia and rallied the non-Malays under the slogan of a Malaysian Malaysia. The PAP was more articulate and forceful than the MCA had been, and the Malaysian Malaysia concept encapsulated the main aspirations of the non-Malays in language, culture as well as equal opportunities to scholarships and to government employment. A Malaysian Malaysia required the features of identity of the nation to be less Malay and more representative of the other races. A Malaysian Malaysia was a rejection of some of the symbols of loyalty insisted on by the Malays. In August 1965, the Tengku decided that the separation of Singapore was necessary to ease the racial tension arising from the PAP's Malaysian Malaysia campaign.

The separation of Singapore did not end the debate and the call for a Malaysian Malaysia was taken up by the DAP (Democratic Action Party) and other non-Malay parties such as Parti Gerakan Rakyaat Malaysia and the PPP (People's Progressive Party). So appealing was such a call that the opposition made significant gains against the ruling coalition, particularly the MCA, in the 1969 elections. The disappointment of the election results and the celebration of opposition supporters led to the worst inter-ethnic riots ever in the country.[18] What aggravated the tension was that the strain in relations between UMNO and the MCA had become evident, and this led to the withdrawal of the latter from the government.

Establishment of a More Malay Character to the State

For twenty months following the riots, the country was ruled by the National Operation Council. By the time the country returned to parliamentary government, changes had been set in motion

both through the creation of new institutions and in amendments
to the constitution that decisively shifted the political balance in
favour of the Malays. Malay political dominance was firmly established. The ruling coalition was retained and the appearance of
sharing political power among the races maintained. But in effect
it was UMNO that dominated and that decided on all major
issues. This dominance was backed by a bureaucracy and an armed
forces that was predominantly Malay. The ruling coalition was
enlarged and this consequently weakened the MCA. The MCA
could no longer claim to be the sole party representing the Chinese
in government and any threat of withdrawal would not have the
same menacing effect as had been the case in 1959 and 1969. The
MCA soon lost the finance and trade portfolios which had given
assurance and access to Chinese business. Within a constellation
of fourteen members, UMNO dominance became more pronounced.[19] With that, an even more Malay character of the state
and of the new symbols of loyalty was insisted upon.

The government introduced the New Economic Policy to re-
dress the economic gap between the Malays and the non-Malays.
Attention was given to creating a Malay commercial class so that
Malay equity participation in the corporate sector would be raised
from 1.9 per cent in 1970 to 30 per cent by the end of the Plan.[20]
A new education policy converted the schools into a largely Malay-
language system and a quota system was introduced to ensure
improved Malay access to higher education. Malay culture was
recognized as the basis of a national culture during a conference
on the subject held in 1971. Only elements from the culture of
the other communities deemed suitable would be accepted into
the national culture.

Business activities became more regulated, and large and
successful Chinese companies came under pressure to restructure
to allow Malay participation. Licences and contracts were largely
reserved for Malays or state-backed Malay enterprises. In other
sectors, the non-Malays complained of restricted appointment and
promotion opportunities in the public service. In education, the
enrolment of Chinese in the local universities fell in percentage
terms. Of continued concern to the Chinese was that Chinese-

medium secondary schools did not receive government financial backing or recognition.

As these changes were taking place, there was observed a strong resurgence of Islam. Calls from PAS (Parti Islam se Malaysia) as well as Muslim leaders associated with UMNO were made for the implementation of the syariah and the setting up of an Islamic state. Many Chinese feared that within such a state their status and identity would be further subordinated. Naturally, there was apprehension among the non-Malays when Dr Mahathir, on taking office in 1981, declared a policy of introducing Islamic values in administration. The establishment of Islamic banking, insurance, and in 1983 the International Islamic University appeared to be determined steps towards a more Islamic character of the state. Moves such as that in 1989 when the Selangor government amended the Islamic Administration Enactment Act granting those who had reached puberty the right to convert without their parents' permission heightened such fears. Non-Muslim religious groups faced increasing difficulties in getting land for temples and churches, and laws were gazetted by states prohibiting the use of certain Malay words for worship.

Chinese Response
In the face of the major restructuring within society the Chinese debated on the most effective adjustments. The options were either to encourage greater communal solidarity or to move towards a less communal posture and to seek new relationships with Malay political and economic power. Both responses were tried out at much the same time. But the initial and instinctive response to develop greater political cohesion within the community gained much attention. At the political front, there was popular support to reform and to revitalize the MCA. In 1973, young Chinese launched the Chinese Unity Movement, believing that Chinese interests could best be defended through a strong communally-based organization to bargain effectively with the Malays.[21] They argued that Malay gains had been achieved because of political unity through UMNO. They therefore hoped to bring back the groups such as the traditional associations and the Chinese educationists which had once provided the popular support of

the MCA. However, the reform effort failed largely because the association and educationists as well as the merchants no longer saw the MCA as being able to represent their interests.

Some Chinese also turned to communal solidarity to defend their economic position that was being seriously eroded by expanding corporate Malay interests. Many Chinese business groups felt threatened because government-backed enterprises such as Pernas, the Urban Development Authority (UDA) and state development corporations had steadily acquired commanding stakes in the country's banking, mining, plantations and trading sectors. Some Chinese, therefore, turned to the traditional associations to mobilize resources and to modernize the networking of Chinese business. The Hainanese, for example, set up Grand United Holdings. The Associated Chinese Chambers of Commerce itself started an investment arm.

Others created new forms, the most significant of which was Multi-Purpose Holdings (MPHB). Initiated by the MCA, the MPHB aimed at protecting Chinese economic interests. Hoping to be like the state-backed Malay PNB (Permodalan Nasional Berhad) it sought to mobilize the resources of the Chinese to retain participation in key economic sectors and to modernize traditional Chinese business. The MCA argued that going back to the dialect associations to help out would keep the Chinese divided, and in any case the associations did not have the skills and resources to match the new Malay institutions. It was thought that with MCA sponsorship the MPHB would be acceptable to the Malays and the other Chinese.[22]

The period 1981–87 was marked by a series of open irritants in inter-ethnic relations. All sides were still adjusting to the post-1969 economic and political changes. Some of the inter-ethnic differences were made more difficult because of the economic recession of the mid-1980s. The Malay political leadership was also going through a phase of uncertainty. Dr Mahathir had just taken over as Prime Minister from Dato Hussein Onn and he had not fully consolidated his leadership within the party. There were to be contests for the deputy President's post in 1982 and 1984, and he himself was later to be challenged.

Business competition entered into inter-ethnic relations and was to become a new source of tension within the coalition. In 1984 MPHB, which held 40 per cent of the UMBC (United Malayan Banking Corporation) shares sought to gain the 10 per cent held by the estate of Chang Ming Tien, which would have given it a controlling stake. UMBC was then the third largest bank in the country. The other major shareholder was Pernas, which had been set up to assist the Malays in trade. The plan came to be known to UMNO and the matter was raised in a heated debate in the 1984 general assembly. MPHB's move was opposed because some delegates saw it as contrary to the goals of the New Economic Policy. The party's youth wing strongly opposed the MPHB's intention. In the end, neither MPHB nor Pernas, the other major shareholder, gained control. But the issue helped Dato Musa Hitam to defeat Tengku Razaleigh Hamzah who was then known to be close to Chinese business groups.

Language and culture continued to be of concern to the Chinese, and these, together with related issues, aroused considerable passion. Changes proposed by the authorities were often seen as threatening the cultural and religious interests of the non-Malays, especially that of the Chinese. What particularly troubled supporters of Chinese education was a provision in the 1971 Education Act which allowed the Education Minister to convert a national-type Chinese-medium primary school into a Malay-medium school. The Dong Jiao Zhong, a body representing Chinese school teachers and management formed in 1954, sought to have the provision removed. The Chinese educationists also campaigned for the setting up of a Chinese-language university. In August 1974, a limited company was formed to start the Merdeka University which intended to provide opportunities for higher education to those coming out of the private Chinese secondary schools. Chinese educationists argued that there was a real need for such an institution, especially as Nanyang University in Singapore was being merged into the National University of Singapore. The application to establish the Merdeka University was turned down and a legal case taken up in the courts was equally unsuccessful.

In October 1987, inter-ethnic tension reached a dangerous point when a decision was made by the Education Ministry to promote non-Mandarin-speaking teachers as senior assistants in national-type Chinese primary schools. Chinese educationists feared that the appointments would be a step towards altering the character of Chinese education, with irreversible consequences. So strongly felt was the concern that leaders of Chinese-based parties within the coalition took up the matter. Senior leaders of the MCA and the Gerakan joined the DAP and educational organizations at a meeting in the Thean Hou Temple to declare solidarity in protecting Chinese education.

In defending Chinese language and culture, there was a continuing consciousness and desire that these features be recognized as part of the Malaysian identity. Chinese educationists rejected criticisms that Chinese language and culture were archaic and alien. They pointed out that Mandarin and the major dialects spoken in Malaysia had acquired Malay terms and features that distinguished them from those used in China and Taiwan. There was also a contention that in its evolution, Chinese culture in Malaysia had become part of the country's heritage and was inseparable from its history. There was therefore strong objection when in 1984 the Malacca state government proposed to develop Bukit China into a commercial area. Bukit China is a sprawling Chinese cemetery that dates back to the fifteenth century and which the Chinese community regards as historically significant. The proposed clearing of part of Bukit China for development was seen as an attempt to obliterate the community's historical presence and links to the nation's identity.

The Chinese also took offence when in 1986 several Malay intellectuals began using the terms *kaum immigran* and *kaum pendatang* when referring to the non-Malays. Some Chinese objected to the use of such terms and believed that these were attempts at distinguishing different classes of citizens. This was, it was argued, inimical to efforts towards full integration of all its citizens. In seeking to popularize the terms, the Malay intellectuals sought to emphasize once again the indigenous Malay character or, as they described it, the definitive features of the state. But some of the retaliatory statements from Chinese leaders, such as the claim that those Malays originating from elsewhere in the archipelago were also immigrants, aroused Malay anger.

The efforts by the Chinese towards political or economic solidarity disturbed the Malays. These moves were viewed as continuing Chinese communal challenge to the new power balance. UMNO, while desiring a coalition partner which enjoyed respectable Chinese support, would now tolerate only domesticated Chinese-based parties without their more communal Chinese links. There could be no return to the seeming political parity of the Alliance Party structure.

The UMNO Youth debate in 1984 over the UMBC shares represented an example of strong Malay reaction to the perceived Chinese economic and political challenge. Even more emotional was the response of UMNO Youth to the October 1987 Chinese school issue. In reaction to the Thean Hou Temple meeting of Chinese leaders, thousands of UMNO youth members held a rally a few days later in support of the Education Ministry's decision at the TPCA stadium. Racial tension heightened so dangerously that there were fears that disturbances similar to that in May 1969 would occur. The crisis was averted when the Prime Minister banned another proposed UMNO rally and ordered the arrest of some 118 people for, among other reasons, allegedly inciting communal feelings.

In the light of these developments, some Chinese leaders suggested that continued Chinese political visibility was no advantage to the community. The option was to adopt a non-communal approach where the interests of all ethnic groups were to be fought for without distinction. They believed that relying on communal solidarity would only encourage racial polarization and retard integration. The formation of Gerakan, the Sarawak United People's Party (SUPP) and the DAP were efforts towards a non-racial political approach. But these parties have been unable to break out of their largely Chinese mould in membership and in articulation of issues. The Chinese character of the non-communal parties has become even more pronounced in recent years with the increase in their membership of the largely Mandarin-speaking. In the MCA, for instance, about 75 per cent of its members are Mandarin-speaking. The leadership of the Chinese-based parties is still largely held by the English-educated but in the future fluency in all three languages of Chinese, English, and Malay would be essential. The lack of progress of the non-communal parties is also due to the preference by the major communities to be represented by other communal parties such as UMNO and MIC.

Reaction to Recent Mahathir Initiatives

The recent policies and gestures from the Malay political leadership under Dr Mahathir are acknowledged as being more open and tolerant and these have been well received by the Chinese community. Certainly, in the 1995 elections, the majority of the Chinese voted the Barisan Nasional to give a mandate to Dr Mahathir and his programmes. Indeed, Chinese-based parties campaigned on the strength of Dr Mahathir's policies. Dr Mahathir in turn acknowledged the community's electoral support. Within the inter-ethnic framework, such demonstration of what some leaders would regard as loyalty to the coalition or to the bargain is helpful to stability and integration.

The Chinese business groups are comfortable with the leadership of Dr Mahathir and his vision of Wawasan 2020. Economic growth and the opening up of international trade and investment links, especially in the Asia-Pacific region, have created new opportunities for Malaysians, particularly the Chinese business sector. Trade procedures have been liberalized and the government is actively promoting and supporting business to expand within the country and overseas. There have been growth in small and medium-size industries (SMI), and many of these SMIs have local Chinese participation. The development of this sector benefits previously neglected areas, such as the former "New Villages" which are pre-dominantly Chinese. The coming in of foreign investments and the setting up of factories by the Taiwanese, for example, have also created business and employment opportunities, especially for the Chinese and Taiwan-educated who had previously been disadvantaged. The Chinese prefer Dr Mahathir's firm and decisive style as this has encouraged a more consistent and predictable implementation of business regulations.

The encouragement given to private business initiatives has been extended to the field of education. Educational opportunities have now broadened through twinning arrangements by local private colleges with foreign universities. Indeed, no issue in the past has caused more anxiety to the Chinese than education and recent changes have opened up new avenues for Chinese educational aspirations. Equally significant, the Chinese have noted a new tolerance in cultural and language matters. Not only have there been statements of assurance but sensitivity to the cultural pluralism of the country is in evidence such as on public functions and on radio and television. Lion dances, banned for a while in the past, are now allowed. Indeed, all sides have displayed sufficient sensitivity to each other so that the expressions of inter-ethnic harmony is consciously made visible and given official approval and backing. This is reflected at the "open house" functions held during festive seasons, and the coining of "Gong Xi Raya" greeting for Aidil Fitri and Chinese New Year, the dates of which coincided in 1996. The Malay and Chinese Chambers of Commerce held a joint "open house" which Dr Mahathir attended, during which he called for Sino-Malay business ventures.

Malay political and economic confidence also allows members of the community to look afresh at some of the old bogeymen. A conference on Islam and Confucianism held at the University of Malaya, Kuala Lumpur, in March 1995 is indicative of such a willingness. Attended by some 200 participants, including a number of internationally renown scholars, the two-day conference was seen to have political significance, not the least because it received the patronage of the Deputy Prime Minister, Dato Seri Anwar Ibrahim, who also delivered the opening speech. As a student leader Dato Seri Anwar had organized demonstrations against the Tengku for being too accommodating to the non-Malays. He later founded Abim, the Islamic youth organization.

In September 1994 Dato Seri Anwar made his first official visit to China. What was different on this occasion was that apart from the courtesy calls and visits to industrial centres, he went to the birth-place of Confucius and later to the tomb of Cheng Ho, the famous Chinese admiral and a Muslim, who had visited Malacca in the early years of the sultanate. Anwar's visit drew the attention of Malaysians not only to the cultural richness of the Chinese civilization but also to the mutual respect demonstrated in China's links with this region. It was, in a sense, a rediscovery of Islam in China and a reminder to the Malays of those early ties that helped secure the rise of the Malacca sultanate. At the same time, it was perhaps an acknowledgement to the Chinese of the community's heritage but at the same time to show that there is not such a great distance between their culture and that of the Malays. Whereas Dr Mahathir had focused on the political and economic concerns of Malaysia-China relations, Dato Seri Anwar drew attention to the cultural aspect.[23]

The various initiatives of Dr Mahathir are not without some opposition. The main critics have come from groups of Malay intellectuals who reflect the more nationalistic or, as some non-Malays would regard them, communal wing within UMNO. Mainly members of universities and literary organizations, they see the position of Malay language and culture under some threat, and the economic and education gains possibly undermined. A number of Malay intellectuals talk of Malay political dominance (*ketuaan Melayu*) and fear that this is being endangered by present trends. They are supported by those who complain that existing developments have benefited only the urban centres and the few Malay rich.

Possibly arising from such a thinking, the matter of the Malaysian Chinese doing business in China was raised as a supplementary question in Parliament on 11 May 1993 by a government back-bencher, who asked whether Malaysian Chinese conducting business in China were motivated by sentimental reasons. This was given very brief mention in the local press.[24] It was a speech on the same subject made the next day by Tengku Razaleigh Hamzah, however, which gained more attention and aroused some controversy. Tengku Razaleigh, in addressing the fourth general assembly of Parti Semangat 46, pointed out that Malaysian Chinese doing business in China should instead be investing at home to help develop the more backward regions. He questioned the priority of the Malaysian Chinese and reportedly raised doubts about their loyalty and sincerity.[25]

It is such statements and sentiments that cause many Chinese to be unsure of whether *bangsa Malaysia*, as they understand it, could truly evolve and gain acceptance. The term *bangsa* is presently used in close association with Malayness and Islam, and except for Dr Mahathir there had not been much comments or elaboration of the idea of *bangsa Malaysia* from many other senior Malay leaders. To the contrary, there has been some insistence by Malay cultural groups that the term for the official language should be *bahasa Melayu* (Malay language) instead of *bahasa Malaysia* (Malaysian language).

Nevertheless, that the subject of the Malaysian Chinese investing in China did not become an issue is a commentary of the prevailing stability of the new power equilibrium within the Barisan Nasional. Since 1988, communal temper has largely cooled and issues that threaten inter-ethnic relations are checked very early by the authorities. Much of this is due to the strengthening of Dr Mahathir's position as leader of UMNO. He has ensured that the executive branch of government is greatly strengthened in relation to the legislative and judiciary. With secure and enhanced power, Dr Mahathir has been able to carry out policies, both domestic and foreign, which many consider as innovative and bold.

The Coming Trends
Given the size of their population and their early participation in the independence movement, the Chinese will still play a significant part in the country's political process. The Chinese form their own political parties and at least three of these are part of the ruling coalition at the federal and state levels. There are six Chinese Cabinet ministers, two state chief ministers, two state deputy chief-ministers, and representatives in state executive committees. The largest opposition party is identifiably Chinese.

Chinese education remains an integral part of the school system and 27 per cent of the total enrolment are in state-supported Chinese primary schools.[26] Nowhere else can there be found a Chinese-language education stream that is part of the public system. About 80 per cent of the Chinese send their children to Chinese primary schools and this high figure has been maintained over the years. There are some 35,000 Malays in these Chinese schools. There are no state-supported Chinese secondary schools but the government allows some sixty private schools to operate. The Dong Jiao Zhong is hoping to start a Chinese-medium New Era College in Kajang, which is intended to provide higher education opportunities for the Chinese-educated and to train teachers for the independent Chinese secondary schools. There are nearly half a dozen widely-circulated Chinese newspapers, and Chinese TV and radio programmes are aired on state and private stations.

Many leaders express the hope that as Malaysia searches for a larger international economic and political role, domestic concerns bounded by ethnic identification can be transcended. Nevertheless, in the changing balance of domestic political power, the format of inter-ethnic co-operation will still be preserved. This is held to be essential to the parliamentary process in Malaysia which, despite criticisms of imperfections, has helped to ensure stability and all sides see little reason for wanting it replaced. The coalition is regarded as the only possible framework of political co-operation and the principal mechanism mediating differences among the races.[27] For the Chinese, it is in the ruling coalition that they have a role in government and thereby some input in policy formulation. Through the MCA, they have a claim to having been part of the historic independence movement. Many Chinese believe that their interest could be safeguarded only within the coalition and through supporting moderate UMNO leaders against those representing more communal demands.

Even UMNO finds the coalition arrangement of some value, especially in the electoral process. Non-Malay votes mobilized by, for example, the MCA are crucial in keenly contested Malay constituencies against the more Islamic PAS in the same manner that disciplined Malay voters have consistently helped Chinese-based coalition parties win many of their seats. More recently, in 1988 the momentum of the new Semangat 46 party challenge to Dr Mahathir was checked when the Chinese voted for the UMNO candidate in Parit Raja, Johor. In Sabah and Sarawak, where no ethnic groups are in the majority, the Chinese are still a deciding factor. Chinese votes have been decisive in changes in state governments in Sabah. In Sarawak, the largely Chinese SUPP, which was previously a powerful left-wing opposition, has helped the coalition to stay in power since joining the state Barisan

Nasional. So important is the inter-ethnic coalition in Malaysia that when it appears to break down, racial understanding is harmed and national stability threatened. Serious tension within the coalition signal to the public that the leaders are experiencing difficulties in accommodating conflicting inter-ethnic interests.

Within the Malaysian political process the main opposition criticisms could be ignored. Electorally, UMNO sees no danger of the opposition coming to power at the federal level. The opposition serves as a convenient political safety valve through which part of the frustration of the non-Malays is vented. Furthermore, non-Malay opposition electoral gains trim the representation of the MCA or Parti Gerakan and through this, weaken their bargaining position within the coalition. Finally, an opposition such as the DAP, when portrayed as a Chinese threat, rallies Malay solidarity.

The politics of the Chinese will continue to be articulated through expressly communal and non-communal parties. But these parties will have a less assertive role. The Chinese recognize the limits to which non-Malay demands can be effectively made; nevertheless, they continue to work within such parameters. There have been changes within the Chinese community, more than 90 per cent of whom are local-born. Many Chinese are fluent in Malay and an entire generation born after independence have gone through the national education system that is Malaysia-oriented. It is not possible yet to identify an essentially Malay-educated group that is large enough and which in orientation is different from the Chinese and the English-educated. The influence of the present generation of Chinese- and English-educated is still strong, while higher education institutions will maintain the continued role of the two groups. The economic growth of China, Taiwan, and Singapore has also enhanced the value of Chinese as a regional business language, while English remains useful for international communication.

Secondly, significant demographic changes are taking place in the country. A lower birth rate is resulting in a decline of the Chinese percentage so that by the year 2020 it is estimated that the Chinese would form no more than 18 per cent of the total population. Equally significant is the increasing urbanization of the Malays. Where Kuala Lumpur, the capital, was once predominantly Chinese, Malays today form nearly half its inhabitants. These two trends are already affecting the electoral pattern. In the 1995 elections, there were fewer urban constituencies which were overwhelmingly Chinese.

The MCA, the only expressly Chinese party in the country, which went through debilitating in-fighting and power-struggles in the 1980s, is striving for a less communal image. It has, for instance, liberalized its membership to allow those with one parent who is Chinese to join. The Tengku Abdul Rahman (TAR) college, which it is closely associated with, enrols a significant proportion of non-Chinese students. The party has also launched the Langkawi Project which aims at providing educational assistance to the rural areas irrespective of race.

Having weak political influence is not new to the Chinese in Malaysia as this was the situation in the early Malay states and during the colonial period. The Chinese are likely to continue to direct their energy and ambition to the economic sphere. As opportunities in the more traditional economic sectors become restricted either because of NEP rules or changing economic demands, some Chinese are venturing into new types of trade and to manufacturing. Manufacturing and high-tech industries have particularly attracted the Chinese, given the thrust of the country's economic development and in a sector where there are less NEP encumbrances. Manufacturing is the largest export earner in the country today, having overtaken palm oil and rubber, and an estimated 80 per cent of the small and medium-size industries are Chinese-owned.

The Chinese will no doubt look to strong political leadership that is supportive of business. Even the Chinese-based parties will still be considered relevant to represent the interests of Chinese business interests. Such indeed was the case in 1985 when the Ministry of Trade and Industry awarded to Satria Utara Enterprise Sdn Bhd, a subsidiary of Pernas, the sole permit to import mandarin oranges for the Chinese New Year. This led to strong protests from the traditional importers who were Chinese, and the matter was resolved through the Chinese-based parties in the coalition. Furthermore, it is through the Chinese-based parties that businessmen find help in dealing with lower level authorities and in establishing contact with Malay business-political groups.

The larger and older Chinese businesses will continue to cultivate political links, perhaps more with powerful Malays and less with overtly Chinese parties. People such as Lim Goh Tong, Lee Loy Seng, Loh Boon Siew, and Robert Kuok are examples of the earlier Chinese whose established businesses were enhanced by opening links with influential Malays. Khoo Kay Peng's Malayan United Industries, Teh Hong Piow's Public Bank, Quek Leng Chan's Hong Leong, the Lion Corporation, Kamunting Corporation, and Sunway Holding represent the more recent business groups which have benefited by establishing connections with important Malay partners.

It has been observed that in recent years Sabah and Sarawak have produced more than a fair number of prominent Chinese entrepreneurs. In Sabah, there are Teh Soon Seng of Aokam and Joseph Lee of CASH, while in Sarawak the more prominent in recent years are Ting Pik Khiing of Ekran and Tiong Hiew King of the Rimbunan Hijau Group. These two states in the political periphery are resource-rich, especially in timber, and given the pivotal political role which the Chinese are still able to play there, allow the Chinese greater economic possibilities. Dialect ties there are still very strong, especially among the Foochows. Some, such as Tan Sri Ling Beng Siew, founder of Hock Hua Bank, belong to the older generation of successful entrepreneurs and demonstrate the dynamism of these dialect networks.

More recently, and at a time when there has been spectacular Malay gains in the corporate sector, there have emerged a number of major companies largely owned by young Chinese but whose rapid diversification and expansion have been credited to powerful Malay backing. These include Westmont Holdings, Promet, the Phileo Allied Group, and Berjaya Corporation. These young Chinese bring with them management and trading skills, and have gained a reputation for corporate daring as they take over old companies and turn them into widely-diversified, though sometimes highly-geared, enterprises. A few of them have gone into ship-building, steel-mills, high-technology industries, and even defence contracts. What distinguishes some of these companies from the earlier ones, however, is their apparent greater dependence on Malay financial and political support.[28]

Besides bringing in management and technological skills as well as some capital, the Chinese will continue to rely on networking, especially that based on dialect, to give them a competitive edge. It is a network that can be traced to the nineteenth century when Penang and Singapore were used as key centres linking the major ports of the region. Today, that link is retained to facilitate business engagements and to help open new opportunities into Vietnam and Myanmar. For instance, Robert Kuok is connected in business to Liem Sioe Liong of Indonesia and the Bangkok Bank group in Thailand, and Liem's Salim and the Lippo groups have expanded their business and investments in Southeast Asia and Hong Kong. Likewise, Joseph Lee of the CASH group has entered into joint ventures with Barito's Prajogo Pangestu of Indonesia.[29] Today, that connection extends to Hong Kong and Taiwan.[30] Networking is viewed as a facilitator to Chinese business in Southeast Asia rather than for cultural solidarity.

Business networking, especially in Malaysia, relies on the maintenance of distinctives that are Chinese. For this reason, at least traditional beliefs and religions of the Chinese remain important. In Malaysia, Islam is not regarded as a part of that Chinese distinctiveness or identity. This may explain why there has not been conversion in significant numbers to Islam among the Chinese, as conversion means abandoning their identity. Islam is identified with the Malays, and the resurgence of the faith is seen by the Chinese as associated with rising Malay nationalism. According to the 1991 census there are an estimated 15,000 Chinese Muslims in the country or 0.4 per cent of the Chinese population. Reports suggest that those who converted have not been fully accepted within the community by the Malays.

Yet, some Chinese see in the universalism taught in Islam a moderating influence upon Malay nationalism. In 1986, for example, some Chinese formed the Chinese Consultative Committee (CCC) to support PAS in the elections. The CCC members were impressed by the willingness of some PAS leaders to consider multilingualism and to review the status of Malay special privileges.

PAS seemed to argue that Islam does not condone ethnic lines as a basis for preferential treatment.

There has been a revival of the various non-Muslim faiths among the Chinese in recent years which, in part, is a reaction to growing Islamic resurgence in the country. There is a strong Buddhist revival movement particularly among the Chinese-educated. Some Chinese-educated, especially the Foochows in Sarawak and in Sitiawan, are Christians. But it is among the English-educated where there was early conversion through the schools, that the number of Christians are larger. Christians total about 1,357,751 or 7.76 per cent in the 1991 census but, despite recent growth, they remain a minority within the Chinese community.

To the young and able Chinese who are fired with more idealism, it is the non-governmental organizations (NGOs) and social movements that they are increasingly drawn to. They share concern about alleviating social conditions and raising aware-ness on global concerns such as the environment, nuclear non-proliferation, and human rights. In approaching such problems, these organizations have generally transcended narrow ethnic preoccupations, and in expressing a more Malaysian perspective, they help promote some integration. There are now more Chinese participating in consumers' organizations and environmental protec-tion movements. They are joined by non-Malay leaders who are frustrated with opposition politics. Lee Lam Thye from the DAP is active in Pemadam, a drug rehabilitation body, and Kua Kia Soong, also from the DAP, is involved in a coalition of concerned NGOs against the Bakun Dam project.

Thus, in the last few years, the Chinese in Malaysia have developed a range of political and economic responses to the changes they face. Though their political role has weakened, their participation remains important in ensuring a multiracial image necessary to maintain stability. In the business sector, they are evolving new relations with major Malay political and economic centres. They are valued for their entrepreneurial skills and for their international business networking. It is possible that some indigenous entrepreneurs, through local joint ventures, could become part of this Chinese networking. Certainly, the present political leadership values the continuance of a multiracial society and considers it an achievement of Malay nationalism, and that it remains valuable in the expansion of Malaysia's regional and international interests. Despite reservations by Malay cultural nationalists, the Chinese distinctiveness and their overseas links are accepted by many Malay leaders as less threatening. China serves no more than a reminder to the local Chinese of the source of their identity and evokes a sentiment little different from that felt by Muslims towards the Middle East.

Notes

1. Michael Blackman et al., *Overseas Chinese Business Networks in Asia* (Canberra: Department of Foreign Affairs in Trade, 1995).
2. Even up to the period of independence, the indigenous Malay community was only approaching 50 per cent of the population.
3. Michael Godley, *The Mandarin-capitalists from Nanyang: Overseas Chinese enterprise in the modernization of China, 1893–1911* (Cambridge: Cambridge University Press, 1981).
4. John Wong, *The Political Economy of Malaysia's Trade Relations with China* (Singapore: Institute of Southeast Asian Studies, 1974).
5. Stephen Leong, "Malaysia and the People's Republic of China in the 1980s: Political Vigilance and Economic Pragmatism", *Asian Survey* 27, no. 10 (October 1987).
6. Stephen Leong, "New Paradigm in Malaysia-China Relations: From Control to Cooperation", *Jetro Sensor*, June 1995.
7. *Star*, 31 May 1993.
8. *Star*, 21 October 1994.
9. Pemegang Amanah Raya Malaysia which operates the Sekim Amanah Saham Bumiputra held 25.83 per cent of Lion Corporation in 1993. *The Kuala Lumpur Stock Exchange Annual Companies Handbook*, vol. xix, Book 1 (June 1993), p. 218.
10. *Star*, 29 May 1995.
11. *Star*, 17 August 1996.
12. *New Straits Time*, 29 August 1996.
13. Soh Eng Lim, "Tan Cheng Lock: His Leadership of the Malayan Chinese", *Journal of Southeast Asian History* 1, no. 1 (March 1960): 29–55.
14. Tan Liok Ee, *The Rhetoric of Bangsa and Minzu* (Clayton, Australia: Centre of Southeast Asian Studies, Monash University, 1988).
15. R. Stubbs, *Hearts and Mind in Guerilla Warfare: The Malayan Emergency, 1948–1960* (Singapore: Oxford University Press, 1989).
16. F.G. Carnell, "Constitutional Reforms and Elections in Malaya", *Pacific Affairs* 27, no. 3 (September 1954): 99–117; Colonial Office (Great

Britain), *Report of the Federation of Malaya Constitutional Commission* (London, 1957); Tun Mohamed Suffian, H. P. Lee, and F. A. Trindadae, eds., *The Constitution of Malaysia: Its Development, 1957–1977* (Kuala Lumpur: Oxford University Press, 1978).

17. Heng Pek Koon, *Chinese Politics in Malaysia: A History of the Malaysian Chinese Association* (Singapore: Oxford University Press, 1988).
18. R.K. Vasil, *The Malaysian General Elections of 1969* (Kuala Lumpur: Oxford University Press, 1972): Karl von Vorys, *Democracy without Consensus: Communalism and Political Stability in Malaya* (Princeton: Princeton University Press, 1975).
19. Felix Gagliano, *Communal Violence in Malaysia 1969: The Political Aftermath* (Athens, Ohio: Ohio Centre for International Studies, 1970).
20. *The Second Malaysia Plan* (Kuala Lumpur: Government of Malaysia, 1971).
21. Loh Kok Wah, *The Politics of Chinese Unity in Malaysia: Reform and Conflict in the Malaysian Chinese Association, 1971–1973* (Singapore: Institute of Southeast Asian Studies, 1982).
22. Bruce Gale, *Politics and Business: A Study of Multi-Purpose Holdings Berhad* (Kuala Lumpur: Eastern Universities Press, 1985).
23. There is recently formed a Malaysia-China Friendship Society with well-known Malay poet, Usman Awang, as President and Lee Lam Thye in the committee.
24. *Star*, 12 May 1993.
25. *Nanyang Siang Pau*, 13 May 1993; and *Sin Chew Jit Pau*, 13 May 1993.
26. In 1984 there were some 1,296 state-supported Chinese primary schools with an enrolment of 588,836. Enrolled in the 60 private schools were 44,656 students. Kua Kia Soong, *The Chinese Schools in Malaysia: A Protean Saga* (Kuala Lumpur: United Chinese School Committees Association of Malaysia, 1985).
27. R.S. Milne, Diane Mauzy, *Politics and Government in Malaysia* (Kuala Lumpur: Federal Publications, 1978).
28. Sally Cheong, *Changes in Ownership of KLSE Companies* (Kuala Lumpur: Corporate Research Services, 1995).
29. Irene Sia, "Robert Kuok: Taipan Incorporated", in *Formation and Restructuring of Business Groups in Malaysia*, edited by Hara Fujio (Tokyo: Institute of Developing Economies, 1993), pp. 57–72.
30. Toh Kin Woon, "Taiwanese Investments in Malaysia: A Macro and Micro Analysis", in *The Development of Bumiputra Enterprizes and Sino-Malay Economic Cooperation in Malaysia*, edited by Hara Fujio (Tokyo: Institute of Developing Economies, 1994), pp. 109–30.

This is a very comprehensive paper. Professor Lee Kam Hing, who is a keen watcher of contemporary Chinese affairs in Malaysia, has done a very thorough job on the subject of the Malaysian Chinese and their identity. There are several points that the paper attempts to highlight:

1. The emergence of China as a giant growth area and the involvement of the "Overseas Chinese" especially from Southeast Asia have renewed suspicions about the local Chinese. In Professor Lee's opinion, there is a kind of uneasiness among the Malays in the peninsula with regard to the issue of the Malaysian Chinese doing business in China. He thinks that the re-emergence of China as an economic and political power is perceived by indigenous Southeast Asians, including the Malays, as encouraging the resinicization of the Chinese in Southeast Asia.

2. Nationalism and religious resurgence of the indigenous people are factors that continue to form parameters for the integration of the Chinese.

3. In Malaysia, inter-ethnic equilibrium is maintained by an inter-ethnic coalition in government. Since the 1950s the so-called inter-ethnic political bargain, which became the basis of inter-ethnic co-operation, has undergone several tests and forms of adaptations to result in a consensus that brought about considerable shifts and adjustments on both non-Malays and Malays.

4. Being a substantially large minority group, the Chinese have been able to retain their identity as Chinese since they are represented at every political level and have a strong hold on

the economy. Both Chinese education and Chinese language have also been assured of their continued existence.

5. The inter-ethnic coalition is regarded as the only workable framework for political co-operation "and the principal mechanism mediating differences among the races". Many Chinese contend that Chinese interests are better safeguarded through political negotiations within the coalition. Any breakdown in the coalition would tend to bring about instability and racial strife.

6. There were several occasions when the coalition was threatened:

   a) One happened in July 1959 when the MCA, under the leadership of UMNO, demanded a third of the seats for the coming elections. (Earlier, the MCA had been allocated 28 seats but demanded that this be increased to 35). The MCA also demanded for the Education Act to be reviewed.

   b) Another occurred during the campaign by Lee Kuan Yew on the Malaysian-Malaysia concept. The concept challenged what Professor Lee calls "the symbols of loyalty insisted on by the Malays".

   c) Another occasion was when the campaign for the 1969 general election became heated over racial issues which, following the announcement of the results of the elections, led to the riots of 13 May.

7. Following the suspension of democracy immediately after the riots, important policy changes were made. A more Malay character of the state was pursued, with new symbols of loyalty being insisted upon.

8. In the opinion of Professor Lee, after the reinstitution of parliamentary democracy in March 1971 the MCA as the effective party to represent Chinese interests was weakened by the enlargement of the Alliance party concept, that is, the formation of the Barisan Nasional.

9. New changes, which included the implementation of the New Economic Policy, caused apprehension among the Chinese. Chinese commercial enterprises came under pressure to restructure in order to accommodate Malay economic participation.

10. The response from the Chinese towards these changes was to forge greater communal solidarity and this gave birth to the Chinese Unity Movement in 1973. The MCA also formed Multi-Purpose Holdings to protect Chinese economic interests.

11. There was inter-ethnic tension between the Chinese and Malays during the period of the recession, particularly between 1981 and 1987. While some Malay intellectuals were using the term *kaum pendatang* to refer to the Chinese, which caused irritation to the latter, some Chinese leaders made statements tantamount to denying the historical claims of the Malays as the indigenous people.

12. By and large, the Chinese community in Malaysia are quite comfortable with Dr Mahathir's style of leadership. His firm control of UMNO has also enabled him to check any inter-ethnic tension that might lead to instability. Under his leadership, Malaysia's economic growth and the opening up of international trade and investment links have created new opportunities for Chinese business.

13. The Malaysian Chinese community are also happy over the broadening of educational opportunities. These changes, says Professor Lee, appear to accommodate Chinese aspirations.

14. The rise of a new breed of Malay entrepreneurs in the corporate world has also enabled inter-ethnic co-operation between Malays and Chinese to take a positive twist. Mahathir's policy seems to encourage economic joint ventures of Malay and Chinese businessmen and this reflects the mood of the country, to promote inter-ethnic co-operation in order to realize the aims of making Malaysia a fully industrialized country by the year 2020.

15. There are also attempts to promote intercultural dialogue between Muslim Malays and Chinese — for example, the conference on Islam and Confucianism.

16. Both the Malay and Chinese political leaderships acknowledge that the multiracial political and economic formats that are benefiting Malaysia recently must be maintained and multi-ethnic co-operation preserved.

17. Although the Chinese will continue to make demands for their community, nevertheless they recognize the limits to

their demands and would accordingly try to accommodate their aspirations within the parameters already acknowledged.

18. Demographic changes are taking place. Professor Lee Kam Hing thinks that by the next century the Chinese population will decline in number because of the lower birth rate. (But I think his figure of 18 per cent for the Chinese population by the year 2020 is too low. According to my sources, it is closer to 29 per cent, with Malays making up 62 per cent of the total population.)

The overall picture that Professor Lee tries to present is that the Chinese in Malaysia today have, since the end of World War II, been able to maintain their Chineseness through making adjustments with existing symbols of Malay polity.

The Malaysian Chinese, nevertheless, as has been rightly pointed out by Professor Wang Gungwu, while willing to adopt the Malaysian national identity, have "at the same time developed a powerful sense of communal identity to assert the community's right to share power in the country".[1] Their ability to assert such right is proven by the fact that UMNO, the party that dominates the Barisan Nasional, has very much accepted the fact that while some semblance of Malay claims to "pre-eminence" should be maintained, Malaysian society is really a multi-ethnic and multi-cultural society.

A clear indication of UMNO's changing attitude is the increased flexibility shown towards the Chinese pertaining to their culture, education and language. Even the appointment of a Chinese to be the Deputy Minister of Internal Affairs and the increasing support given to Sino-Malay economic co-operation could be interpreted as signs of greater inter-ethnic tolerance. Under the strong leadership of Dr Mahathir, UMNO has also consistently addressed issues regarding nation-building from a multi-ethnic perspective. This explains the fact that Chinese culture is now quite liberally accepted as part and parcel of the Malaysian culture. No longer does one hear of Malay politicians protesting at the inclusion of the Chinese dragon dance or lion dance at functions officiated or attended by Malay senior ministers, including the Prime Minister himself or his deputy. Perhaps this wind of change is not only due to a shift in policy by UMNO but also is a consequence of Chinese steadfastness in the struggle to assert their communal rights.

There is also less politicization of such issues as the national culture and the national language by UMNO leaders. As a matter of fact, even if such issues have from time to time been raised by Malay cultural organizations, they no longer receive the same response or the same attention as they used to in the seventies or early eighties. The fact that UMNO has allowed the English language to play a very significant role in the development of a modern Malaysia is another indication of the changing attitude of UMNO. This is not to say that there are no critics from certain quarters within the Malay élite to UMNO's stand on the issues of Malay language and culture. But the emergence of a new breed of Malay political élite whose economic base and educational background are different from the political leaders of the fifties and sixties, has brought changes not only to the political culture of UMNO but also given birth to new perspectives on ideas of nation building of which the Chinese are part and parcel.

The crucial issue in the eyes of many Malay intellectuals in Malaysia today is the question of nation building. By nation building, they mean the creation of a Malaysian nation out of the diverse ethnic groups. The first time the issue of nation building cropped up was in January 1991 when a group of Universiti Kebangsaan Malaysia (UKM) lecturers wrote a memorandum to the Prime Minister upon the expiry of the New Economic Policy suggesting that the issue of nation building be taken up and to have it linked with an economic policy that would replace the NEP. The thrust of the argument in that memorandum was to emphasize the need for an economic policy that would continue to give attention to rural poverty while advocating a shift in policy towards industrialization. The end of the NEP brought apprehension to Malay intellectuals especially when the privatization concept was increasingly gaining acceptance in government circles and among the top leaders of UMNO. They were unsure of what the effects of privatization of education would have on Malay educational opportunities and the role of the Malay language as a tool for nation building. There was fear that Chinese economic predominance would again push the Malays into economic and educational regression.

The much criticized NEP was, however, replaced by the New Development Policy (NDP). The cornerstone of the NDP was privatization. Inherent in the new economic philosophy was the emphasis on growth and the modernization of the Malaysian economy. The strategy was a shift from a mixed economy to one that is industrial-based. In order to achieve this, Malaysians are constantly reminded that there are strategies that they will have to adopt if Malaysia is to achieve the status of a fully modern nation state by the year 2020. There are challenges and hurdles that Malaysians will have to face, one of which is the creation of a united Malaysian nation, or what is termed *bangsa Malaysia.*

Thus far, it seems that the ideas that were outlined by Dr Mahathir's Vision 2020 speech, which he delivered to the Malaysian Business Council Meeting in early 1991, have received undivided support from the Chinese community. Nation building in the Mahathir era does not entail the restriction of Chinese economic activities, as pointed out by Professor Lee Kam Hing. Neither would policies that attempt to enforce assimilationist tendencies, such as the pursuance of a national culture and a one-language policy, benefit the country in the long run, especially if one realizes that to achieve Vision 2020 not only would inter-ethnic harmony between the Chinese and Malays need to be sustained but the vital role that the Chinese business community can play in the pursuit of industrialization, given their wealth and economic strength, industriousness and educational skills, also need to be recognized.

To quote Professor Wang Gungwu again, "The Chinese have never had a concept of identity, only a concept of Chineseness ..."[2] I think when one discusses the identity of the Malaysian Chinese one cannot but recognize this fact. Political pressure exerted by the Malay majority in the late sixties and the seventies was perceived by the Malaysian Chinese community as an attempt to put Chinese culture and Chinese language under threat of extinction. This resulted in the struggle to project a Chinese communal identity. Hence, the strained relationship between the Chinese and Malays in the late seventies and mid-eighties.

The present political setting, however, appears to have diluted the fear and tension. Nevertheless, to many indigenous Southeast Asians, including the Malays, the "communal identity" still persists especially in the wake of a greater awareness among Southeast Asian Chinese of the re-emergence of China as an economic giant and a superpower. In Malaysia, many Malay cultural activists are dismayed that their vision of creating a Malaysian nation built on Malay polity and culture is no longer acceptable to the present Malay political élite. In this sense, Professor Lee is quite correct to say that the newly-found confidence of the Malay corporate élite, which also happens to be the group that is now holding the reins of Malay political leadership, has enabled it to accept the reality that a multi-ethnic and multi-cultural Malaysia is the only basis for nation building and, thus, the only alternative for a better future both for the Malays and the country.

Notes

1. Jennifer Cushman and Wang Gungwu, eds., *Changing Identities of the Southeast Asian Chinese since World War II* (Hong Kong University Press, 1988), p. 4.
2. Ibid., p. 1.

Chapter 4

The Ethnic Chinese in Myanmar and their Identity

Mya Than

Introduction

The purpose of this study is to explore and analyse the ethnic Chinese in Myanmar and their identity in terms of their attitudes towards the nation-state and their relationships with the indigenous people and with China. As the Chinese immigrated into Myanmar in several waves, their concepts of nation-state and their identity probably changed from time to time, or wave to wave. There are many reasons for overseas Chinese migration. Some immigrated for political/security reasons (such as civil wars or political oppression; for example, the *panthay* rebellion in 1873), some for economic or commercial reasons (business and employment opportunities, famines, for geographical reasons and for easier communication), while others were for social reasons (over-population in their home countries, racial and cultural affinities, connection with host countries, stimulus of pioneers in their home towns, and development of migration agencies) (for details, see Hicks 1995, chapter 2).

Chinese immigration into Myanmar is almost as old as the country's history. Thus, later generations of migrants and the descendants of migrants who were born in the country would have different attitudes from those long resident in the country. Moreover, their political, economic and social positions would influence their definitions of their identity and their attitudes towards the nation of their residence and towards the indigenous ethnic groups.

Therefore, this chapter will discuss briefly the historical and demographic development of the ethnic Chinese in Myanmar and their political, social and economic positions in the country. Then, it will explore their identity — in other words, how the Chinese view their Chineseness, whether they consider themselves as "indigenous ethnic Chinese" or "Southeast Asians" or "Overseas Chinese", their assimilation into or integration with other indigenous groups and their attitudes toward the People's Republic of China (PRC), also in the historical perspective. In order to have a complete picture, the attitudes of the indigenous ethnic groups towards the ethnic Chinese will also be examined. As Myanmar now practises an "open-door" policy and recently attained observer status in ASEAN after acceding to the organization's Treaty of Amity and Cooperation, the chapter will also address the role played by the ethnic Chinese in this regionalization process.

For the purpose of this study, the term "ethnic Chinese" will be used to mean "Chinese who have immigrated into Myanmar and their descendants", or "a group of people in Myanmar of Chinese ancestry with cultural affinity", or just "individuals of substantial Chinese ancestry who observe some important cultural rituals, such as ancestor worship, Chinese New Year celebrations, funeral rites, and so on", although Professor Wang Gungwu (1981) has different definitions for "ethnic Chinese". In addition, as the name of the country of Burma has been officially changed from the "Union of Burma" to the "Union of Myanmar" in June 1989, for those events pre-dating the name change, the original name "Burma" is retained in order to preserve the chronological order; while for those events which post-date the name change, the name "Myanmar" is used. (Since June 1989, the term "Burmese", for the citizens of Burma, has been replaced with "Myanmar" and the term "Burman", an ethnic group of Burma, with "Bamar".)

The Ethnic Chinese in Myanmar

Chinese from Guangdong and Fujian in China emigrated into Burma in the Song (960–1279 AD) and Ming (1368–1644 AD) dynasties (East Asia Analytical Unit 1995, p. 61). However, the numbers were few until the Yuan (1271–1368 AD) dynasty when Chinese businessmen expanded their businesses on a more permanent basis. As Myanmar has a common border of more than 2,000 kilometres with Yunnan, Chinese immigration into Myanmar might even have been earlier than historical records show. After the British colonization of the region, the Chinese arrived via Malaysia, which was then called Malaya. Hence, in terms of the routes they took, there are two types of Chinese in Myanmar — Mountain Chinese and Maritime Chinese. Mountain Chinese are those who came from Yunnan by taking the mountain road while the Maritime Chinese came by sea via Malaysia. According to local Myanmar, there are two kinds of Chinese — "*Leto*" (literally, short sleeve) and "*Letshe*" (long sleeve), depending on their occupations, generally like blue-collar and white-collar. *Leto* Chinese were mostly carpenters, coolies and farmers whereas *Letshe* used to be traders, bankers and brokers. According to Chen (1976), the Cantonese are referred to as *Leto* while the Fukianese are *Letshe*.

According to dialects, there are in Myanmar, Yunnanese, Cantonese, Hokkien and Hakka. Apart from these, there are local ethnic Chinese called Kokang Chinese who live along the Yunnan-Myanmar border and speak Mandarin. The ethnic Chinese in upper Burma are mostly Yunnanese, Hokkien and Kokang while Hokkien and Cantonese are found mostly in the lower part of Myanmer along the Ayeyarwady (Irrawaddy) delta, including Yangon, and Tanintharyi (Tenaserrim) coast.

During the pre-war period, the population of ethnic Chinese in Myanmar numbered about 193 thousand in 1931, which was about 1.3 per cent of the total population of the country (Table 1). This figure is less significant compared to that of Indians which accounted for about 5 per cent of the total population in

TABLE 1

Chinese Population in Myanmar, 1931–83

(In thousand)

Year	1931	1941	1953	1961	1973	1983
Chinese	194	—	300[@]	350[#]	227	234
Total	14,670	16,824	19,100	21,530[*]	28,921	35,307
Chinese as (%) of total	(1.3)	(—)	(1.6)	(1.6)	(0.8)	(0.6)

[@] Skinner (1950)
[#] Purcell (1965)
[*] *UN Demographic Yearbook 1962*

SOURCE: Censuses of India and the Union of Burma.

the same period. Out of these 193 thousand ethnic Chinese, about 54 per cent were, according to the 1931 census of India, born in Myanmar.

The size of the Chinese population just before World War II was estimated at 20 thousand by Harvey, as quoted in Purcell's (1965, p. 42) work. This was even after "most of racketeers brought in by the Burma Road had gone off to Shanghai". Soon after World War II, there was a sharp increase in Chinese immigration, especially from Yunnan. They were mostly from the Kuomintang (KMT) faction of the Chinese army and those who fled Yunnan when the communists took over power. The size of the ethnic Chinese community increased to about 300 thousand, which was about 1.6 per cent of the total Myanmar population of 19.1 million in 1953.

According to Skinner (1950), about half of the total Chinese population of Burma was found in and around the Ayeyarwady (Irrawaddy) delta, including Yangon (50,000) and Mawlamyine (15,000). The proportions of the various dialect groups were roughly as follows: Hokkien 40 per cent, Cantonese 25 per cent, Yunnanese 20 per cent, Hakka 8 per cent, and Hainanese 3 per cent (p. 3).

As border areas have always been difficult to control because of the terrain, the increasing Chinese immigrants from Yunnan could not be checked, despite the government's concerted efforts.

Thus, it is estimated that there were 350,000 ethnic Chinese in Myanmar in 1961, which is equivalent to slightly more than 1.6 per cent of the total population during that period. However, the size of this community seems to have been declining since the 1970s, probably caused by two factors. Firstly, the nationalization of private firms in 1964, including industries, trading houses, and banks, especially those owned by ethnic Indians and Chinese. About 300,000 Indians and 100,000 Chinese left the country after 1962 (Smith 1994, p. 63). Secondly, a new citizenship law which "discriminates" against the ethnic races of foreign origin was introduced in 1982. As a result, many ethnic Chinese left the country, mostly going to Taiwan, the United States, Hong Kong and Australia. There is the possibility that some Chinese were also registered under the "mixed foreign and Burmese" category in both censuses. Therefore, the number of ethnic Chinese in the censuses of 1973 and 1983 seems to be underestimated. The ethnic Chinese in 1973 numbered 227,000, which is about 0.8 per cent of the total population, whereas in 1983, the number was 234,000 which accounted for about 0.6 per cent of the total. The sex ratio also declined from 113.5 in 1973 to 106.8 in 1983 (Table 2).

Currently, one source has estimated the size of the ethnic Chinese community, or those who are of largely Chinese ancestry at 15 to 20 per cent (East Asia Analytical Unit 1995, p. 61), which seems to be overestimated, whereas Smith (1994) under-estimated it at 400,000 (p. 64). A more realistic estimate of the Chinese population would be about 2 to 3 per cent of the total 45 million. The East Asia Analytical Unit also estimated that 20 per cent of Myanmar's ethnic Chinese live in Yangon, with another 20 per cent in the Shan States, and 13 per cent each in the Bago and Ayeyarwady regions. Mandalay and Tanintharyi account for the rest (p. 62).

However, compared to some Southeast Asian countries, the size of the Chinese population in Myanmar is small.

In terms of origin, almost 45 per cent of the Chinese in Burma in 1931 were Fukianese or Cantonese, about 21 per cent were Yunnanese including a small number of *Panthays* (Muslim Chinese), and the rest were from elsewhere in China south of the Yangtze.

TABLE 2

**Percentage Distribution of Racial and Ethnic Groups,
by Sex: Burma, 1973, 1983**

Group	Total		Males		Females		Sex ratio	
	1973	1983	1973	1983	1973	1983	1973	1983
Burman	68.0	69.0	67.6	68.9	68.2	69.1	98.0	98.3
Shan	8.9	8.5	9.0	8.5	8.9	8.5	100.1	98.2
Karen	6.6	6.2	6.6	6.2	6.6	6.2	97.9	98.4
Yakhine	4.4	4.5	4.5	4.5	4.4	4.5	100.1	99.4
Other indigenous	6.7	6.5	6.7	6.5	6.6	6.5	99.1	99.5
Mixed Burmese	1.5	1.3	1.5	1.4	1.5	1.3	102.7	101.8
Chinese	0.8	0.6	0.9	0.7	0.8	0.7	113.5	106.8
Indians and Pakistan	1.9	1.4	2.1	1.4	1.8	1.3	113.1	104.5
Other foreign races	1.2	2.0	1.3	2.0	1.2	1.9	105.1	100.9
Total	100.0	100.0	100.0	100.0	100.0	100.0	100.0	100.0
Number	28,085	34,125	13,963	14,122	16,940	17,185		

SOURCE: Calculation based on Union of Burma Censuses (1973 and 1983) by I. Khin Maung.

It is estimated that, presently, Yunnanese and Kokang account for about 30 to 40 per cent of the total ethnic Chinese in Myanmar.

Nation-building and the Positions of the Ethnic Chinese

Myanmar, like Malaysia and India, was under British colonial rule for more than a hundred years. This colonial period generated political and economic alienation, especially among the young Bamars (Burman). The separation of modern economic opportunities and traditional activities and of the sources of power shared by the British and Indians in Myanmar, led young Bamar leaders of the post-independence period to identify themselves with nationalism, socialism and Buddhism. These three elements have been the basis of the national ideology during the nation-building period since Myanmar gained its independence from the British.

Like Myanmar, other single nation states, which were once autonomous political entities under the colonialists, have emerged in Southeast Asia since World War II. "The fundamental concern of these nations is how to be economically and politically viable entities after having been exploited for decades and even centuries of colonialism, and how to compete in a world dominated by imperialist forces which keep the Third World nations underdeveloped and dependent on them" (Tan 1988, p. 140).

During the process of nation-building, the establishment of racial harmony was an important factor, especially in Myanmar where there are seven major ethnic groups, namely, Shan, Kachin, Chin, Karen, Mon, Yakhine (Arakanese) and Kayah, and more than 130 minor ethnic minorities. This was because during the colonial period, the Bamar group was kept isolated by the British from most of the other indigenous ethnic groups. Hence, Burma in 1948 formed the "Union" — a unitary state which is in fact "the fusion of the different ethnic peoples into a nation with a set of overarching common goals and aspiration" (Steinberg 1982, p. 47). Thus, Myanmar has been a multi-cultural, multi-ethnic and multi-religious society for most of its history.

As in other Southeast Asian nations, nation building in Myanmar has had significant consequences on Chinese cultural identity although, unlike Malaysia or Indonesia, the number of ethnic Chinese was very small, forming only about 1.6 per cent of the country's population. Some political and social factors forced the Chinese minority to be assimilated into Bamar society as they were considered, along with the Europeans and Indians, to be exploiting the indigenous people. They were seen by the locals as rich, and the economy of the country was perceived to be mostly under their control. Successive Burmese governments therefore tried to restrict their "economic power" and to limit Chinese education. At some stages of modern history, they have also become the "convenient scapegoats for economic difficulty in the country". As a result of nation building and later, so-called "socialist-nation-building", the Chinese in Myanmar had only two options: either leave the country, or assimilate. Those who stayed behind had no alternative but to integrate or assimilate into the Myanmar society. Since then, their political, social, and economic positions have changed significantly throughout the post-war modern history of Myanmar.

In sum, let me quote Tan (1988), "Other than having to look after their own cultural, economic and political interests, the Chinese also have to think about their identity and even be concerned with the identity of their future generations. Being Chinese can no longer be taken for granted. Indeed they even have to redefine their own view of Chineseness" (p. 141).

Economic Position

Unlike in other Southeast Asian countries such as Malaysia, Thailand, Indonesia, Philippines, Cambodia, Laos and Vietnam, the ethnic Chinese in Myanmar did not occupy a prominent role in commerce in pre-war days. As Table 3 (a) and (b) shows, they were obviously in third place after the Europeans and Indians during the colonial period. Most of the Chinese were merchants, manufacturers, brokers and millers. According to the 1931 census, 41 per cent of the Chinese were traders and merchants, 38 per cent were carpenters and workers in metal and leather, 9 per cent were semi-skilled workers, and 6 per cent were in agriculture and the forest sector (Purcell 1965, p. 45). In almost all the cities and towns, there were Chinese general merchandise shops, and many sole agents for petroleum products were found to be Chinese.

TABLE 3a

Business Firms in Rangoon by Types of Business and by Nationality of Ownership

(In per cent)

		Total	E	I	C	B	U
1. Merchants	1895	121	23.1	47.1	19.9	9.9	0
	1930	659	9.7	57.8	19.7	7.9	4.9
2. Manufacturers	1895	7	42.9	28.6	28.5	0	0
	1930	80	18.8	23.8	10.0	16.2	31.2
3. Brokers & Dealers	1895	64	7.8	23.4	26.6	37.5	4.7
	1930	229	20.1	48.4	11.8	6.6	13.1
4. Service	1895	191	86.9	7.3	5.2	0.6	0
	1930	256	37.1	28.9	6.3	14.8	12.9
5. Bankers & Money	1895	31	0	96.8	0	3.2	0
Lenders	1930	29	13.8	82.8	0	0	3.4
6. Owners and Millers	1895	20	75.0	0	20.0	5.0	0
	1930	103	19.4	34.9	22.3	11.7	11.7
7. Agents and Insurance	1895	15	86.7	13.3	0	0	0
Companies	1930	47	49.2	29.6	4.2	6.4	10.6
8. Contractors	1895	29	44.8	20.7	31.0	3.5	0
	1930	69	36.2	39.1	4.3	7.3	13.1
9. Shopkeepers	1895	16	37.5	43.8	18.7	0	0
	1930	—	—	—	—	—	—
10. Traders	1895	111	15.3	45.0	17.1	22.6	0
	1930	—	—	—	—	—	—
11. Partners	1895	50	74	14	12	0	0
	1930	—	—	—	—	—	—
12. Distributors and	1895	—	—	—	—	—	—
Suppliers	1930	31	22.6	38.7	12.9	6.5	19.3
13. Extraction	1895	—	—	—	—	—	—
	1930	4	100	0	0	0	0
14. Import/Export	1895	—	—	—	—	—	—
	1930	316	29.8	52.8	8.6	2.5	6.3

E = Europeans
I = Indians
C = Chinese
B = Burmans
U = Unidentified

SOURCE: *Khin*, June 1970.

TABLE 3b

Business Firms in District Towns by Lines of Business and by Nationality of Ownership

(In per cent)

		Total	E	I	C	B	U
1. Merchants	1895	192	6.8	25.5	9.4	56.8	1.6
	1930	641	9.7	37.5	16.1	34.7	2.0
2. Manufacturers	1895	2	50.0	50.0	0	0	0
	1930	39	33.4	12.8	5.1	15.3	34.4
3. Brokers and Dealers	1895	39	0	12.8	5.1	82.1	0
	1930	231	3.5	3.5	42.8	47.6	2.6
4. Service	1895	137	46.7	40.9	1.5	10.9	0
	1930	233	11.6	24.0	4.3	35.6	24.5
5. Bankers and Money Lenders	1895	30	0	90.0	0	6.7	3.3
	1930	35	14.3	51.4	0	34.3	0
6. Owners and Millers	1895	3	0	0	0	100.0	0
	1930	239	7.5	11.7	10.0	65.8	5.0
7. Agents	1895	42	38.1	42.9	4.8	11.8	2.4
	1930	58	15.5	13.8	8.7	62.0	0
8. Contractors	1895	27	33.3	37.0	18.5	11.2	0
	1930	124	7.3	50.8	20.1	21.8	0
9. Shopkeepers	1895	26	34.6	46.2	0	19.2	0
	1930	96	1.1	53.1	12.5	33.3	0
10. Traders	1895	221	4.5	13.6	17.6	63.8	0.5
	1930	644	0.2	23.0	10.6	65.7	0.5
11. Import/Export	1896	—	—	—	—	—	—
	1930	20	15.0	40.0	15.0	15.0	15.0
12. Distributors and Suppliers	1895	—	—	—	—	—	—
	1930	10	10.0	60.0	0	30.0	0
13. Extraction	1895	—	—	—	—	—	—
	1930	4	100.0	0	0	0	0
14. Partners	1895	—	—	—	—	—	—
	1930	—	—	—	—	—	—

E = Europeans
I = Indians
C = Chinese
B = Burmans
U = Unidentified

SOURCE: *Khin*, June 1970.

They even ran illicit opium and gambling dens, tea-shops, liquor-shops, and so forth.

To promote their common interests, the ethnic Chinese businessmen in Rangoon formed a Chamber of Commerce at the beginning of the twentieth century. "The Chinese Overseas Bank, the Bank of China, and Chinese Insurance, shipping, rice, and mercantile firms maintained five branches along the Burma Road, and the payment of Chinese customs could be made through these branches" (Purcell, p. 46). In short, the pre-war colonial economy was largely controlled by foreign nationals and capital, mainly by the Europeans, the Indians and then the Chinese.

However, World War II changed the situation significantly. Soon after Burma gained independence in 1948, the government pursued a policy of indigenization in both administrative and economic affairs as part of the nation building process. With this aim, the government nationalized some major industries such as timber, transport, and oil. It also gave a larger share of retail trading and importing to Burmese nationals through import-licensing and quotas. This nationalization and indigenization policy affected the Indians more than the Chinese.

During the post-war period, according to Skinner (1950), more than 40 per cent of all ethnic Chinese were traders and merchants. Chinese as well as Indian retail shops were found in almost all the towns and cities of the country. The Indians, however, began returning in ever greater numbers to their homeland after the war, and the position of the Chinese traders thus improved. In the larger cities, they had their own Chamber of Commerce and all the major firms were members. In addition, there were numerous trade organizations and guilds, usually called *t'ung yeh kung hui*, which represented the various trades in which the Chinese participated (p. 25).

"When new industrialization in the form of import substitution industries began to catch on in the late 1950s, Indian participation was marginal. Most of the new industries were initiated by the Bamar, Sino-Bamar, or naturalized Chinese businessmen" (Khin 1993, p. 644). This was because the Chinese community had already accommodated the changes demanded by the indigeni-zation process, and adopted Burmese names, dress and language even before the government started to pursue this policy. Since then the ethnic Chinese began to take the place of many Indian shopkeepers, as the number of Indians greatly declined. "But they did not have a grip of the rice trade as they had in Siam, Indochina, and the Philippines, this being very largely in the hands of the Indians — mostly Marwaris, Maimanis, etc. The Chinese were active bidders for fishery and ferry rights in many streams" (Purcell, p. 45).

Then came the military regime which took over power after the *coup d'etat* in 1962. The new regime introduced the "Burmese Way to Socialism" which called for a stronger approach to nationalization and indigenization of the economy. After the introduction of the Enterprise Nationalization Law of 1963, almost all retail, wholesale, and import trade, (and later) manufacturing businesses and the banking sector were taken over by the government. Although these actions affected both foreigners and Burmese businessmen, it was the Indians and Chinese businessmen who were the hardest hit. As a result, many Indians (about 200 thousand of them) and a small number of Chinese businessmen left the country. Moreover, in response to the threat of the Cultural Revolution instigated by some pro-China ethnic Chinese groups, anti-Chinese riots broke out in some cities. This resulted in serious damage to Chinese businesses in several cities.

However, as the Burmese Way to Socialism gave birth to the booming black market in the late 1960s, the ethnic Chinese again took these opportunities and played a dominant role in it. In the seventies and early 1980s, as the government relaxed some of its rigid economic policies, the ethnic Chinese once again became overwhelmingly active in the service and cottage industries. In Rangoon, more than half of the shops in various big markets were estimated to be run by them.

In terms of the labour force, the Chinese accounted for 0.8 per cent of the total labour force in 1983, which was a decline from 0.9 per cent in 1973 (Table 4). However, in absolute numbers, they increased by 12.5 thousand. It is interesting to note that although the ethnic Chinese population accounted for about 0.6 per cent of the total population in 1983, their contribution to the labour force as a percentage of the total was 0.8 per cent.

TABLE 4

Labour Force, by Race and Sex, 1973 and 1983

Race and Sex	1973		1983		Absolute Change 1973–83	Percentage Change 1973–83
	Number	Percentage	Number	Percentage		
Total	9,367,054	100.0	12,199,979	100.0	2,932,925	30.24
Burmese	6,113,095	65.3	8,484,690	69.5	2,371,595	38.79
Male	4,103,376	(67.1)	5,481,149	(64.6)	1,377,773	33.57
Female	2,009,719	(32.9)	3,003,541	(35.4)	993,822	49.45
Other Indigenous	2,805,689	29.9	3,182,163	26.1	376,474	13.41
Male	1,800,087	(64.2)	1,921,321	(60.4)	121,234	6.73
Female	1,005,602	(35.8)	1,260,842	(39.6)	255,240	25.38
Mixed Parentage	112,485	1.2	133,635	1.1	21,150	18.80
Male	80,463	(71.5)	91,622	(68.6)	11,159	13.86
Female	32,022	(28.5)	42,013	(31.4)	9,991	31.20
Chinese	81,724	0.9	94,212	0.8	12,488	15.28
Male	58,004	(71.0)	62,594	(66.4)	4,590	7.91
Female	23,720	(29.0)	31,618	(33.6)	7,898	33.29
Indian & Pakistani	157,918	1.7	152,996	1.3	-4,922	-3.11
Male	135,230	(85.6)	118,251	(77.3)	-16,979	-12.55
Female	22,688	(14.4)	34,745	(22.7)	12,057	53.14
All Others	96,143	1.0	152,283	1.2	56,140	58.39
Male	85,752	(89.2)	129,750	(85.2)	43,998	51.30
Female	10,391	(10.8)	22,533	(14.8)	12,142	116.85

SOURCE: Calculation by I. Khin Maung, based on Union of Burma Censuses (1973 and 1983).

In 1988 when the present military regime, the State Law and Order Restoration Council (SLORC), took over power, the "open door" policy was introduced. The private sector was encouraged and the law on foreign direct investment (FDI) was promulgated. Today, the country's ethnic Chinese are again at the forefront in Myanmar's economy. The majority of retail, wholesale and import trade, including cross-border trade and big restaurants, are run by them or by mixed Chinese-Bamar; and the largest supermarket in Yangon is operated by an ethnic Chinese group. More importantly, the government does not differentiate between ethnic Chinese and other Myanmar citizens, or between their respective companies, in employment policies or purchasing requirements (East Asia Analytical Unit 1995, p. 63). Much of the foreign direct investment (FDI) entering the country is channelled through ethnic Chinese networks throughout Southeast Asia (East Asia Analytical Unit 1995, p. 64). On the other hand, many wealthy Chinese in Yangon tend to have investments outside the country, especially in Singapore.

Some observers have found the reason for the success of the ethnic Chinese in Myanmar. "Myanmar, like China, legal and other 'soft' infrastructures are still being developed, and good connections are essential for doing business. The ethnic Chinese have social and business structures which operate well in the absence of sound legal and other structures; they have a propensity for developing international connections. They are therefore at their most competitive in countries such as Myanmar" (ibid, p. 60).

In sum, it can be said that the ethnic Chinese have contributed to the economic development of the country to some extent.

Political Position

Historically, the relationship between Myanmar and China is not as long and close as that between China and Indochina. China occupied Indochina for more than a millennium, while in Myanmar, apart from a few invasions from China, there has been no political interference between the two since 1767. This was mainly due to the difficulty of communication between the two countries because of the mountain ranges and rivers along the 2000-kilometre-long border. This is also the reason why despite the affinity of their races, Chinese culture has never had much influence on Myanmar. It has been far easier for Myanmar to communicate with India by sea and as a result, Indian culture has had much influence over Myanmar culture, especially religion.

However, "it was only in 1940–41, the deputy ministers and other officials of KMT came into Burma and behaved as if they owned the place" (Purcell 1965, p. 47). Moreover, in 1945, Chinese armies came into northern Burma and behaved as if Burma belonged to them since schools and training centres in Chungking used maps showing all northern Burma and parts of Assam as *China Irrendenta* (ibid, p. 48). Again in 1949, large fragments of the defeated armies of the KMT occupied some areas in the northeast of Myanmar for some time. This problem was later resolved with United Nations assistance.

It is important to note that Burma was the first non-communist country to recognize the People's Republic of China (PRC) in 1949. Border disputes between the two countries were settled amicably, and Myanmar pursued the only-one-China policy. The two countries strictly followed the policy of peaceful coexistence until 1967 when outbursts of the Cultural Revolution significantly damaged the relationship between the two countries. Moreover, until the early 1980s, China supported and gave refuge to the armed Communist Party of Burma. Presently, China is one of the few countries that give full political and economic support to the present regime in Myanmar.

As an ethnic group, unlike in some of the Southeast Asian countries, the Chinese in Myanmar have never played a dominant role in the country's politics although their social position improved gradually throughout the country's history. During the days of the Burmese kings, unlike other foreign residents, the role of the Chinese in the country was simply commercial. That role did not change even in the colonial days. However, in the colonial parliament, and in the Rangoon Municipal Administration, there were one or two representatives from the Chinese community.

During the war with Japan, some ethnic Chinese, mostly Sino-Bamar, actively participated along with other ethnic groups. It was only after World War II that their offspring began to be employed as civil servants, technicians, doctors, military officers and so on, but there were only a very few in politics. As China was divided into two — that is, mainland China and Taiwan, or in other words, communist and non-communist — so also were their supporters in Burma divided. The Burmese called the supporters of mainland China *tayoke ni* (red Chinese), and the other group, *tayoke phyu* (white Chinese). There were a few clashes between them. As Burma was a strong supporter of mainland China and because of KMT aggression in the early 1950s, *tayoke phyu* in the country were tolerated but closely watched by the then democratically elected government. In those days, whenever an important person from China visited Burma, prominent *tayoke phyu* leaders would be detained for the duration of the visit. Since some Sino-Bamar and ethnic Chinese had participated in the war against Japanese invasion, a few of them were given important positions in government and in the political parties in the newly independent state of Burma.

Until it was nationalized in the 1960s, the Chinese press in Burma also played an important role in politics. Out of four Chinese dailies and weeklies, a few were politically oriented as they were funded by some political parties.

Since the military government took over power in 1962, political participation by the ethnic Chinese has become marginal although there exist a few high-ranking Sino-Bamar military officers.

Social Position
Unlike other ethnic groups of foreign origin, the ethnic Chinese have a special place in Myanmar. In other words, the ethnic Chinese are more socially acceptable to Myanmar than other foreigners. This is because of racial affinity, language affinity with the Shan, one of the native races, and the ethnic Chinese' easy adoption of Myanmar language, dress and local customs. Many have also changed their Buddhist sect from Mahayana to Theravada Buddhism. Table 5 shows that in 1983 more than 82 per cent of the ethnic Chinese were found to be Buddhists. It is interesting to note that, despite these racial affinities with the Chinese, the Burmese have stronger cultural ties with India, especially in religion owing to the communication factor in the early days of Myanmar's history.

TABLE 5

Population by Race and by Religion, 1983

(In thousand)

Race	Buddhist	Christian	Hindu	Muslim	Others	Total
Burmese	23,220	46	3	254	9	23,532
Chinese	192	5	—	3	33	233
Indians	116	19	144	140	9	428
Others	6,992	1,608	27	912	2,071	9,932
Union Total	3,0520	1,678	174	1,309	2,122	34,125

SOURCE: Union of Burma Census 1983.

In feudal times, many Indian Brahmins served the Burmese kings as astrologers and advisors, whereas the Chinese were just traders.

During the colonial period, the role of the Chinese as traders/ merchants did not change although their economic position improved. They diversified into manufacturing and the services sectors although they were in third place, following the Europeans and Indians (see Table 3a and b). Their representatives, although few, could be found in the colonial Burma Legislature and the local administration in the big cities. In Yangon, Chinese businessmen voiced and raised their common interests through the Chambers of Commerce; one of them, the Burmese Chinese Chamber of Commerce, was established in 1910.

After World War II, there were six Chinese chambers of commerce. Apart from these, there existed many clan/dialect associations in most of the cities and big towns, as most of the ethnic Chinese lived in the urban areas.

Table 6 shows the distribution of the rural-urban population by race. According to the table, the shares of the ethnic Chinese population in both the urban and rural areas to total population declined significantly by about four to five times. This was probably because of an increase of Bamar and other indigenous races and racial identification during the census. Table 6 also indicates that most of the ethnic Chinese lived in the urban areas.

As was mentioned earlier, the social position of the ethnic Chinese in terms of employment up to World War II did not

TABLE 6
Rural and Urban Population by Race
(In per cent)

Race	1931 Census		1953/54 Census		1973 Census	
	Rural	Urban	Rural	Urban	Rural	Urban
Myanmar			97.0	82.0	99.5	97.3
Chinese			1.0	6.0	0.2	1.4
Indians & Pakistanis			2.0	9.0	0.2	1.2
Others			0.0	3.0	0.1	0.1
Total	100.0	100.0	100.0	100.0	100.0	100.0

change much, that is, their role was mainly in the economic sectors, not in the political nor administrative sectors. Unlike in some Southeast Asian countries, after the war, not a few of the Chinese in Burma replaced the Indian professionals and administrators who left Burma. Most of these ethnic Chinese were from the second or third generation of Chinese immigrants, were educated in Burma and had adopted Burmese names and dress. A few of them held important political and military posts in the post-independence period but more of them were involved in merchandise, commercial, manufacturing and services sectors.

The government allowed the ethnic Chinese to establish their own temples, cemeteries, clan or dialect associations and Chinese schools in almost all the cities and towns. In the heart of Chinatown near the centre of Yangon, two famous Cantonese and Hokkien temples built in the year 1890 and 1900 are still being visited by well-wishers and worshippers. As far as religion is concerned, they have been free to practise their own throughout history. It seems that they have more freedom than the Muslim community although the successive constitutions have given them equal status. There is also no restriction on their cultural affairs but the Chinese community has played down its activities since 1964 in order not to attract much public attention.

The post-independent government allowed the Chinese community to open their own schools to teach the Chinese language and disseminate Chinese culture. According to the 1931 census, the literacy rate of the Chinese population was about 41 per cent. There is no doubt that this rate has increased significantly in the post-independence period. In the post-war period, there were twenty-eight Chinese schools in Rangoon alone. Out of these, eight were middle or secondary schools while the rest were primary. Some Chinese schools in Rangoon and Mandalay were ranked among the top high schools in the country in terms of academic achievements, sports, and disciplines. With the exception of the primary schools, Chinese, Burmese and English languages, along with other academic subjects were taught in these secondary schools. There were altogether 180 Chinese schools in the rest of the country, with most of them primary schools.

However, after 1967, due to nationalization measures and serious anti-Chinese riots in response to the spillover effect of the Cultural Revolution in China, many Chinese businesses and homes were damaged and many traditional associations and schools were banned. Chinese schools were forced to close. Since then, the ethnic Chinese have kept a low profile in all economic, social and political sectors. The hardest blow to the ethnic Chinese community was the promulgation of the Citizenship Law in 1982. Many of their children were not allowed to attend professional tertiary educational institutions, such as medical, engineering, agricultural and even economics colleges. Many students of Chinese origin who were already studying in these institutions at the time were expelled. A few holding important political posts were also forced to resign.

Now that the country has opened up its economy and is plugged into the regional network, especially to ASEAN and China, the role of the ethnic Chinese in the social and economic spheres has improved significantly.

Legal Status
There have been significant changes in the legal status of the Chinese community throughout Myanmar's recent history because of the bitter pre-war experience of exploitation by aliens in the country and racial unrest. As far as the legal status of foreigners and non-indigenous citizens of Myanmar is concerned, the successive governments have tried to define it through various

constitutions and citizenship acts/laws, such as the Foreigners Registration Act of 1940, the 1947 Constitution, the 1948 Union of Burma Citizenship Act, the Union Citizenship (Election) Act of 1948, the 1974 Constitution, and the 1982 Burma Citizenship Law.

During the days of the Burmese kings, the status of foreigners was defined by the kings based on their whims and fancies, and on a case-by-case basis. The British colonialists encouraged immigrants because of the labour and capital shortage. Although the registration of foreigners was properly kept, there was in practice no clear definition of the legal status of foreigners and citizens of the country.

Under the Burmese government after the war, the line between foreigners and citizens was clearly defined. According to Section II of the 1947 Constitution, citizenship would be granted to:

1. every person both of whose parents belong or belonged to any of the indigenous races of Burma;
2. every person born in any of the territories included within the Union, at least one of whose grandparents belongs or belonged to any of the indigenous races of Burma;
3. every person born in any of the territories included within the Union of parents both of whom are, or if they had been alive at the commencement of this Constitution would have been, citizens of the Union; and
4. every person who was born in any of the territories which at the time of his birth was included within His Britannic Majesty's dominions and who had resided in any of the territories included within the Union for a period of not less than eight years in the ten years immediately preceding the date of the commencement of this Constitution or immediately preceding 1 January 1942 and who intended to reside permanently therein and who signified his election of citizenship of the Union in the manner and within the time prescribed by law.

Most of the Indians and Chinese who had not been permanent residents before World War II but were recent migrants or itinerant workers fell into the fourth category. All those who fell under the first three categories quoted above automatically became citizens of the Union of Burma (for details, see Taylor 1993). Ethnic Chinese who belonged to the third category cited above became "full-fledged" citizens of Burma. However, those who belonged to the fourth category had to apply to become citizens by 30 April 1950, according to the Union Citizenship (Election) Act of 1948. A few ethnic Chinese even contested in general elections in the newly independent Burma.

However, the situation has changed dramatically since 1962 when the military took over power in Burma. The then ruling military "Revolutionary Council" declared the 1947 Constitution null and void. Only when the Revolutionary Council handed over power to the Burma Socialist Programme Party in 1974 was a new constitution promulgated. In the 1974 Constitution, there exists one article, Article 145 of Chapter XI, which mentions citizenship matters. It specifies that:

a. All persons born of parents both of whom are nationals of the Socialist Republic of the Union of Burma are citizens of the Union.
b. Persons who are vested with citizenship according to existing laws on the date this Constitution comes into force are also citizens.

According to section (b) quoted above, most ethnic Chinese who were already citizens of Burma were constitutionally recognized as citizens.

Although the 1974 Constitution guarantees equal rights to all citizens, there exists political "discrimination" among the citizens. In Chapter XII, Article 177, paragraph (a) a distinction is drawn between the political rights of citizens differentiated in Article 145, which states as follows: only those citizens "born of parents both of whom are also citizens" can be elected to the national legislature, the Pyi Thu Hluttaw, or the lower level state organs of power, the various levels of the People's Councils. "In effect, the Constitution (of 1974) draws a distinction between those who became citizens more than a generation back and those who did not" (Taylor 1993, p. 678).

Then in 1982, the Burma Citizenship Law was promulgated. This law, in effect, underscores the distinction between the two groups of citizens drawn by the 1974 Constitution. The objective of this law was to clarify the positions of the immigrants and their descendants as well as defend the security of the state. This was in line with the speech made by U Ne Win, the then chairman of the ruling party, at a party meeting held on 11 December 1979, referring to persons of mixed blood: "Because of their mixed parentage, the descendants of alien-Burmese unions, like full aliens, could not be fully trusted because of their alleged foreign contacts and possible external economic or political interests".

According to the 1982 Burma Citizenship Law, there are three categories of citizens.

1. Full citizens: Nationals who are the descendants of residents of the country before 1823, that is, citizens at the time the legislation came into force; or persons who are born of parents, either one or both of whom were citizens at the time of birth.
2. Associate citizens: Persons who "apply for the citizenship under the Union of Burma Citizenship Act, 1948".
3. Naturalized citizens: Persons who have yet to apply but are eligible to apply for citizenship under the Burma Citizenship Act of 1948.

The difference between these three groups is more a political one. The first group has, officially, full rights as citizens. They are entitled to all rights and privileges accorded to full citizens except for those rights specifically promulgated by the state from time to time. However, as a small non-indigenous ethnic group, the Chinese are less equal compared to other indigenous ethnic groups like the Shans or Kachins, in the sense that the Chinese do not have a special administrative area designated to them. On the other hand, Bamar, as the largest indigenous ethnic group, has a special position because of its population size and historical dominance.

Compared to the 1982 Burma Citizenship Law, the citizenship legislation enacted in 1948 seems to be relatively liberal for the ethnic Chinese in Myanmar. The interesting remarks on this law made by Taylor (1993) are as follows:

> The 1982 legislation had been criticized both inside and outside Burma for its allegedly racist features. The Burma Communist

Party condemned it as an act of racial bigotry, a "narrow-minded, bourgeois and racist manifesto". Since Indians and Chinese in Burma are known to have expressed anxiety about their status as have others who are aware of their mixed origins. However, for most people the legislation has made little difference. Those without citizenship, either legal or illegal foreign residents, are not concerned about the new law as it does not change their status at all. Those excluded from full citizenship are aware that the decision taken on their status is political and not racial in nature. As all power of decision rests with Ministers on the recommendation of their subordinates, there is relatively little an individual can do but to use whatever personal influence he or she may have to effect a favourable decision. As under the previous arrangements, the poor and the illiterate will face the greatest barriers to citizenship for themselves and their children" (p. 680).

In sum, since 1962, it seems that the political, economic and social autonomy of the ethnic Chinese has declined significantly.

However, since 1988, when the present military regime took over power, the legal status of the ethnic Chinese has again become ambiguous. Their position, at least in commercial affairs, may be stronger now as a result of the opening up of the country's economy. However, the National Convention for drafting the constitution is being held in Myanmar, and it is too early to assess the outcome of the convention regarding the legal status of the ethnic Chinese.

It is interesting to note the impact of citizenship legislation on the registered number of foreigners residing in Myanmar, which is shown in Table 7. According to the table, the largest number of foreigners registered in Myanmar was in 1970 before the 1974 Constitution was introduced. Since then, the number has declined significantly. The number of Indians started to decline in the 1960s whereas the number of Chinese started to do so only in the 1970s. It seems that legislation for citizenship throughout the years have affected the Indians more than the Chinese as the former decreased about three times while the number of Chinese registered as foreigners declined by about one and a half times only. This may be because the Chinese are more easily assimilated into Myanmar society compared to other non-indigenous ethnic groups.

TABLE 7

Number of Registered Foreigners

	1961	1970	1975	1981	1991	1994
Indians	108,738	81,301	58,459	55,740	40,956	36,590
Pakistanis	26,250	19,336	11,569	8,799	5,414	4,622
Chinese	81,766	128,052	114,666	99,296	70,558	57,785
Others	9,999	24,596	11,569	22,901	14,955	14,721
Total	226,753	253,285	179,863	186,786	131,883	118,718

SOURCE: *Statistical Year Books*, various issues.

The Ethnic Chinese and their Identity

According to Tan (1988), "an ethnic identity has three major components, namely, the label, the objective aspects (such as languages and customs) of the identification, and the subjective experiences of that identification. The last component includes the self-perception as well as the social and psychological meanings of being a Chinese" (p. 140). Ideally, in Myanmar, three factors must be considered in identifying whether a person is an ethnic Chinese or not. They include ethnic and cultural norms — namely, ancestry, culture, and Myanmar citizenship.

As ancestry and Myanmar citizenship are given factors, the cultural component is the most important one for identifying the ethnic Chinese. For the cultural component, Professor Wang's (1981) concept is useful for the purpose of this study. According to him,

> By cultural here, I am referring to the inclusive way it is used in cultural anthropology, that is, everything related to traits which were learned and transmitted by and to members of society, including knowledge, beliefs, morals, customs, religions and law. These traits were similar in nature to those found in the traditional Chinese sense of identity. But the new cultural identity went further. Unlike what I have called historical identity, which was largely based on past cultural values and which depended on the persistence of these values among overseas Chinese communities, the new awareness of culture recognized the function and usefulness

of modern non-Chinese cultures from which Chinese communities could learn new ways of ensuring their prosperity and success.

However, since the above is too broad, Chinese ethnic identity is defined for the purpose of this study, as follows: as long as they follow their cultural customs and rituals such as New Year celebration, ancestral worship, funeral rites and so on, and if they consider themselves as ethnic Chinese, then they are identified as ethnic Chinese. Currently, in Myanmar, unlike in other countries, written language and dress are not significant components of Chineseness.

However, there seems to be a greater extent of assimilation and integration of the ethnic Chinese into Myanmar society. One contributing factor is mixed marriage. The offsprings of mixed marriages usually incline to the side of their current environment (host country). However, there seems to be a custom for the male offspring of such unions to assume the Chinese race and for the females to assume the race of the mother.

Nevertheless, the degree of assimilation (or Chineseness) depends on many other factors. Firstly, it depends on where they live and which school they attended. Those Chinese who live in the Chinatown area are less assimilated into Myanmar society than those who live outside Chinatown. In other words, those who live in Chinatown observe Chinese cultural traditions or speak the Chinese language (dialects) more than others. Ethnic Chinese who live in the small towns are also more readily assimilated than those in the cities. Moreover, those who have Myanmar education are almost completely integrated into the surrounding environment, whereas those who have Chinese education are less assimilated. In sum, those Chinese who live in small towns or outside Chinatown in the cities and who had Myanmar education and do not observe or observe only a few Chinese traditional rituals are identified as Bamar. Those who belong to this group and are married to Myanmar are no longer Chinese in the eyes of the Chinese or Myanmar. They are considered native Myanmar.

At the community level, there are three factors to identify Chineseness or to measure the extent of assimilation, namely, Chinese education, clan or dialect association, and Chinese mass media.

In the past, the Chinese schools played a very important role in teaching language and passing on "values" to the younger generations. Many textbooks were imported from China, Singapore and Hong Kong. Since the mid-1960s, however, Chinese schools in Myanmar together with other private schools, including mission schools, have been nationalized and Burmanized. Since then, the teaching of the Chinese language and culture have not been allowed and all Chinese children have had to attend Burmese schools.

As far as the Chinese media is concerned, there were four Chinese dailies and three weeklies in the country, which constituted the only Chinese press before nationalization was carried out in 1964/65. The circulation of the dailies in the early 1950s was estimated at about 12,000 (Skinner 1950). Since there were no Chinese radio stations in the country, the Chinese dailies picked up news from foreign radios such as Radio Peking. With the nationalization and Burmanization of the mass media, the Chinese media disappeared. Recently, the Chinese community in Yangon produced a daily newsletter which contained mainly prices for the day's trading in the main commodities in Yangon.

There are still many Chinese associations such as clan associations, dialect associations, regional associations (for example, the Fukian association, and the Guandong association), the Chinese Chamber of Commerce, temple associations and even the so-called secret societies in Myanmar. However, unlike in the days of pre-military rule in the 1960s, they keep a low profile.

During the 1950s, there were more than eighty clan associations in Rangoon alone. They are still active in Myanmar although not on the scale of the post-independence period. In earlier days, probably until the early 1960s, they organized the transfer of remittances to mainland China and gave business capital at marginal interest rates to poorer members. Some clan societies still teach Chinese martial arts and organize lion dance groups. They also take care of the old destitute and homeless and thus pass Chinese values to members of their clan.

Chinese temples remain very significant institutions to disseminate and promote Chinese culture. They help in performing funeral ceremonies, ancestor worship, and some also keep the ash-urns of the deceased. Many of them collect money and give out scholarships to students and help the poor. There are also secret societies which disseminate martial arts to members and help the weaker ones.

Before they were banned, the Chinese Chambers of Commerce in Yangon not only functioned as lobby groups for Chinese businessmen, but also helped the Chinese community to observe traditional Chinese culture. After 1988, the Chinese Chamber of Commerce in Yangon, founded in 1910, functioned on a *de facto* basis. These associations are still popular within the Chinese community in Myanmar but they tend to focus on welfare and social activities.

This shows that out of the three pillars supporting the identity of the ethnic Chinese, only one has survived, which in turn suggests that the Chinese in Myanmar are very well assimilated into Myanmar society — in other words, they are well Myanmarized.

At the national level, the ethnic Chinese, as in other Southeast Asian countries, consider Myanmar as their national identity in terms of their political and legal status but without losing their consciousness of being Chinese.

More importantly, as the national identity of Myanmar is made up of two factors, nationalism and Buddhism, it is not difficult for the Chinese to be identified as Myanmar at the national level.

An important question to be asked then is when they cease to be ethnic Chinese. According to my interviewees, both Chinese and Bamars, many of Chinese origin have assimilated into Myanmar society so well that they have not only changed their names and dress but also do not speak the dialects or perform any Chinese cultural rites, and therefore are no longer Chinese. These ethnic Chinese are completely assimilated into the Myanmar society, so much so that they do not even bother to observe fundamental Chinese customs. Most of them belong to the younger and modernized generation, or were educated in Myanmar schools, or live in small towns or outside the Chinatowns of the cities, or have married into Myanmar families. In other words, even though they have Chinese blood, if they do not observe Chinese customs and do not speak their language, they cease to be Chinese since their identity is closely related to Myanmar culture.

For some, the reasons would be political, economic, or social. During the post-1964 (after the nationalization of businesses) and post-1974 (after the introduction of the new socialist constitution) periods, even for those who consider themselves as Chinese, they would when asked identify themselves as Sino-Bamar when they do not want to be identified as Chinese, especially for official purposes. This was probably reflected in the 1983 national census.

Nowadays, as in most countries, due to the invasion of Western culture, the assimilation process through mixed marriages, and political and social pressures imposed by the state, the degree of Chineseness has declined in relative terms. Despite this trend, especially since 1990 when the Myanmar Government began to allow foreigners to invest in the country, "Chineseness" appears to have been revived. This may be because many Chinese investors from the neighbouring countries such as Singapore, Thailand and Malaysia are setting up businesses in the country, and this situation demands increased contacts with local Chinese groups of various dialects. As a consequence, many Chinese who hid behind the "national identity" for some time have now openly come out to announce their "cultural identity" to the world.

As regards ethnic Chinese-Myanmar relations, Purcell (1965) was right when he said, "Many persons of Chinese race in Burma had long regarded themselves as Burmese citizens and had no more interest in China than US citizens of the second or third generations have in their European ancestral homes" (p. 42). Even in the times of the Burmese kings, "they were, in spite of their character of middlemen, instinctively recognized by the Burmese as of close kindred in blood, and were not classified by them with the *kalas* or other foreigners, though that term included every race of India proper, of Western Asia, and of Europe" (ibid, p. 60). Purcell even found that, "To a greater extent than in Siam, Malaya, or Indochina, the Chinese in Burma came to regard the country as their home" (p. 69). This attitude was confirmed by Wee (1972) that so long as the Chinese are willing to become Burmese nationals and adopt Burmese names, they will have equal economic opportunities as their Burmese brethren.

Lastly, we will look at the issue of how other ethnic groups, especially Bamar, see them. Like the concept of Chinese identity, the attitudes of other ethnic groups towards the Chinese also vary, depending on the political and socio-economic situation. During the pre-war period, when the Chinese were in third place behind the Europeans and Indians in the economic sphere, the Bamars' attitude towards the Chinese was relatively not as prejudiced as they were towards other resident foreigners, although the Chinese were also considered as "exploiters" during the recession years.

In the post-war and nation-building period, as the Chinese became more prepared to assimilate themselves into the society than the Indians and because of racial and cultural affinities, many Bamar considered them as *pauk phaws*, or siblings. Although greater assimilation of the major indigenous ethnic groups into a supra-ethnic Myanmar nationality has not occurred, many ethnic Chinese have been readily assimilated. However, as their economic power and political inclinations towards mainland China and Taiwan became more apparent in the late 1950s and early 1960s, some Bamars, especially those in power and in business, viewed them as "guests" who were exploiting the country's resources. Despite this, unlike other indigenous ethnic groups like the Karens or Shans or Kachins, the ethnic Chinese did not pose a security threat to the government, and therefore the government's attitude towards them was more benign.

Since 1990, the ethnic Chinese are once again playing a more dominant role in the economy. They are being treated as equals and competitors. However, in Mandalay where the Chinese, mostly non-Burmese-speaking Chinese from the border areas, control commercial life and the income gap is widening, there exist "negative" attitudes towards the Chinese there.

Conclusion

Based on the above findings, the prospects of ethnic Chinese integration in the national and regional sphere will be discussed here.

As mentioned earlier, those Chinese in Myanmar who could not integrate into Myanmar society had left the country at various times for many reasons: political, economic, and social. Those ethnic Chinese who remained are so well integrated into the host society that it is sometimes difficult to distinguish between them and other ethnic groups such as the Bamar, Shan, Karens, and so on. This is because most of the ethnic Chinese speak the local language, dress like the locals and mix easily with the local people. They have also contributed to the development of the country. They participate in traditional Myanmar festivals and most of them follow the Myanmar Buddhist way of life, which allows spirit and ancestral worship. (At the world-famous Shwedagon pagoda in Yangon, one can find temples erected by the ethnic Chinese.) Many Chinese now live outside the Chinatown areas of the cities while many Myanmar also live in the Chinatown areas. Most of the ethnic Chinese can speak the Myanmar language and have adopted Bamar names and dress. More importantly, like most Myanmar people, they are generally Buddhist. There have also been more mixed marriages between the Chinese and the Bamars. Thus, this has fostered integration of the Chinese into Myanmar society.

However, those Chinese who recently migrated from the border areas to Mandalay find it difficult to assimilate with the local people because of their different languages, customs and levels of wealth. The central quarters of Mandalay have been transformed into a booming business centre with hotels, restaurants, shops, foreign business offices and modern buildings many of them owned by the "new-wave" Chinese. Only some native-owned businesses like printing presses, shoe shops, garment shops and cheroot factories are left. Some critics have even gone so far as to describe the situation in Mandalay as a plural society as in the colonial period "in which alien social groups dominate the society and economy at the expense of economic hardship and economic decay for the Burmese" (Mya Maung 1994, p. 459). If the income gap between the ethnic groups, especially between the native Bamar and the ethnic Chinese, continues to widen further, the possibility of undesirable social consequences cannot be ruled out. This will be a negative factor for national integration.

Another issue is whether the ethnic Chinese in Myanmar have become "Southeast Asians" or "Overseas Chinese". As far as the ethnic Chinese in Myanmar are concerned, it is true that they have become less "Chinese" than their forefathers as a result of adopting Myanmar culture more and more. There is also an affinity between Bamar and Chinese culture so that many Bamar are worshipping the Goddess of Mercy (Guanyin) while many Chinese regularly visit pagodas and monasteries.

However, even though most of the local-born Chinese are almost completely assimilated into Myanmar society, they are more "Southeast Asian" than other Myanmar people in the sense that they are networking through their "Chinese" connections or "ethnic networks" based on mutual economic interests and cultural affinities, such as dialect groups and some traditional customs (for details, see Suryadinata 1995). Today, Myanmar's ethnic Chinese seem to be at the forefront of the country's economy. Much of the foreign investment now entering Myanmar is channelled through ethnic Chinese networks (East Asia Analytical Unit 1995, p. 64). Moreover, the identity of the younger generation of ethnic Chinese, especially the youth, is probably more like that of their counterparts in other Southeast Asian countries in terms of dress, body language, values and attitudes.

To conclude, more in-depth studies on the ethnic Chinese in Myanmar and their identity are needed since values and attitudes are involved and there is so far a vacuum in this area. It is hoped that this chapter, despite its many limitations, will serve as a ground-breaking study or as an exploratory one for those scholars who wish to pursue further in-depth studies on the ethnic Chinese in Southeast Asia.

References

Chen, Yi-Sein. "The Chinese in Rangoon during the 18th and 19th Centuries". In *Papers on Asian History, Religion, Languages, Literature, Music Folklore, and Anthropology*. Ascona, Leiden: Artibus Asia, 1976.

East Asia Analytical Unit. *Overseas Chinese Networks in Asia*. Department of Foreign Affairs and Trade, Parkes ACT, 1995.

Fitzgerald, Stephen. *China and the Overseas Chinese: A Study of Peking's Changing Policy 1949–70*. Cambridge: Cambridge University Press, 1972.

Khin Maung Kyi. "Indians in Burma: Problems of an Alien Subculture in a Highly Integrated Society". In *Indian Communities in Southeast Asia*, edited by K.S. Sandhu and A. Mani, pp. 625–66. Singapore: Times Academic Press and Institute of Southeast Asian Studies, 1993.

———. *Journal of Burma Research Society (JBRS)* L111 (June 1970).

Mya Maung. "On the Road to Mandalay: A Case Study of the Sinonization of Upper Burma". *Asian Survey*, no. 5 (May 1994).

Purcell, Victor. *The Chinese in Southeast Asia*, 2nd edition. London: Oxford University Press, 1965.

Shozo, Fukuda. *With Sweat & Abacus: Economic Roles of Southeast Asian Chinese on the Eve of World War II*, English edition. Singapore: Select Books, 1995.

Skinner, G.W. *Report on the Chinese in Southeast Asia*. Michigan University Microfilms, Cornell University, December 1950.

Smith, Martin. *Ethnic Groups in Burma*. London: Anti-Slavery International, 1994.

Steinberg, David I. *Burma: A Socialist Nation of Southeast Asia*. Colorado: Westview Press, 1982.

Suryadinata, Leo, ed. *Southeast Asian Chinese and China: The Politico-Economic Dimension*. Singapore: Times Academic Press, 1995.

Tan, Chee-Beng. "Nation-building and Being Chinese in a Southeast Asian State: Malaysia". In *Changing Identities of the Southeast Asian Chinese since World War II*, edited by Jennifer Cushman and Wang Gungwu. Hong Kong: Hong Kong University Press, 1988.

Taylor, Robert. "The Legal Status of Indians in Contemporary Burma". In *Indian Communities in Southeast Asia*, edited by K.S. Sandhu & A. Mani. Singapore: Times Academic Press and ISEAS, 1993.

Wang, Gungwu. *Community and Nation: Essays on Southeast Asia and the Chinese*. Singapore: Heinemann Educational Books (Asia) Pte. Ltd., 1981.

Wee Mon-Cheng. *The Future of the Chinese in Southeast Asia: As Viewed from the Economic Angle*. Singapore: University Education Press, 1972.

Comments by
Khin Maung Kyi on
"The Ethnic Chinese in Myanmar and their Identity"
Presented by Mya Than

The papers presented at this meeting principally deal with the problems of large Chinese migrant groups who happen to hold strong economic dominance in the countries of Southeast Asia in which they are domiciled. Burma's case is entirely different from the experience of the other Southeast Asian countries.*

Mya Than has done an admirable job of welding all the recent facts together to present the existing state of ethnic relations with regard to the Chinese in Burma. However, this writer feels that ethnic Chinese problems should be more incisively interpreted in the larger context of national integration and identity, the historical experiences of the Burmese nation, and the relative economic position of the Chinese *vis-à-vis* other ethnic groups, either foreign or local. This paper will therefore complement Mya Than's paper.

The migrant ethnic Chinese population in Burma was historically very small compared with those in other countries in

---

* In this paper, the more commonly known term "Burma" is used instead of the recently introduced "Myanmar" to denote the country. It should be noted that Myanmar and Bamar are interchangeable terms: Bamar is more colloquial whereas Myanmar is more confined to literary or court usage. The reason why Burma is preferred here is that Burma or Bamar connotes the whole people of Burma including all ethnic groups whereas Myanmar is more confined to the Myanmar ethnic group, the largest group of all and its language. In 1930, when the nationalist "Our Burma" movement was founded, all Burmese leaders agreed that from then on Bamar would be used to represent the whole country including all ethnic groups among which Myanmar was only one. Burma or Bamar was not restricted to the colonial period either. Early European travellers mentioned the country as Birma. The Thais also called it Phama. Only the Chinese used Myein, probably because Sino-Burmese historical relationships were mostly formal and through the Burmese Court. The Court of Ava, the Burmese Court, used the term "Myanmar".

Southeast Asia. For example, Thailand had a large proportion of ethnic Chinese before their active integration into Thai society. In Burma, however, the Chinese formed only 1.3 per cent of the total population in 1930, whereas the more ubiquitous Indians made up 7 per cent of the total population. The Chinese and Indian proportions in total population shrank to 0.6 per cent and 0.4 per cent respectively by 1973, as a result of the very extensive nationalization of businesses; most Indian businessmen and many well-to-do Chinese left the country between 1962 and 1970.

Another important pattern to note is that most Chinese migrants came to Burma after the annexation of Burma by the British in 1986. Merchants, tradesmen and labourers came to work in the coastal cities like Moulmein, Tovoy, Mergue and Rangoon first, and then spread later into the hinterland. It should also be noted that most Sino-Burmans, even the first generation children of mixed Chinese and Burmese parentage would have registered or presented themselves as Burmese. This would have reduced the number of Chinese in the population census in later periods when the intense integration process was being introduced. Mya Than has reported how the blending of the Chinese and their descendants with the mainstream Burmese was very easily and conveniently done.

The next point to note is that Chinese migration took place through maritime rather than land routes although Burma has a very long land frontier with China. It would have been expected that Burma with its sparse population and abundant resources would be a candidate for waves of Chinese migration from the North. This never happened. First, the ethnic northern tribes and ethnic groups who lived in Yunnan province served as a buffer against Chinese migration. In fact, the tribes in Yunnan and the northern tribes in Burma belong to the same ethnic group. In addition, the distance between the main population centres of China and the Burmese frontiers, and the difficulty of transport and lack of established routes further restricted migration by land. When upper Burma, the only remaining part of Burma still under Burmese rule, was annexed by British India in 1886, the migration of Chinese nationals from either China or other settlements in the East to Burma became difficult, whereas Indians from India could freely travel to Burma without any documentation or visa as Burma had became a province of India.

The degree of economic dominance of a foreign ethnic group domiciled in a country is directly related to the relationships between the host people and the immigrants. Historically, Chinese traders were operating in Burma since the early days of the Pagan period (AD 1000 to 1300), and the Silk Road probably passed not far from Burma. Border trade between Burma and China thus existed for a long time. In fact, the last Burma-China War was fought because of trade disputes in the border areas. Under the Burmese kings, ethnic Chinese merchants enjoyed a comparative advantage over other nationalities in dealing with the Burmese court because they were familiar with the methods and protocol of the Burmese court. External trade was done through royal or state monopolies. Apparently, the Chinese as agents of the crown had almost total control over the export of lac, cotton and other agricultural products. These comparative advantages were wiped away when Burma was placed under Indian administration. Indian merchants who were familiar with Western administration, machinery and its laws gained dominance in commerce and trade in Burma. In fact, Furnivall in his unpublished manuscript on "Economic History of Burma", describes very clearly the loss of Chinese dominance in Burma's external trade after the annexation of Burma.

Under the British administration, the importance of the role of the Chinese in internal trade and business gradually declined. As Table 3a in Mya Than's paper indicates, between 1895 and 1930, Chinese businesses in three sectors, namely, manufacturing, brokerage and contracting, out of six types of businesses they were active in, declined. Their relative shares as a proportion of establishments owned by the Chinese in these categories of business had shrunk from 28.5 to 10 per cent in manufacturing, from 26.6 to 1.8 per cent in brokerage and from 31 to 4.3 per cent in contracting. On the other hand, Indian businesses improved their position substantially in the six categories of businesses, out of the total of eight categories they were active in. In each of these categories, they controlled a large proportion of the business.

TABLE A

**Business Firms in Small Towns by Line of Business
and Nationality of Ownership**

(In per cent)

Line of Business	Year	Total Number	Nationality of Ownership				
			E	I	C	B	U
Merchants	1895	236	6.4	16.9	12.3	64.0	0.4
	1930	770	3.8	38.3	13.1	44.2	0.6
Manufacturers	1895	1	100.0	0	0	0	0
	1930	12	0	25.0	0	75.0	0
Brokers and	1895	28	0	3.6	7.1	85.7	3.6
Dealers	1930	185	1.6	15.7	16.2	57.8	8.7
Services	1895	30	66.6	23.3	0	10.1	0
	1930	181	11.6	30.9	10.0	38.6	8.9
Bankers and	1895	6	0	33.3	33.3	33.4	0
Money-Lenders	1930	21	33.3	14.3	0	52.4	0
Owners and	1895	7	14.3	42.9	0	42.8	0
Millers	1930	313	5.8	13.4	4.5	75.3	1.0
Agents	1895	15	40.0	6.7	13.3	40.0	0
	1930	32	6.3	25.0	15.6	49.9	3.2
Contractors	1895	16	6.3	37.4	31.3	18.7	6.3
	1930	210	1.5	4.9	19.2	38.4	0
Shopkeepers	1895	15	20.0	60.0	6.7	13.3	0
	1930	436	0.3	52.2	18.3	28.9	0.3
Traders	1895	128	3.9	16.4	13.3	63.3	3.1
	1930	1,854	0.3	15.5	12.6	71.5	0.1
Import/Export	1895	n.a.	n.a.	n.a.	n.a.	n.a	n.a.
	1930	3	0	0	33.3	0	66.7
Distributors and	1895	n.a.	n.a.	n.a.	n.a.	n.a.	n.a.
Suppliers	1930	2	0	50.0	0	50.0	0
Extraction	1895	n.a.	n.a.	n.a.	n.a.	n.a.	n.a.
	1930	7	85.7	0	0	0	14.3
Partners	1895	n.a.	n.a.	n.a.	n.a.	n.a.	n.a.
	1930	n.a.	n.a.	n.a.	n.a.	n.a.	n.a.

NOTE: E = European   C = Chinese   U = Unidentified
      I = Indian   B = Bamar   n.a. = not available

SOURCE: *Burma Trade Directory*, 1895 and 1930.

However, in the case of businesses in the small towns, the picture is quite different. In 1930, out of ten categories of businesses, in which all three communities — Indian, Chinese and Burmese — were operating, the proportion of Indian businesses had declined in three categories, namely, banking and money lending, owners and millers, and shopkeepers, but in other types of businesses, they held the same position as in 1895, or improved substantially in some cases. On the other hand, Chinese participation had declined in banking and money lending, but was maintained or improved in other categories. On the whole, however, their share of business establishments was next to the Indian and Burmese communities. However, the Burmese share of business establishments improved markedly in seven categories. They occupied a dominant position in merchandizing, manufacturing, banking and money lending, brokerage and dealership, and trading although on a reduced scale in some areas. This indicates that Burmese business, having been exposed to Western business methods for thirty-five years, had improved their skills and competence.

Mya Than also mentioned the prevalence of Chinese businesses in the small towns. It is true that in certain businesses, the Chinese were dominant, especially in storekeeping, medical stores, coffee shops, noodle shops, restaurants, pig butchery, village shops, and liquor and opium dens. They also owned rice mills and participated in trade but this field was largely controlled by European and Indian firms. The tea shops, restaurants, and stores, did not compete with the local businesses or impinge on the lives of the majority. The fact that Burmese business in the small towns enjoyed a relatively prominent position in some areas over other groups probably lessened the impact of the Chinese intrusion on these communities.

The lesser role of Chinese businesses in the Burmese economy compared with other foreign ethnic groups such as the Europeans and Indians could also be explained by the change in the direction of trade after the annexation of Burma. Table B indicates that the percentage of export trade that went to India increased progressively up to the beginning of World War II from 20.6 per cent in

TABLE B

Burma's Export by Country

(In per cent)

	West		Asia and Far East			Total	
Year	U.K.	Else-where	India	Straits Settlement	Else-where	%	'000 of Rupees
1868–69	65.8	2.0	25.1	5.3	1.8	100	32,662
1883–84	36.9	20.9	20.6	18.3	3.3	100	68,770
1897–98	12.9	23.8	44.9	12.6	5.8	100	139,084
1910–11	10.8	19.4	35.8	9.1	24.9	100	323,600
1920–21	12.7	8.2	51.6	7.7	19.8	100	535,409
1930–31	9.2	12.1	40.6	7.1	31.0	100	541,995
1939–40	13.6	5.8	60.9	4.6	15.1	100	530,987

SOURCE: J.S. Furnivall, "Economic History of Burma", Tables Vol. I – X.

1883–84 to 60.9 per cent in 1939–40, while exports to the Straits Settlements declined from 18.3 per cent in 1883–84 to 4.6 per cent in 1939–40. The British share of Burmese exports too fell from 36.9 per cent to 13.6 per cent in the same period, establishing India as the dominant trading partner for Burma.

Likewise, Burma's imports from the Straits Settlements where the Overseas Chinese businesses operated more prominently, declined from 12.9 per cent of total imports in 1883–84 to 2.6 per cent in 1939–40 (Table C). On the other hand, India's hold on Burma's imports remained strong throughout 1868–69 to 1930–40, when 50 per cent of imports to Burma came from India. The United Kingdom, Europe and others made up about 30 to 40 per cent of Burma's imports throughout the period, indicating the importance of manufactured goods that came from these industrially advanced countries.

Within this context, Indian businesses had a very strong hold on the Burmese economy. The business network and knowledge they had accumulated were far more important than the knowledge and network of the Chinese merchants in the Far East.

The problem of ethnic integration or assimilation in Burma goes back a long way. Burma, besides Vietnam, has had a long

TABLE C

Burma's Imports by Country
(In per cent)

| Year | West | | Asia and Far East | | | Total | |
	U.K.	Else-where	India	Straits Settlement	Else-where	%	'000 of Rupees
1868–69	37.1	1.1	51.1	9.4	1.3	100	27,588
1883–84	38.7	1.6	45.2	12.9	1.6	100	60,145
1897–98	35.7	5.1	44.9	8.6	5.7	100	101,241
1910–11	31.6	10.4	42.4	4.6	11.0	100	186,497
1920–21	28.0	12.9	45.7	2.3	11.1	100	370,518
1930–31	23.7	14.1	41.9	2.7	17.6	100	283,424
1939–40	17.2	10.8	55.4	2.6	14.0	100	251,603

SOURCE: J.S. Furnivall, "Economic History of Burma", Tables Vol. I – X.

history of often tumultuous relations with China. Ever since Burma's ethnic groups comprising linguistically and culturally similar groups of Tibeto-Burmans moved slowly down to the plains of the Irrawaddy, the Myanmar ethnic group, the most energetic and aggressive of all, had been trying to weld all the diverse but related ethnic groups into a single nation, while at the same time warding off often forceful overtures from China. Burmese history has recorded incessant struggles in uniting and integrating the Burman races. Each time a Burman empire was established, the break-up would follow after a few generations of rulers. The Burmans first absorbed and assimilated the earlier Proto Burman kingdom of Pyu and later conquered the Mon Khmese kingdom of Pegu in the South. But rebellions and re-establishment of new Mon kingdoms ensued, culminating in a brutal put down, by the Burmese, of the last Mon rebellion in 1756. The Burmans also had to contend with new waves of immigrating Shans. The weak Burmese empire after the Tartar invasion in 1283 had to absorb and co-opt rising Shan rulers to the Burmese fold, and Shan princes were accepted as the new kings of Burma. They, on their part, accepted and followed the traditions, titles, and language of the Burman courts and chose to rule as Burman kings. The coming of the British as the new colonial rulers interrupted the whole process of integration and assimilation before it was completed.

On the other hand, in external relations, the Chinese figured prominently. While the Burmans had only a cultural relationship with India, China had directly attempted to intervene in the affairs of Burma. The Chinese Army came down to Burma four times, the last in 1769 when the invading Chinese army was roundly defeated by the Burmese forces. Although the Chinese claim for suzerainty or tributory rights over Burma was never established, successive Chinese governments persisted in holding on to the idea of the Burmese kingdom as a tributatory state, even including Upper Burma as part of China in their maps, until the Sino-Burma border agreement was signed in 1961.

Such being its historical experience, Burma has been very careful in dealing with its powerful neighbour. Its strategy has been to maintain a cordial and non-threatening relationship, particularly avoiding a situation that China may construe as threatening to its security. At the same time, successive governments in Burma had been quite apprehensive of possible Chinese interference in its internal conflict. Maintaining its own internal unity and stability, and being watchful of the migrant Chinese community had been the central core of this strategy. Under General Ne Win, the nationalization of all foreign schools, and the introduction of the Burmese language as the medium of instruction in all schools, together with the nationalization of all businesses, was thought to effectively neutralize the possibility of Chinese ethnicity rearing its head again in Burma. Thus, the Chinese born in Burma in the last twenty-five years have been effectively Burmanized.

However, this situation has been rapidly undergoing change under the guise of an open-door policy that the present military regime has been pursuing. Three elements are rapidly changing the situation. First, the small Chinese settlement in the Burmese border state of Kokang, a member of which happened to secure the rulership earlier under Chinese patronage, has been swelling in its ranks with remnants of the Kuomintang who had fled from communist China since 1951. This fully- or half-Chinese community has taken control over opium cultivation and trade, and probably earns as much foreign exchange as the Burmese government itself receives from its foreign exports. Their ranks have been recently reinforced by economic migrants coming down from the more northern parts of China. These economically powerful pure ethnic Chinese groups have bought their way into Burma by conniving with corrupt local officials in the border region. They have also almost taken over the business centre of Mandalay, the traditional city of Burma, by buying up choice property in the town areas and pushing the Burmese population to the outskirts.

Their strength has been further enhanced by Burma's continuing dependence on the cheap and sub-standard consumer goods from China and their control of this trade. As Yunnan and the neighbouring provinces develop new and nascent industries, Burma with its hunger for consumer goods has become a potentially captive market for these new industries to introduce or export new products through open border trade, thus enjoying both scale effects and experience curve advantage. The money from the drug business has also increased the power of this new breed of *towkays* and *lawpans*.

Added to this is the increase of Chinese capital coming from the countries of Southeast Asia. Though there is nothing intrinsically wrong with foreign direct investments coming into and investing in a country, the tipping of the balance of economic power of one ethnic group, with strident ethnic overtones, over indigenous ethnic groups could court problems in its wake. As Mya Than has rightly pointed out, the resurgence of ethnicity and awareness of ethnocentricity is rising again in Burma. The ringing bells of ethnic networking in the Chinese diaspora in Southeast Asia, as espoused by some Southeast Asian leaders may not help allay the fears of the indigenous people about their economic future. For them, the power of the "Lords of the Rim" and the rising might of the "new Middle Kingdom" may seem very real and formidable. For the best interest of Burma's development, investments from many different countries and sources should be welcomed and encouraged, both to get the best competitive deals and to prevent dependency on a few sources. Under the present political circumstances, however, options are more or less limited.

Burma's ethnic Chinese problem has had much deeper roots than those in other countries of Southeast Asia. Burma faces both the ethnic Chinese and China's problems. Managing ethnic Chinese problems in Burma with a reasonable level of negative impacts requires an intricate balancing of different requirements and interests, the needs of free trade, the demands of local indigenous development, real or implied threat of the powerful neighbour, and the impending rise of native resentment. The problem has been further compounded by the interruption in the process of national integration itself, while consensus and unity among the political forces have still to be achieved.

A well-known authority on Burma, J.S. Furnivall, in his preface to the seminal work on *Political Economy of Burma*, first published in 1931, recognizing the then imminence of Burma's independence, its lack of preparation for the task, its reigning problems of ethnic diversity, and the sheer task of nation building, had this to say:

> If, as is but too probably, the obstacles prove insurmountable, the end of British influence in Burma can be only a matter of time and, after a period of anarchy more or less prolonged, our descendants may find Burma a Province of China. China has a great civilisation and it is quite possible that the absorption of Burma by the Chinese will be the best destiny for Burmans. Then the European visitor looking at Burman lads playing Burmese and Association football will probably reflect that at least one valuable element of Burmese civilisation outlasted British rule and that there is one good thing we gave them. But this will be an inglorious, if not unfitting, memorial of British rule in Burma.

It may sound harsh, condescending or even demeaning to Burmese patriotic ears, but fifty years after independence, the most promising Southeast Asian candidate for development has become the most backward and retrogressive in the region. It would be up to the Burmese and their leaders to prove Furnivall's prophesy to be not true after all.

References

Furnivall, J.S. *An Introduction to the Political Economy of Burma*, 3rd edition. Rangoon: Burmese Advertising Press, 1957.

————. "Economic History of Burma", Tables No. 1–X. Unpublished manuscript.

Khin Maung Kyi. "Western Enterprise and Economic Development in Burma". *Journal of Burma Research Society* 53, Pt.1 (1970): 25–52.

Kyaw Thet. *History of Union of Burma*. Rangoon: People's Stores Corporation, 1960.

Chapter 5
The Ethnic Chinese as Filipinos

Teresita Ang See

Introduction

In the past decade, especially after the introduction of the open-door policy in China and the influx of investments from Chinese all over the world into China, there has been rising interest in the phenomenon of what many writers call the "Overseas Chinese" or the "Chinese overseas." There has been quite a number of international conferences held which are focused on the topic. Likewise, a plethora of publications about the Chinese outside mainland China, specifically about the Chinese in Southeast Asia, has emerged. The government of Australia even went to the extent of commissioning a study on *Chinese Business Networks in Southeast Asia*,[1] one of the better researched works on the topic in recent years. However, the interest, albeit a much welcome one, can also have serious implications especially for the Chinese in Southeast Asia, depending on how this interest is manifested or expressed. Among some writers nowadays, there seems to be an increasing trend to lump all the ethnic Chinese together into "a grand conspiracy" to form a so-called "Third China" or "Greater China" powerful enough to tip the economic balance scale against the United States and Japan.

One glaring example is the three-part series published in *San Jose Mercury News*[2] of California on 27–29 June 1994. The series deliberately twisted a lot of facts and exaggerated figures that tended to overstate the role of the ethnic Chinese in their own country's domestic economy and to substantiate the authors' thesis of a supposed "new yellow peril". The series was written by Lewis M. Simmons and Michael Zielenziger and carry statements like: "Overseas Chinese have a lock on much of Asia's economy, how do they do it? Through a vast network of family businesses run on trust and intuition." The last part, on 29 June on, "The consequences of indifference" emphasizes the central thesis that gives us an inkling of why the three-part series was written in the first place. The blurb says: "The United States and Japan slept as Chinese influence grew in Asia. Even now, they're barely aware of the challenge." Another example is Sterling Seagrave's *Lords of the Rim: The Invisible Empire of the Overseas Chinese.*[3] Seagrave writes: "Be so subtle that you are invisible. Be so mysterious that you are intangible. Then you will control your rivals' fate." Sun Tzu in the *Art of War* also writes, "and no group has taken his advice more to heart than the Overseas Chinese, a vast, highly interconnected network of fifty-five million expatriate Chinese who control up to two trillion dollars in assets, and not only dominate the Pacific Rim but are making increasing inroads into the West." Like the story in *San Jose Mercury News*, Seagrave warns: "The longer term outlook is that the Overseas Chinese will greatly increase their commercial lead over the rest of the world — and if the West does not prepare for that possibility, it is in for a major shock." Both used words such as "a vast interconnected network, expatriates dominate the economy" to promote the idea that these ethnic Chinese are a homogeneous group invisibly linked together ("controlling two trillion dollars in assets") with a common agenda of displacing America's and Japan's economic superiority. Others use language such as "borderless empire", "Chinese diaspora", "offshore China", "Greater China", and the like. In fact, the use of China-centric terms such as "Chinese overseas" or "Overseas

Chinese" itself reflects back to the Cold-War era when these Chinese were considered "yellow perils". Wittingly or unwittingly, these writers are promoting ideas that may have dangerous implications for the ethnic Chinese in their own countries.

Convening a workshop with a theme such as "The Ethnic Chinese as Southeast Asians" is most timely and the convenor, Dr. Leo Suryadinata, deserves to be congratulated for his perceptiveness in pushing for a discussion of such a concept. Serious scholars on the study of the ethnic Chinese in recent years have posited the qualification that the Southeast Asian Chinese are indeed no longer *Huaqiao* or sojourners, much less "overseas Chinese or "Chinese overseas". They are, in fact, Southeast Asians, albeit of Chinese origin. They are responsible to their respective Southeast Asian countries and are not homogeneously lumped together to form a vast interconnected network to serve China, much less to dominate the local economies of their own countries. The sojourners of the past have now become Thais, Malaysians, Indonesians, Singaporeans, or Filipinos, each one distinct from the other. As for the Chinese in the Philippines, they can be Ilocanos, Tausugs, Bicolanos, Samals, Manilans, Negrenses, and so forth without discarding the truth that they are of Chinese origin.

Convening such a workshop also recognizes a uniqueness common to these Southeast Asian nations — the presence of a substantial number of ethnic Chinese in their midst. Apart from similarities in geography, history, culture and race, Southeast Asia as a region is also home for the biggest number of ethnic Chinese outside of mainland China. Hence, a workshop on the ethnic Chinese as Southeast Asians holds even greater and more far-reaching significance. Because of their common experiences, Southeast Asian countries have formed themselves into a regional grouping and they are now playing an increasingly important role in the global economic and political arena. If we consider the presence of the ethnic Chinese as a uniqueness of these Southeast Asian countries, can such a presence also be tapped to exert a more crucial influence on the growing importance of Southeast Asia as a region? At the outset, I mentioned the growing importance of the role of the ethnic Chinese in Southeast Asia and people have increasingly paid greater attention to this fact. I would now like to posit this question: while each of the ethnic Chinese populations identify with their respective Southeast Asian countries, can they, at the same time, be encouraged to identify themselves also with Southeast Asia as a region, and can each be tapped to exert greater influence for and on behalf of Southeast Asia? In short, can the presence of the ethnic Chinese be a unifying factor serving Southeast Asian interests rather than the more far-fetched claim of a Southeast Asian "overseas Chinese enclave" serving a Greater China?

Since I am from the Philippines, I am to talk about the Chinese Filipinos or the ethnic Chinese as Filipinos. After exploring the question of whether they are Chinese or Filipinos, allow me to go back and relate it to the theme of the workshop, "The Ethnic Chinese as Southeast Asians" and raise the question: can they eventually also identify themselves as Southeast Asians in much the same way as the French, Germans, British, Spaniards and others identify themselves as Europeans? However, before I start discussing the identity of the Chinese Filipinos, let me briefly review the Philippine colonial experience and the formation of the Filipino nationality which is a late nineteenth century phenomenon. Likewise, I will discuss some crucial historical factors and government policies that served to retard the process of integration and to constrain the ethnic Chinese from finally identifying themselves as Filipinos. These factors are: the Philippines' relations with China and the Philippine Government's policy on citizenship; the pro-Taiwan and pro-China factionalism in the community; the colonial experience and the divide-and-rule policy in particular; and lastly, the colonial legacy of discrimination, negative perceptions and stereotypes about the ethnic Chinese.

Filipino National Identity and Nationhood

The emergence of the Philippines as a nation with a national identity is relatively recent, a late nineteenth century phenomenon, in fact. Even in the middle of the twentieth century, some scholars still said that the Philippines was a country in search of a national identity. The many revolutionary uprisings against the Spanish government that occurred towards the end of Spanish rule at the turn of the century were launched by a highly fragmented society.

They were prodded not by a national consciousness or aspiration for the country to be freed from the shackles of colonial rule but more for parochial concerns of the regions where the uprisings occurred, or for the personal grievances of the leaders of the uprisings. Historian Renato Constantino writes: "The growth of the concept of nationhood was coterminous with the development of the concept of Filipino."[4] With this historical background, it is easy to understand why the identification of the ethnic Chinese as Filipinos is a late twentieth century phenomenon. Father Miguel A. Bernad, a Jesuit historian, writes: "In the course of the past four hundred years (over three hundred under Spain, a half century under America, and three decades under our own independent government) a national unity has emerged in which people of different regions and of different linguistic groups do not consider themselves merely Tagalogs, Visayans, Pampangos, Ilocanos, Bicols, and so on, but first and foremost as Filipinos. However, this unification of the country into one nation and one people has not been completed. There are still minority groups within the country who do not yet feel at home within this union. When every member of a minority group feels that he is, first, a Filipino, and only secondarily a member of his ethnic group, the task of unification will have been completed."[5]

The people who propagated the consciousness for a national identity and the idea of a Filipino identity and nationhood were the Ilustrados, mainly Chinese mestizos who formed the middle class and who were able to receive and be influenced by the more liberal Western ideas during their studies or exile abroad. Prominent Filipinos in both the reform and revolutionary movements were almost all of Chinese descent although they joined the revolution as Malay Filipinos and not as Chinese mestizos. Historian Dr. Antonio Tan succinctly states the Chinese mestizos' contributions to national development: "The Chinese mestizos were an important element of Philippine society in the 19th century. They played a significant role in the formation of the Filipino middle class, in the agitation for reforms, in the 1898 revolution, and in the formation of what is now known as the Filipino nationality."[6] Moreover, the Philippines, made up of 7,100 islands, has always been a culturally pluralistic society. It has tolerated the existence of different cultural communities in as many linguistic divisions, from the Cordillera and Sierra Madre mountains' tribal minorities in the north to the Muslim minorities in the south. Thus, under this cultural pluralism, the recognition of the ethnic Chinese as a cultural minority should have been a much smoother process, but other barriers, like the lack of citizenship and other factors to be discussed below, have been responsible for the Chinese being considered alien minorities for a long time.

The Ethnic Chinese and China
Up to 1975, the Philippines had diplomatic relations with Taiwan and had very close relations with it. The Philippines recognized Taiwan's jurisdiction over a hundred thousand alien Chinese permanently residing in the country, and allowed it to closely supervise the affairs of the Chinese community. Taiwan exercised rights of supervision over the so-called Chinese schools, in terms of curriculum, textbooks, and even hiring and training of teachers through the General Association of Chinese Schools (校总). Taiwan also actively involved itself in the affairs of the Federation of Filipino-Chinese Chambers of Commerce (菲华商联总会) and in the Grand Family Association (宗联), a federation of family associations all over the country.[7]

In June 1975, however, the Philippines established diplomatic relations with the People's Republic of China (PRC) and thus turned away from Taiwan. In preparation for this, the Philippines had to address two main issues: the question of the allegiance of the local Chinese, and the fear of the Chinese possibly becoming tools of communism. Thus, two Presidential Decrees (P.D.) specifically addressing these problems were promulgated by then President Ferdinand Marcos before diplomatic relations were established. The first was P.D. 176, promulgated in 1973 to implement the constitutional provision on the Filipinization of all alien schools. The second was Letters of Instruction (LOI) 270 issued on 11 April 1975 just two months before the establishment of diplomatic relations with China. LOI 270 paved the way for the mass naturalization of the resident Chinese by administrative means. Both decrees had quite significant and far-reaching impact on the Chinese community, particularly in hastening the integration of the local Chinese into mainstream society.[8]

Before the mass naturalization process, the ethnic Chinese could obtain citizenship only through the judicial system, since the Philippine Constitution adopted the *jus sanguinis* (citizenship by blood) as against *jus soli* (citizenship by birth) principle of citizenship. The judicial process of naturalization was a time-consuming, onerous and extremely expensive process since it was fraught with graft and corruption. Therefore, it left a sizeable number of ethnic Chinese (no matter if they were born and educated in the Philippines) with Chinese (at the time, Taiwan) citizenship. The Philippine Government facilitated the mass naturalization of the local Chinese because of its fears that if allowed to retain their Chinese citizenship after diplomatic relations with the PRC were established, these Chinese would owe allegiance and be subjected to the direct supervision and control of the PRC, a communist country, thereby creating a possibility of their adopting or being influenced by the communist ideology.[9]

The facts, however, showed that the government's fears were misplaced. An understanding of the Chinese community would show that the local Chinese are basically capitalist, profit-oriented businessmen — antithetical to communism. They are as against communist ideology as most Filipinos. The question of allegiance at that time, however, was a chicken-and-egg issue. The Philippine Government hesitated in granting citizenship to the local Chinese because it doubted their loyalty. On the other hand, the local Chinese argued that they could not freely give political allegiance to a country which they did not belong to. This issue was thoroughly debated upon during the 1971 Constitutional Convention's deliberations on the adoption of the *jus soli* as against the *jus sanguinis* principle of citizenship.[10]

When the government finally saw its way to granting easy access to citizenship through LOI 270, a greatly accelerated integration process was easily seen. The local Chinese, young and old, availed of this process. Without doubt, this mass naturalization gave great impetus to the integration of the local Chinese. What the Philippine Government failed to realize at that point was that the majority of the local Chinese were already native born, they grew up in the Philippines, were educated in Philippine schools, had no first-hand experience of China, and had known no other country except the Philippines. What had held them back from fully identifying themselves as Filipinos was the lack of citizenship. When citizenship was granted, therefore, political identity was established and the barriers to full commitment to citizenship were finally lifted.[11]

The establishment of diplomatic relations with China itself was also of great significance. In fact, it can be considered a turning point in the history of the Chinese in the Philippines because of its far-reaching implications in affecting the consciousness and orientation of the older generation Chinese. Just before the establishment of Philippine-China diplomatic relations, China regained its rightful position in the United Nations. China thus achieved a new status and became a player of consequence on the international stage. For a while, there was widespread euphoria among the Philippine Chinese who pinned high hopes on the diplomatic relations with China. They believed that with a "great China" to support them and to protect their interests, their days of being underdogs were over. With such a powerful mother country and its embassy officials to depend on, their problems could all be solved. This China-oriented outlook and ethnocentrism verging on outright cultural chauvinism was typical of the older generation Chinese who had strong loyalties to China and who longed for a strong mother country to help and protect them. They admired the gunship diplomacy of the West and wished that China could do the same.[12]

For the Taiwan-oriented faction within the local Chinese community, the uncertainties regarding Taiwan's political future, especially after the Philippines severed its political ties with Taiwan, left many in limbo. Unwilling to commit themselves to China whose communist system was opposed to their capitalistic way of life and beliefs, many decided that it was time to hitch their fortunes with the Philippines. Out of habit, many of them, until now, are pro-Taiwan in sentiment but they also realize that they have only themselves to depend on to work out their future in the Philippines. In recent years, many of these Kuomintang-oriented sympathizers have modified their outlook and this has been reflected in their speeches. They have started to talk about the long range interests of the greater society and the need to identify with the mainstream.

However, it did not take long for these Chinese to wake up to the reality that China's "protection" and support cannot be granted as a matter of course. Due to its anti-hegemony stance and its avowed policy of non-recognition of dual nationality and non-interference in local affairs, China, no matter how strong, cannot live up to the expectations of the local Chinese especially since many of them are already Filipino citizens. China's cautiousness and reluctance to interfere and to involve itself in the affairs of the local Chinese (which, admittedly, are internal affairs of the Philippines) even after diplomatic relations were established was a rude awakening to many of these China-oriented older generation Chinese. In their disappointment, many came to realize that their survival depended not on China's greatness but on the Philippines' own future. They started to open their eyes to the fact that their interests could not be separated from the interests of Philippine society and that the so-called local Chinese problems were directly related to the problems of the larger Philippine society and as such, could only be solved within the boundaries of Philippine society.[13]

This has been demonstrated most clearly in recent years. As the spate of kidnappings menaced and traumatized the ethnic Chinese community, they tried to pin their hopes on Taiwan and China. They thought that Taiwan could put economic pressure and China could put political pressure on the Philippine government to solve the problem. It was an even ruder awakening when China stuck to its principle of non-interference in internal affairs and Taiwan also refused to lift its hands in relation to the kidnapping problem except to help in the prosecution of one kidnapping case where the victim was a Taiwanese. Ironically, in this Taiwanese case, it was later discovered that the one involved in the kidnapping was Colonel Reynaldo Berroya, the former head of the government's anti-kidnapping task force himself.[14] Colonel Berroya was convicted of kidnapping in 1995 but the case is still on appeal.

Pro-Taiwan vs. Pro-China Factionalism

The historical reality of a long and intimate relationship with Taiwan preceding diplomatic relations with the PRC also gave rise to a phenomenon in the Philippines that has no parallel in Southeast Asia — a split in the Chinese community into two clashing factions, one with a pro-China orientation and the other with a pro-Taiwan orientation. The existence of these two factions and the bitter and active rivalry between them has no equal in Southeast Asia. There are five Chinese-language dailies with a total circulation of about 35,000 in the Philippines. Two of these dailies are pro-Beijing, two are pro-Taipei, and one is a fence-sitter. There are also two rival factions in the fire-prevention brigades, and there are family associations, like the Cua-Chua, the Co, and the Lim Associations, which are split into two factions. Chambers of Commerce, which should have been involved only in business matters, are not exempted from this factionalism. There are other groups — literary groups, athletic groups, music clubs, and even schools — that have clearly defined leanings. The situation sometimes verges on the ridiculous. On their respective foundation anniversaries on 1 October and 10 October, the two factions rival each other in the number of congratulatory newspaper advertisements they get, the number of guests and government officials in their respective receptions, and so on. Any worthwhile projects launched by one group would be boycotted by the other group. Some prominent businessmen even leave the country to avoid meeting with the Chinese ambassador at official gatherings. In recent years, however, this active rivalry has been growing weaker as more and more of the pro-Taiwan factions are making a beeline to the lucrative China market; it is nevertheless still a contentious issue that has divided the community and affected its stand on various pressing issues that affect them directly.[15]

However, this ongoing cold war is confined only to a very small sector of the Chinese community, mostly the older genera-tion businessmen who, unfortunately, still hold leadership positions and wield power and influence in the community. The younger generation, however, are not even aware of the existence of these petty intrigues and senseless animosities among the professed leaders of the community. They would find what their elders are fighting for an irrelevant issue which is of no concern to them because their concern lies with their future in the Philippines. Way back in 1970, Dr. Robert Tilman had concluded in his study of the Philippine-Chinese youth: "The problems, frustrations, prejudices, follies, faults, hopes and aspirations are about the same, whether the students be Chinese or Filipino."[16]

In addition to the factionalism, for the past several decades since the war, the older generation Chinese have clung stubbornly to their ethnocentrism and cultural chauvinism. They have laboured hard to perpetuate their Chineseness. The saying "Once a Chinese, always a Chinese" was a ruling passion among them. Yet, no matter how hard they tried to resist the changes brought about by their environment, their efforts have been futile and they have learned that integration is a natural sociological phenomenon which nobody can prevent. In fact, the process of detachment from China as a nation started from the beginning of the twentieth century when many of the Chinese fulfilled their dreams of economic success, and dreams of returning home to China gradually vanished. Most importantly, after 1949, when China closed its doors to the outside world, the local Chinese finally realized that there was no more going home and that the Philippines was the only country where they and their future generations would live. Contrary, therefore, to the fears that diplomatic relations would be a stumbling block to integration, facts have proved that even the older Chinese have come to realize that their destinies cannot be separated from the Philippines and that it is the Philippines, not China, which has a decisive influence on their future. From events in the past two decades, the local Chinese have realized that only by working hand in hand with the Filipinos for the greater national interest rather than for narrow self-interests of their parochial community can their own future be assured. This realization, in turn, was greatly instrumental in hastening the process of integration.

Legacy of Colonial Experience

The more than three centuries of Spanish rule and five decades of American occupation left indelible marks on the Philippines, espe-cially in the relations between the ethnic Chinese and the native

Filipinos. True to the dictum of divide and rule, both the Spaniards and the Americans separated the ethnic Chinese from the Filipino mainstream. The Spaniards put up a physical barrier by confining the Chinese in their exclusive enclave, the *Parian*, and the Americans perpetuated a psychological barrier by encouraging the Chinese to live a separate existence by having their own schools, press, chamber of commerce and other associations. Both colonizers, as well as the short-lived Japanese rulers, exploited to the hilt the art of scapegoatism — blaming the Chinese for the economic ills that befell the country caused by their maladministration and ineffective economic policies. The deliberate anti-Chinese policies of discrimination and the tendencies of the colonial administration to blame the ethnic Chinese for their own failed policies are legacies which have been passed on and perpetuated to the present.[17]

Many Social Distance surveys[18] and studies on ethnic prejudices have been conducted in the past. Although they differ in degree, they have a common finding — that the Chinese, just like the Muslims in Southern Philippines, lie low in the social distance scale. In the studies using semantical differences, both the studies of Weightman and Berreman[19] came up with these adjectives: the Chinese are business-minded, good in mathematics, rich, industrious, thrifty, dynamic, and persevering. On the negative side, most of these attitude and behaviour surveys reveal that the native Filipinos resent the Chinese for being exploiters, abusive employers, shrewd businessmen, and tax evaders, and for the prevalent belief that the Chinese control the economy. An analysis of both the positive and negative images of the Chinese leads to one conclusion — all the traits mentioned are economic in nature. They are a reflection of the supposed "business success" of the Chinese. In fact, they intensify the myth that all Chinese are businessmen or to say it more bluntly, the Chinese are all "economic animals". More importantly, they reinforce the image of "economic power" held by the local Chinese, which further elicit envy and distrust of the native Filipinos.

In my past papers on these biases and stereotypes, especially the paper on the "Images of the Chinese in the Philippines", I have pointed out that these stereotypes are based on prejudices and misunderstanding borne mostly out of some unfortunate personal experiences and grudges. Most importantly, the traits such as abusive employers, exploiters, and tax evaders, are true of any race and can be blamed on irresponsible and opportunistic businessmen and not on the Chinese as a racial trait.[20] Most of these social distance and attitude surveys were conducted in the sixties and seventies and it would be useful to conduct new surveys. With so many changes happening among the ethnic Chinese, it would be worthwhile to find out if perceptions about them have changed. Among 120 respondents in a survey my students conducted informally in 1989,[21] there seems to be much improvement in attitudes towards the ethnic Chinese in that the majority answered that they did not mind having a Chinese as a business partner, a neighbour, a friend or even as a spouse. The negative attitudes about them are again confined mostly to business practices, like being secretive and paying low salaries.

Most of the dynamics of animosity are concentrated in Metropolitan Manila and among the middle class. In a study in 1971, anthropologist John Omohundro observed that: "Not all regions and social strata of Filipinos feel the same way about the Chinese but there is little careful inquiry into variations within the country. It is popular knowledge that the Ilocano-speaking regions of Luzon are the most anti-Chinese, whereas the Muslim Filipinos of Mindanao are considered in the main very tolerant. The Ilongo and Cebuano-speaking people of the central Philippines, popularly considered easy-going people, harbour less animosity and express it less than the Tagalog speakers of Manila. It remains to be shown that these popular conceptions are a social reality."[22]

Undercurrents of racism and latent racial animosity have always lain below the surface but they have not really been problematic except on occasions when politicians deliberately exploit the issue and fan racial unrest to serve their own ends. In recent years, during elections especially, some candidates or interest groups would deliberately fan anti-Chinese prejudices by campaigning against candidates with "short" surnames. In 1995, there were campaign posters such as *"Sa Intsik na nga ang ekonomiya, pati ba naman ang politika? (The economy already belongs to the Chinese, even politics too)?"* This was led by Jun

Ducat, a businessman who purportedly heads Kalipi (*Kadugong Liping Pilipino* or Filipinos of same blood and race). The irony is that this anti-Chinese campaign was targetted at candidates who have been Filipinos for three generations, and whom nobody would acknowledge to be an ethnic Chinese — such as the present Manila Mayor Alfredo Lim, or the Congressman of Tarlac and uncle of President Corazon Aquino, Representative Jose Yap.[23] The same campaign posters resurrected the old slogan, "The Philippines for the Filipinos", reminiscent of the earlier "Filipino First" campaign immediately after independence from the United States and the establishment of the new Republic. At that time, nationalism was equated with being anti-foreign and anti-Chinese.

In recent years, we have again witnessed anti-Chinese and racist acts especially after every economic crisis spawned, for instance, by an oil price increase or a rice shortage. The government's tendency to divert attention away from real problems by blaming the Chinese traders is an age-old practice but it is nevertheless still dangerous and demoralizing for the local Chinese. Worse is the fact that other sectors may deliberately exploit this latent racism for their own ends. Sociologist Dr. Rodolfo Bulatao says: "Childhood prejudices and narrow loyalties may be diluted and overlayed with specific concerns as one matures, but they remain latent and capable of being mobilized unwittingly or by design. The less aware the public is of these underlying cleavages, the more explosive their potential, and the less adequately ethnic tensions are handled, the more difficult it will be to create one national unity out of the country's various ethnic components."[24] This warning, especially on the unwitting or deliberate mobilization of latent hostilities, cannot be ignored and there have been increasing signs that the "ethnic Chinese" can be utilized to divert attention from more pressing national issues, as had happened countless times in the past.

This can be clearly seen in the anti-Chinese mass rally that took place in Angeles City on 5 July 1986, just a day after the announcement of American withdrawal from Clark Air Base in Angeles City. Slogans and posters scattered all over the city blamed the Chinese for the high prices of goods and suggested that instead of sending the Americans out, the Filipinos should unite to send the Chinese out of the country. In 1995, the convenient practice of scapegoatism found its target among the big Chinese Filipino rice traders. Because of the failure of the government's own agricultural policies that resulted in a rice shortage and the fact that measures to alleviate the rice shortage through importation were not put in place immediately since it was election time (May 1995), the shortage became a full-blown crisis. The old bogey of a so-called "rice cartel" of Chinese rice traders was resurrected deliberately and the rice crisis was blamed on them. This was done even though the government knew all the while that out of the seven members of the alleged "rice cartel" three were no longer in the rice business since 1990. These traders became tired of always being the butt of the blame whenever something went wrong with the supply of rice (which they called a "political foodstuff"). This act of diverting attention away from the real problem and conveniently blaming others has dangerous repercussions for the Chinese community. It intensifies feelings of vulnerability and jolts the confidence of the ethnic Chinese in continuing their businesses in the Philippines.[25]

Adding to the fears and unrest among the ethnic Chinese are the repeated pronouncements by President Fidel V. Ramos' political adviser himself, General Jose Almonte, which has been interpreted to be racist. For example, Almonte was quoted by the *Straits Times* (Singapore) as saying: "Our so-called Taipans, they're not as big as the Taipans of Hong Kong or maybe Singapore, but they claim that, between them, they can pay our indebtedness and that is about $30 billion. That's a lot of money. Now, it's all right if this was acquired through means acceptable to the national community, but they were not, and we must get them to show a greater responsibility to the community." In another interview in Congress, General Almonte was quoted as saying: "The problem of insurgency is no longer in the mountains of the Sierra Madres and Cordillera but in the boardrooms of Binondo and Makati." Binondo is the acknowledged financial and distribution centre of the Chinese Filipinos while Makati is the financial and commercial centre owned by the Spanish Filipino élites and home to most of the multinational companies.[26]

While the earlier surveys prevalently showed the economic nature of the prejudices, the social image, leaves much to be desired. Many of the surveys showed that the Chinese are considered "unassimilable", that they are clannish, that they refuse to marry Filipinos, that they are a dirty and noisy people, and other similar negative impressions. The image of the Chinese as "*Intsik Beho or Intsik Tsekwa*" is still prevalent in Philippine literature.[27] The myth that "Once a Chinese, always a Chinese," is, unfortunately, also still a prevalent belief. Gregorio F. Zaide, writing in *Political and Cultural History of the Philippines*, summed up the prevalent anti-Chinese sentiments this way: "The Chinese were obnoxious because they were economically dominant, strange because they were culturally alien, repulsive because they were culturally clannish and disloyal because they were politically unreliable."[28] But, do realities fit this image? Rapid changes have occurred, especially among the young local-born Chinese. The accusations of "unassimilability" of the Chinese can be easily refuted by looking at the socio-cultural changes that have occurred among the younger generation of Chinese Filipinos. The changes are described more fully in the following pages on socio-cultural integration.

In consonance with these changes, even the image of the Filipinos in the minds of the Chinese has changed. Among the older generation Chinese, personal contacts they have had with Filipinos are limited to their workers, their employees, their maids at home, corrupt policemen and firemen, Bureau of Internal Revenue agents and City Hall inspectors who harass them regularly, and politicians who befriend or lambast them depending on personal conveniences and purposes. Hence, the image of the Filipino in their consciousness is also negative. Likewise, the economic disparity or class differences between the majority of the Filipinos who still live below the poverty line and the predominantly middle class ethnic Chinese is a reality that often intensifies this negative attitude from both sides. Now, with the younger generation Chinese having personal Filipino friends in school, at work, and in their neighbourhood, a deeper and more intimate relationship is formed which gives rise to a generally more positive image of the Filipinos in their minds.[29]

Taking these historical realities, like Philippine-China relations and the legacy of discrimination as a background, we realize that the process of integration among the ethnic Chinese has actually happened under such disadvantageous or adverse circumstances. Let us now go to the main discussion on the ethnic Chinese as Filipinos. First, I would like to emphasize that the ethnic Chinese in the Philippines is not a homogeneous or cohesive group and I will also point out that it is not accurate to use only the urban Metropolitan Manila Chinese as our yardstick in tackling the whole issue of the Chinese as Filipinos.

Diversity and Complexity

Historically, the largest concentration of ethnic Chinese has always been in Metro Manila, or in the City of Manila specifically. Out of the 800,000 to 850,000 ethnic Chinese all over the Philippines, forming roughly 1.2 per cent of the population of 68 million, more than half can be found in Metro Manila and the other half of this number are concentrated in the areas bounded by Binondo and a part of the congested districts of Tondo, San Nicolas, Sta. Cruz and Quiapo. Added to this heavy concentration of ethnic Chinese in Metro Manila is the fact that the greater number of Chinese associations — whether chambers of commerce, home-town, family or clan, alumni, arts, literary, or religious — are also concentrated in Manila; in fact, they are predominantly located in Binondo, or the so-called "Chinatown" district. Hence, when people talk about the ethnic Chinese in the Philippines, they often refer to the Chinese in Manila. In short, the Chinese Manilans are considered to be the representatives of the entire ethnic Chinese population in the country. In addition to this, the definition of ethnic Chinese, in practice, is further narrowed down to refer mostly to the traditional leaders of the Chinese community — the so-called *qiao ling* (侨领) — who come predominantly from the leadership ranks of traditional Chinese organizations. When the Chinese community is mentioned or events in the Chinese community are reported, people often jump to the conclusion that these refer only to the so-called *qiao ling* and their activities because they are mainly what appear in the Chinese-language dailies.[30]

Likewise, researchers and scholars have also focused their studies mostly on the Chinese in Manila and these studies are often made to reflect the situation of the entire ethnic Chinese population in the Philippines. The truth, however, is that the Chinese Manilans, much less the group made up only of the *qiao ling,* can hardly represent the entire Chinese population in the Philippines. As we explore the one unifying identity of the ethnic Chinese as Filipinos, we should bear in mind that there exists a vast continuum of differences and uniqueness among the ethnic Chinese in different parts of the country made up of 7,100 islands. Studying the ethnic Chinese as Cebuanos, Ilonggos, Ilocanos, Pangasinenses, Tausugs, Zamboanguenos, and so forth would certainly bring out the pitfalls of generalizing about the Chinese in the Philippines.

In fact, even among the Chinese Manilans, there also exist vast differences. Just take citizenship as an example. There are those who already have Filipino citizenship and can be legally considered Filipinos, or Filipino citizens. However, there exists a pocket of Chinese who are still non-Filipino in citizenship. Should they be included in our topic "The Ethnic Chinese as Filipinos" or should they be left out? If they are to be left out, we should remember that among these non-Filipino citizens, there are those who cannot even speak Chinese, who grew up only in Filipino neighbourhoods, have only Filipino friends and for all intents and purposes are like any other Filipino except for the lack of citizenship. Is it fair to consider them aliens and not as Chinese Filipinos? Take the case of the scholar of Rotary Club in Cotabato who was sent to the United States on a one-year exchange scholarship. Upon arrival back at the Manila International Airport after a year, she was detained by the immigration and refused entry to the Philippines because she did not have a re-entry permit. The girl never knew that as a Chinese passport holder, she was considered an alien and needed to apply for a re-entry permit to come back to the only country that she knew. Even the immigration agents did not know what to do with her. They wanted to deport her to Taiwan but the girl did not know anyone there, she did not even speak Chinese and never had any Chinese-language education. In fact, she only learned that she was a Chinese citizen (by virtue of her father being Chinese) when she was applying for a Filipino passport and was denied one. She was detained by the immigration for several days while the Rotary Club made arrangements to prove that she was a permanent resident of the country.[31]

On the other hand, among those who possess Filipino citizenship, the degree of Filipinoness compared to their Chineseness also vary greatly. Added to this, the dimension of the new immigrants from China, Hong Kong or Taiwan must also be considered. To what extent and what criteria can be used to consider the latter group as Chinese Filipinos? Are they within the scope of this study? This illustrates the fact that it is really quite difficult to use citizenship to make generalizations as to who are Chinese Filipinos. This is particularly true if we factor in the corruption in the Philippine bureaucracy and the reality that there are many ways, legal and extra-legal, by which Filipino citizenship can be obtained, especially among the new immigrants.

Just the issue of citizenship alone illustrates the complexity of studying the Chinese Manilans. Moreover, we should bear in mind that they are not truly representative of all the Chinese in the Philippines, much less be lumped together with the ethnic Chinese in other parts of the country, especially in the provinces and in the rural areas. On the other hand, the complexity also serves to emphasize the need to explore in depth the uniqueness, the differences and the varying levels or degrees of being Filipinos. These differences can be seen in age or generation, levels of education, cultural background (such as whether they participate in traditional Chinese organizations or not), degree of language proficiency, social and economic status, personal experiences, lifestyle, attitudes and orientation, as well as their sense of identity and belonging. To many Filipinos and foreigners, the Chinese community in the Philippines appears to be a homogeneous one, instead of the complex and diversified population that it really is. In fact, even the definition of ethnic Chinese leaves a lot of confusion. Here, I use the well-accepted sociological definition that the ethnic Chinese are people with a measurable degree of Chinese parentage, have undergone a minimum Chinese language education, can understand and speak a bare minimum of Chinese dialect, still have close contacts with the Chinese community and have retained some Chinese customs and traditions enough to consider themselves and be considered by others as Chinese. It is acknowledged that 10 per cent of the Filipinos have Chinese blood in them but only about 1.2 per cent can really be considered ethnic Chinese.[32]

For the purposes of this study, I conducted a survey on "Ethnic Identity of the *Tsinoys*"[33] (*Tsinoy* is a colloquial term increasingly used now to refer to the *Tsinong Pinoy* or Chinese Filipinos). The 510 respondents gathered from schools, civic organizations and alumni and parents associations are mainly from Metro Manila (80 per cent), with some from the provinces (20 per cent). The ages ranged from 17 to 60 and I subdivided the ages according to Philippine demographic groupings. Henceforth, this survey will be referred to as the 1995 Identity Survey when cited, in comparison with an earlier survey done among 381 students in 1988.

Let me now highlight some major points of diversity among the ethnic Chinese population in the Philippines:[34]

1. Based on citizenship, as mentioned above, the main difference is among those who are Filipino citizens and those who are not.

2. Among those who do not have Filipino citizenship, some hold China (PRC) passports, Taiwan (ROC) passports, Hong Kong passports or British identity cards. Then there are those who hold U.S., Canadian, Australian or Singapore passports. One striking irony is the fact that some were born locally and have never been to China. If they have not gone abroad and therefore have no need for passports, their only identification papers are their birth certificates, to prove that they were born in the Philippines, and the Alien Certificate of Registration (ACR) and the Immigrant Certificate of Registration (ICR) issued by the Bureau of Immigration of the Philippines, if they had registered themselves; they are, *de facto*, stateless.

3. Among the holders of PRC or ROC passports, the newcomers and older immigrants, and the local-born and China-born must also be further differentiated. Of the China-born, those who came in before the fifties or before the Pacific war are

certainly different from those who came in later in the seventies, eighties or nineties in terms of their sense of identity and belonging. Then again, they are also different compared to the Chinese passport holders who were born in the Philippines and grew up in the Philippines. Among the Taiwan (ROC) passport holders, apart from the real Taiwanese themselves, there are those who have dual nationality, like the Chinese Filipino overseas contract workers who, for the convenience of working in Taiwan, also applied for Taiwan citizenship despite the fact that they already hold Filipino citizenship.

4. Among those who have Filipino citizenship there are also differences. Some are natural born Filipinos (that is, both parents or the father or mother are Filipino citizens at birth); while some are naturalized citizens (including those who applied under judicial means and those who applied under the administrative decree of Marcos in 1975). Besides these are those who obtained Filipino citizenship fraudulently but who are, nonetheless, considered legitimate Filipinos. The 1995 Identity Survey showed that more than 70 per cent of the ethnic Chinese were natural born (see Table 1).

It is interesting to note that when broken down into age groups, the youngest age bracket of 17 to 21 years showed the highest number of natural born citizens (82.6 per cent). This is the generation born after 1975 of parents who acquired citizenship through LOI 270, the decree facilitating naturalization promulgated by then President Marcos.

TABLE 1

How Citizenship is Acquired

	Freq.	Percentage
Chinese citizens	20	3.9
Natural born Filipino	369	72.3
Naturalized Filipino	110	21.6
Others [2 Brits., 2 Amer.]	4	0.8
No answer	7	1.4
Total	510	100

TABLE 2

How Citizenship is Acquired

(By age)

Age	Chinese Citizens	Natural Born Filipino	Naturalized Filipino	Filipino by Election	Others	No Answer	Total
				Citizenship			
17–21	2.6%	82.6%	11.5%	0.3%	6.0%	2.3%	100%
22–32	6.7%	67.6%	24.1%	0.9%	0.9%	0.0	100%
33–45	5.3%	28.1%	54.4%	10.5%	1.8%	0.0	100%
46–Above	0.0	28.0%	52.0%	20.0%	0.0	0.0	100%
No Age	12.5%	56.3%	31.3%	0.0	0.0	0.0	100%

5. Based on ethnic origin, no matter what the citizenship is, there is a big difference among Filipino citizens whose parents are pure Chinese and those who have mixed parentage. The mestizos are naturally more Filipinized than those who hail from pure Chinese racial stock. The 1995 Identity Survey showed that among those who are Filipino citizens, 55.9 per cent had parents who were pure Chinese and 32 per cent Chinese mestizos. This jives with the earlier survey of 1988 where more than 50 per cent of the student respondents said that they would not mind getting married to Filipinos. It was also a confirmation of the earlier premise that the rate of intermarriages was on the rise.[35]

TABLE 3

Racial Origins

	Freq.	Percentage
Pure Chinese	285	55.9
Chinese Mestizos	163	32.0
Others	50	9.8
No Answer	12	2.3
Total	510	100

6. Based on educational level and cultural background, whether or not the person was a Filipino citizen, those who were educated in the Philippines were naturally more greatly influenced by the Philippine environment, and their sense of belonging and attachment to the Philippines was deeper compared to those who were educated in China or outside the Philippines. In fact, studies have pointed out that native-born ethnic Chinese who are educated in Philippine schools are no different from Filipinos. In contrast, those who are educated in China, Taiwan or Hong Kong are naturally much more sinified.

7. Based on age or generational differences, except for some isolated cases or isolated influences, generally, the younger the generation, the more Filipino they become. The older the generation, the greater the Chinese influence especially considering the fact that the ethnic Chinese make up only 1.2 per cent of the population.

8. Based on geographical location, there are differences between the Chinese in Metro Manila and the provincial Chinese. Those who live in Metro Manila are further differentiated between those in the so-called Chinatown area and those in the suburbs. Even in the case of the provincial Chinese, those who come from Cebu, Iloilo, Bacolod, Davao and other bigger urban areas are different from those who come from the rural villages. The degree of interaction and relationship with Filipinos would naturally influence their affinity with the Filipinos as well as their sense of identity as Filipinos.

9. Based on social and economic status, business or profession, the differences affect the degree of interaction and relations with Filipinos which in turn also influence their identity as Filipinos. The élites and the lower classes who have closer relations with Filipinos are more Filipinized compared to those who socialize or interact only with fellow Chinese.

10. Based on social activities, those who are members of traditional Chinese organizations and are active in the affairs of these associations are more exposed to Chinese community events and are better represented in affairs and concerns of the community. In contrast, those who are active members of

Filipino civic groups and organizations are more exposed to the Filipino social milieu and have closer relationships with the Filipinos.

11. Based on hometown origins, the Fujianese, making up 85 per cent of ethnic Chinese, are different from the Cantonese although the cultural differences are not very distinguishable to outsiders. Some have observed that among the younger generation, the cultural divide between Filipinos and Chinese may at times be narrower than that between Fujianese and Cantonese.

Identity and Integration

Whatever the differences or diversities, the most important criteria for gauging the Filipinoness of the Chinese would be their sense of identity and the degree of their integration into Philippine society. This can be viewed from the standpoints of socio-cultural, economic, and political integration. These points have been discussed thoroughly in several of my past papers. My central thesis is that integration has happened among the Chinese in the Philippines, dramatically so among the younger local-born generation. This is so among the Chinese Manilans but even more so among the Chinese in the provinces. The evolution of the Chinese from itinerant traders and seafarers to become sojourners or *Huaqiao* and later immigrant permanent residents has been a long, difficult historical process. The dramatic changes that have taken place among the younger generation born in the country after the Pacific War may have happened in a shorter period historically, but they are no less significant.[36] When asked "What country do you call your home?" in the 1995 Identity Survey, 97.3 per cent of the 510 respondents said that the Philippines was their home (see Table 4).

There was no significant difference in the answers of those from the provinces and those from Metro Manila, and when broken down according to age distribution, the differences were also slight.

When asked, however, on whether they forsee themselves as staying on in the Philippines, only 69.6 per cent answered "yes" (see Table 6). The reasons given (for staying) were mostly: this is

TABLE 4

What Country Do You Call Home?

Country	Freq.	Percentage
Philippines	496	97.3
China	6	1.1
Others/No Answer	8	1.6
Total	510	100

TABLE 5

What Country Do You Call Home?
(By address and age)

	Philippines	China	Others/ No Answer	Total
Address				
Metro Manila	96.8% 6	1.7%	1.6%	100%
Provinces	97.3% 0	0.0	2.7%	100%
No Address	100%	0.0	0.0	100%
Age				
17–21	96.7%	1.9%	1.3%	100%
22–32	98.1%	0.0	1.9%	100%
33–45	98.2%	0.0	1.8%	100%
46–above	96.0%	0.0	4.0%	100%
No Age	100%	0.0	0.0	100%

the only country that I know; this is where my family, friends and relatives are; and this is where I find good opportunities. Those who answered that they do not forsee themselves staying cited the peace and order situation and the worsening problems in the country as their main reason for wanting to leave. Those in the provinces (73.6 per cent) had a slight edge over those in Metro Manila (66.2 per cent) in their desire to stay on. The older people were more prone to taking the option of leaving compared to the younger ones.

TABLE 6

Do You Forsee Yourself Staying on in the Philippines?
(By address and age)

	Yes	No	No Answer	Total
Overall	69.6%	21.4%	9.0%	100%
Metro Manila	67.9%	22.0%	10.1%	100%
Provinces	75.3%	21.9%	2.7%	100%
No Address	73.3%	16.7%	10.0%	100%
Age				
17–21	65.1%	24.3%	10.5%	100%
22–32	63.9%	25.9%	10.2%	100%
33–45	91.2%	7.0%	1.8%	100%
46–Above	88.0%	8.0%	4.0%	100%
No Age	87.5%	6.3%	6.3%	100%

The answers of those who consider the Philippines as home and those who forsee themselves staying on are quite revealing and disturbing. The penchant for going abroad either to work or to immigrate is equally strong, whether one is a native Filipino or a *Tsinoy*. Dr. Robert Tilman found the same answers in his survey in the late sixties and a much publicized youth survey conducted recently by the advertising agency McCann-Erickson also showed the prevalent dream of leaving the country. This is an alarming trend that Philippine policy-makers must address.[37]

Other concrete examples of the many aspects of integration that have taken place at the political, cultural, social and economic levels include the following.

The Socio-cultural Level. The Filipinized ways of the younger generation have always been their elders' bane. Much has been done to improve Chinese language education and to give impetus to cultural renewal and invigoration. The influence of the environment, however, proves to be too strong. The fact that the ethnic Chinese make up only a very small percentage, both relative to the total Philippine population and in absolute numbers, is a deciding factor in the socio-cultural make-up of the younger generation who are more at home in the Westernized Filipino rather than the purely Chinese cultural milieu. The ethnic barriers that separated their parents from their Filipino peers are no longer as visible.

Another indicator of socio-cultural integration is seen in the fact that more and more young Chinese have native Filipinos as their close personal friends. Likewise, more and more of them are joining Filipino cause-oriented groups and other civic organizations like the Jaycees, the Rotary Club, and the Lions Club, instead of joining purely Chinese organizations concerned only with narrow interests of the Chinese community. Professional organizations nowadays are also teeming with active Chinese members and officers. Among them are the Writers Association of the Philippines, the University Student Councils, the Filipino businessmen's groups, professional associations like the Philippine Medical Society, Association of Architects, Certified Public Accountants, and the like. In fact, many young Chinese-Filipinos have been so successfully integrated into the Filipino social milieu that they are no longer aware of the possibility of any strains in Filipino-Chinese relations. Perhaps, because many of their close personal friends are Filipinos, they would tend to dismiss or ignore the existence of a "Chinese-problem."[38]

The historical reality that 90 per cent of the local Chinese are already native-born citizens who have gone to Philippine schools, joined Filipino organizations, and learned to speak Tagalog and English as their first languages naturally has a tremendous effect on the present ethnic identity. That the younger ethnic Chinese have long lost their ability to speak Hokkien (the *lingua franca* of the Chinese community) is a fact which many Chinese parents lament about; but many Filipinos are not aware of it. How much this language facility has deteriorated is substantiated by both the 1988 survey[39] (see Table 7) and the 1995 Identity Survey (see Table 8). About 13 per cent can speak Hokkien or Mandarin, 44 per cent can speak Filipino, 10 per cent can speak a local dialect and, 31 per cent can speak English. Adding those who can speak English, Filipino and a local dialect together gives a total of 85 per cent. The younger the generation is, the weaker is the ability to speak Hokkien. The same is true with the provincial Chinese

TABLE 7

Language Ability, 1988

	Percentage
Fluent in Filipino	85
Fluent in Hokkien	47
Speak Hokkien only at home	10
Speak a mixture of Filipino and Hokkien at home	77

whose ability to speak a local dialect (47.9 per cent) is better than their ability to speak Filipino (24.7 per cent) but the ability to speak Filipino is better than the ability to speak Hokkien (6.8 per cent).

Many Filipinos still do not see this reality and other tremendous changes that have happened to the ethnic Chinese community since the war. Even the older generation Chinese sometimes deny this reality and collectively lament the loss of identification with China among the younger generation.

The Economic Level. The integration of economic interests is something inevitable because most of the businesses of the ethnic Chinese are domestic. Unlike multinational companies which have companies in other parts of the world, most of the companies of the Chinese Filipinos are local or domestic companies whose profits are ploughed back into the Philippine economy. Regardless of their citizenship, the local businesses owned by the ethnic Chinese can be considered only as Filipino businesses, integral parts of the national economy, subject to and affected by local laws, sustained by Philippine economic growth, or overwhelmed by Philippine adversities and calamities. In short, whatever affect Filipino businesses affect them and vice-versa.

Moreover, since 1975, when easy access to citizenship was provided through a decree of former President Marcos, many young Chinese have become Filipino citizens, and more and more of them are moving out of traditional business and going into the professions. Without citizenship, they could not practise any of the professions so most of them flocked to business courses. Now,

TABLE 8

Language Spoken at Home, 1995

	Filipino	English	Hokkien	Mandarin	Local	Others	No Answer	Total
Overall	43.7%	30.8%	12.2%	0.8%	10.4%	0.2%	2.0%	100%
Metro Manila	47.7%	32.9%	13.8%	1.1%	3.7%	0.3%	0.5%	100%
Provinces	24.7%	13.7%	6.8%	0.0	47.9%	0.0	6.8%	100%
No Address	41.7%	38.3%	8.3%	0.0	6.7%	0.0	5.0%	100%
Age								
17–21	53.0%	29.6%	6.9%	0.7%	8.6%	0.3%	1.0%	100%
22–32	44.4%	32.4%	14.8%	1.9%	5.6%	0.0	0.9%	100%
33–45	10.5%	36.8%	22.8%	0.0	24.6%	0.0	5.3%	100%
46–Above	12.0%	16.0%	32.0%	0.0	28.0%	0.0	12.0%	100%
No Age	31.3%	43.8%	25.0%	0.0	0.0	0.0	0.0	100%

young Chinese have become successful in new fields in the arts and sciences — law, literature, journalism, art, music, mass communication, and even Philippine studies, social work, and so forth. These courses and/or careers have been chosen by people who have wholeheartedly accepted their being Filipino and whose lives will be lived in the Philippines. One will not take up social work or mass communications, for instance, if one does not have a sense of belonging to Philippine society.

In a paper on the "The Myths of Ethnic Chinese Economic Miracle", presented at the 1994 Hong Kong International Confer- ence on Chinese Overseas, researcher and banker Go Bon Juan cited the objective and subjective conditions that accounted for the success of the ethnic Chinese in business. He explained that conditions such as the location of these businesses in the Southeast Asian countries at a time when the business climate was most conducive for growth far outweighed the subjective conditions of the culture and tradition of these Chinese. His observations un- doubtedly support our argument that the full integration of Chinese businesses into the Philippine economy redounds principally to the country's domestic economy.[40]

The Political Level. Since the citizenship decree of 1975 which allowed the majority of the ethnic Chinese to gain the legal dis- tinction of being Filipino citizens, the greatest barrier to political integration has been lifted. Issues of national concern affect them as greatly as they affect other Filipinos. In contrast, concerns in China affect them only peripherally or indirectly. From the legal standpoint, the majority (85–90 per cent) of the ethnic Chinese in the country are already Filipino nationals and thus can be considered Filipinos. Therefore, whatever contributions they have made to the economy, politics, society or culture, legally speaking, can be said to be their contributions or obligations as citizens of the country.

In the 1995 Identity Survey, one of the questions asked was whether they agreed that the ethnic Chinese should keep out of politics; only a small 9 per cent said they agreed while 79 per cent disagreed. In the same vein, the majority (74.1 per cent) agreed that the ethnic Chinese had the right to pressure the government to attend to problems that confront the community while 10 per cent said that they had no right to do so (see Table 9). The degree of political integration can also be seen in the fact that many Chinese now completely identify themselves as Filipinos. In recent elections after the dictatorial regime of former President Marcos was deposed, many of the local Chinese participated in the electoral process not just as voters but as candidates themselves. The list of ethnic Chinese candidates who ran in the national and local elections was quite impressive. When Senator Ninoy Aquino was murdered upon his arrival at the Manila International Airport, young Chinese felt the tragedy as deeply as their Filipino brothers. Many of them also joined the Filipinos in keeping vigil at EDSA during the peaceful people's power revolution of February 1986. They staked their lives too for they keenly and sincerely felt that it was also their birthright that they were fighting for.[41]

In many issues that affect the national interest, it is heartening to realize that many of these young Chinese would consider the Philippine interest as their paramount concern, even if they conflict with the Chinese community's interests, with China's interests, or with Taiwan's interests. This can be seen from several events where there was a clear dividing line between the older generation China-oriented or Chinese-community-centred Chinese and the younger generation Philippine-oriented Chinese. For example, during the elections which catapulted President Corazon Aquino into power, many Chinese households were caught in conflict over who to vote for. Most of the older Chinese would say that despite what Marcos did, he had always been good to the Chinese, he had suppressed many of the anti-Chinese tendencies of his officials and had created opportunities and a more peaceful climate for the Chinese to make money and earn profits. Moreover, the Chinese were grateful for the citizenship decree promulgated by Marcos. Not many realized that the decree was issued out of expediency and in preparation for diplomatic relations with China. However, the young would argue that Marcos was not good for the Philippines and what is not good for the Philippines would never be good for the Chinese also. They lamented over the shortsightedness and narrow mindedness of their elders who considered only their selfish interests. In many instances, the dilemma was resolved only with

TABLE 9
Political Participation

A. The Chinese should keep out of politics			
	Agree	Disagree	No Answer
Overall	9.0%	79.0%	12.0%
Age			
17–21	9.2%	75.0%	15.8%
22–32	10.2%	81.5%	8.3%
32–45	10.5%	86.0%	3.5%
46–Above	0.0%	92.0%	8.0%
No Age	6.3%	93.8%	0.0%

B. The Chinese can pressure the government			
	Agree	Disagree	No Answer
Overall	74.1%	10.0%	15.9%
Age			
17–21	67.8%	9.2%	23.0%
22–32	78.7%	13.0%	8.3%
32–45	87.7%	10.5%	1.8%
46–Above	100%	0.0%	0.0%
No Age	75.0%	18.8%	12.3%

the households having a split vote — the older ones voting for Marcos, and the young ones voting for Cory Aquino.[42]

Another manifestation of the increasing detachment towards events in China is shown in their knowledge about Filipino political leaders, compared to Chinese leaders. The respondents were asked to rank the leaders in order of how well they knew them. The ranking from the most well known to the least known were: Dr. Jose Rizal, former President Ferdinand Marcos, Mayor Alfredo Lim (of the City of Manila), Senator Nikki Coseteng (an ethnic Chinese Senator), Senator Edgardo Angara (Senate President), Mao Zedong, Sun Yat Sen, Deng Xiaoping, Li Peng, Jiang Ze Min. It is not at all surprising that the last two received only about 0.5 per cent recognition. The same was true of the problems in Philippine society that the respondents were concerned with. Understandably, peace and order was the topmost concern but next in rank were problems of poverty, inefficiency and corruption in the government, unequal distribution of wealth — much as any Filipino would have answered the questions.

Religion and Objective Factors. Apart from socio-cultural, economic and political integration, another factor that helped as a unifying factor between Filipinos and Chinese is the absence of religious animosity. In other countries, differences in religion can be a factor that retards integration but in the Philippines, the majority of the ethnic Chinese are Catholics and Protestants although some observe their faith only nominally. In the 1995 survey 82.9 per cent professed to be Catholics or Christians (see Table 10). For the small sector (2 per cent) who practise Buddhism, Taoism or folk Chinese religion, it is interesting to note that religious syncretism is quite prevalent also. It is usual for the Chinese to practise Christianity while at the same time also observe many of the Chinese folk customs and rituals. Chinese Buddhist and Taoist figures side by side with Catholic images of the Virgin Mary and Jesus Christ are common sights in many Chinese households and stores. Life rituals from birth to death are a mixture of Filipino and Chinese ways.[43] In fact, the 1995 survey showed that only 40 per cent still practise ancestor worship (see Table 11) and the younger the age, the less they practise such rituals.

TABLE 10

Religion

	Catholic	Christian	Buddhist	Islam	Atheist	No Answer
Overall	70.0%	12.9%	2.0%	0.2%	0.2%	0.0
Age						
17–21	71.3%	13.7%	1.0%	0.3%	0.3%	13.4%
22–32	65.9%	13.6%	1.1%	0.0	0.0	19.3%
33–45	75.9%	8.6%	3.4%	0.0	0.0	12.1%
46–Above	76.0%	4.0%	16.0%	0.0	0.0	4.0%
No Age	10.0%	30.0%	0.0	0.0	0.0	60.0%

TABLE 11

Do You Practice Ancestor Worship?

	Yes	No	Occasionally	Parents Only	No Answer
Overall	40.0%	36.9%	0.2%	21.0%	2.0%
Age					
17–21	34.9%	42.8%	0.0	20.4%	2.0%
22–32	41.7%	31.5%	0.0	24.1%	2.8%
33–45	54.4%	22.8%	1.8%	21.1%	0.0
46–Above	64.0%	32.0%	0.0	4.0%	0.0
No Age	37.5%	18.8%	0.0	37.5%	6.3%

By and large, however, the objective reality that the ethnic Chinese live their lives in the Philippines, carry on their businesses or practise their professions in the country, already provides the condition for their integration with the mainstream society whether they are conscious of it or not. For example, as mentioned earlier, government policies, political developments, the business climate, and economic issues of the country affect the ethnic Chinese directly as they live and conduct their businesses there. Subjectively, some of them (especially the older generation) may still consciously refuse to identify themselves with the Philippines and the interests of the Filipinos, but objectively, it increasingly appears to be a matter of fiat and not by subjective choice owing to the conditions surrounding their presence in Philippine life. However, though the objective conditions show the extent of integration and the degree of identification as Filipinos, many may not be conscious of the changes nor be aware of the semantical differences, as shown in Table 12. When asked how they identified themselves, the older respondents answered that they were Filipinos of Chinese descent. They probably had exposure to literature on integration and social changes (particularly the regular publications of Kaisa like the fortnightly *Tulay* (Bridge) in English and Filipino, and the weekly Chinese supplement in *World News, Integration* [融合]).

It appears that many, especially the young, student sectors are sure of the significant differences between a Filipino of Chinese descent and a Chinese who happen to be a Filipino citizen. Hence, in the blank for Others, some answered, I am a Chinese Filipino, a *Tsinoy*, and so forth, with an understandable lack of awareness of semantical differences. But at least, only 1 per cent answered "I am a Chinese."

Likewise, to test the extent of ties the respondents still had with China, they were asked on whether they or their parents had made contributions to China. For those who answered the question, a high 93.7 per cent said that they had donated to the Philippines and almost the same number said they had *not* made contributions to China (see Table 13). However, the answers are not significant because of the extremely high number (60 per cent) of respondents who failed to answer the question for some reason. Some belong to the younger group who may not know if their parents had made contributions to China, while some of the older ones failed to answer perhaps because of the fear that the question was sensitive.

In an earlier article, I mentioned the fact that whenever a visiting basketball team from China competes with a local team, the young people in the audience would always cheer the Philippine team while their parents would cheer for the visiting China team. This is confirmed by the survey results where 75.9 per cent of the respondents said that they would support the Philippine team while 15.9 per cent said that they favoured the China team (see Table 14). The younger groups and also the provincial respondents would also favour the Philippine team.

TABLE 12

How Do You Identify Yourself?

A. Overall	Overall	17–2	22–32	B. Age 33–45	46–Above	No Age
I am a Filipino of Chinese descent	1.2%	62.2%	51.9%	77.2%	80.0%	56.3%
I am a Chinese who happen to be a Filipino citizen	30.2%	31.3%	36.1%	17.5%	16.0%	37.5%
Chinese of Filipino descent	0.2%	0.3%	0.0	0.0	0.0	0.0
Others:	5.7%	5.2%	9.2%	3.6%	4.0%	0.0
Any of two given choices (0.2%)						
Both Filipino and Chinese (0.2%)						
Chinese-Filipino (0.2%)						
Chinese (1.0%)						
Filipino-Chinese (1.0%)						
Filipino (2.5%)						
Tsinoy (0.6%)						
NA	0.4%	0.0	0.9%	1.8%	0.0	0.0
No Answer	1.2%	1.0%	1.9%	0.0	0.0	6.3%

TABLE 13

Contributions to China

	You donate to China	Parents donate to China	Parents donate to RP
Yes	4.7%	17.5%	
No	32.5%	18.2%	
Never	0.0	0.0	2.7%
Occasionally	0.0	0.0	22.5%
Often	0.2%	0.0	11.6%
No Answer	62.5%	64.3%	63.1%

TABLE 14

Which Team Do You Want To Win?

	RP Team	Chinese Team	Any	None	No Answer
Overall	75.9%	15.9%	0.2%	0.4%	7.6%
Age					
17–21	81.9%	11.5%	0.3%	0.3%	5.9%
22–32	73.1%	20.4%	0.0	0.9%	5.6%
33–45	63.8%	20.7%	0.0	0.0	15.5%
46–Above	44.0%	32.0%	0.0	0.0	24.0%
No Age	68.8%	31.3%	0.0	0.0	0.0%

A Question of Acceptance

It should also be mentioned here that despite its success the integration process has not always been smooth and there have been resistance from the Chinese community. On the other hand, there has also been resistance to fully accept the ethnic Chinese on the part of the Filipinos.

At the turn of the century, the increasing repressions and cruelties of the Spanish authorities and later on of the American colonizers drove the local Chinese into a strong spirit of communalism. Chinese institutions such as schools, the press, and other associations were set up as agencies of communal mobilization.[44] At the same time, the national political awakening of the Chinese in China elicited a strong response from the local Chinese, which further intensified their Chineseness. The schools and press especially became strong media for cultural renewal. However, after the war, the standard of Chinese education slowly deteriorated. Education is the foremost weapon the Chinese can think of to pull the young Chinese back from the tide of integration and preserve the Chinese cultural heritage. No matter what their political orientations are, the local Chinese are united in their views that the Chinese education of their school children must be safeguarded. They harbour only one hope — that their descendants would continue to retain their Chineseness and remember that they are descended from the Yellow Emperor in China.

In the past decade, many of the Chinese leaders frantically looked for ways to fund projects to improve the teaching of the Chinese language. Seminars on Chinese language and culture have been organized, and teachers have been sent to Taiwan and China for skills improvement, but again, environmental forces are stronger than the conscious will. Chinese language education has continued and will continue to deteriorate despite these efforts because of the objective reality that the Chinese are a small part of the total Philippine population and integration will continue to happen whether they accept it or not. Because of the failure of the Chinese schools to strengthen the Chinese identity of the young Chinese and the far-reaching effects of the mass naturalization decree on the eve of diplomatic relations with the People's Republic of China, the younger generation Chinese have moved further on in the continuum of deculturation.[45]

It must be pointed out that the process of becoming Filipino is not a one-sided process. It has another equally important facet — the Filipinos' or Philippine society's acceptance of one's being a Filipino and belonging to mainstream Philippine society. Only after this full acceptance and recognition is given to the ethnic Chinese would they be able to fully contribute to the country and participate fully in the concerns of Philippine society as Filipinos.

Three decades ago, to postulate "the ethnic Chinese as Filipinos" may shock a number of people. In the past two decades, however, dramatic changes have occurred in the composition, orientation, and status of the ethnic Chinese. Are they now more readily or easily accepted as Filipinos and as equal partners is a question that must be seriously explored. As mentioned earlier, my recent studies have shown that there still exist some undercurrents of racism and latent hostilities but these are borne mostly out of some isolated, unfortunate, personal experiences. I would theorize that unless these latent hostilities are exploited frequently by unscrupulous persons for their own personal agenda, there seems to be little danger now that the issue of racism would again explode to the extent of what happened in earlier years, especially in the nascent years of Philippine independence.

But, the initiative for an ethnic Chinese to be considered a Filipino must come from the Chinese himself. There must be a complete identification with the Philippines and affinity with the concerns of the Filipino people. The initiative to educate the ethnic Chinese, especially the older generation and the new immigrants, about the Philippines and the Filipino way of life must come from the ethnic Chinese themselves. In thoughts and in deeds, they must be completely Filipino, fully attuned to Philippine life, legally, emotionally, and mentally. It is for this reason that an organization devoted to the active promotion of integration, such as the Kaisa Para Sa Kaunlaran, exists and has made much progress in being a bridge of understanding between Filipinos and Chinese. Much effort has been exerted into making Filipinos aware of the changes that have taken place in the ethnic Chinese community and to encourage the latter to get involved and meaningfully participate in the concerns of Philippine society. Unless there is a secret political agenda to deliberately ostracize the ethnic Chinese, efforts to promote their full acceptance as Filipinos should succeed.

Conclusion

From the beginning, when the Chinese sailed the southseas as immigrant *huaqiao*, they have been going through a gradual process of de-sinicization. Leaving their ancestral homes was an initiation to this de-sinicization. The process became more and more entrenched and far-reaching as the years went by because it was a natural historical development. The result is that the ethnic Chinese are becoming more and more un-Chinese. This natural phenomenon cannot be prevented, and in fact, need not be prevented.

As the Chinese Filipinos cross the ethnic lines and come to identify themselves more as Filipinos, their cultural traditions also gradually become part of the greater national tradition. The result is mutual enrichment and enhancement of the positive elements in each culture. This healthy interchange can promote greater goodwill among people. Just as in early days when Chinese products were a prime commodity for exchange in the international market, Chinese human elements have also become agents of change that would bring greater enrichment and development to the Filipino nation.

The new identity that has emerged is a direct by-product of integration, a historical force that has occurred spontaneously and naturally under objective conditions in Philippine society itself. It is the Philippine soil, the Philippine social environment that has given birth and nurtured the new generation of Chinese Filipinos who comfortably accept their identity as Filipinos yet remain proud of their Chinese heritage. They are not just Chinese who live in the Philippines (菲律宾华人) but have actually become Filipinos of Chinese descent (华裔菲人) who are a living part of the country, with their roots sunk deeply into Filipino soil. The future is in their hands and the future direction of the local Chinese community will largely depend on them.[46]

Finally, we have mentioned that all Southeast Asian countries share some racial, historical and geographical affinity as well as the unique presence of the ethnic Chinese in their midst. Can this uniqueness be tapped to strengthen the development of Southeast Asia as a region? More concretely, can the web of relations spawned by the ethnic Chinese as Southeast Asians be tapped to have a greater influence economically, culturally and politically on the region? Since Southeast Asia has the greatest concentration of ethnic Chinese in the world, they can be tapped to play a historical role of uniting the region and spur a more concerted effort to develop the region.

Perhaps this can be the ultimate achievement of such a conference as "The Ethnic Chinese as Southeast Asians". It is reasonable to expect the ethnic Chinese, after learning to identify themselves with their individual Southeast Asian countries, to one day also learn to identify themselves with the interests of Southeast Asia as a region, rather than unite to form a mythical "invisible empire" for the interests of China.

Notes

1. *Chinese Business Networks in Southeast Asia*, Research output of the East Asia Analytical Unit (Department of Foreign Affairs and Trade, Commonwealth of Australia, 1995).

2. Lewis M. Simmons and Michael Zielenziger, *San Jose Mercury News*, 27–29 June 1994. The first part dated 27 June 1994 is titled "All in the Family", and the blurb says: "Overseas Chinese have a lock on much of Asia's economy, how do they do it? Through a vast network of family businesses run on trust and intuition." The second part on 28 June is titled "The Chinese Connection" and the blurb says: "Lured by the promise of profits and pulled by ancestral ties, overseas Chinese are pouring billions of dollars into China and driving its phenomenal economic development." Most of the graphs and figures quoted in the article were exaggerations that tended to overstate the ethnic Chinese portion in the domestic economy of Southeast Asia.

3. Sterling Seagrave, *Lords of the Rim: The Invisible Empire of the Overseas Chinese* (London: Bantam Press, 1995), p. 1 and p. 5.

4. Renato Constantino, *A Past Revisited* (Quezon City: Renato Constantino, 1973), p. 151.

5. Miguel A. Bernad, S.J., "Philippine Culture and the Filipino Identity", in *The Filipino in the Seventies — An Ecumenical Perspective*, edited by Vitaliano R. Gorospe, S.J. and Richard L. Deats (Quezon City: New Day Publishers, 1973), pp. 9–10.

6. Antonio Tan, *The Chinese Mestizos and the Formation of the Filipino Nationality* (Manila: Kaisa Para Sa Kaunlaran, Inc., 1989).

7. Chinben See, "Chinese Organizations and Ethnic Identity in the Philippines", in *The Chinese Immigrants — Selected Writings of Prof. Chinben See*, edited by Teresita Ang See (Manila: Kaisa Para Sa Kaunlaran, Inc., 1994), pp. 164–77. See also, Theresa C. Cariño, "State Ideology, Policies and Ethnic Identity: The Case of the Chinese in the Philippines", in *The Ethnic Chinese — Changing Relations and Identities in Southeast Asia*, edited by Teresita Ang See and Go Bon Juan (Manila: Kaisa Para Sa Kaunlaran, Inc., 1994), pp. 149–55. See also various souvenir programmes of the organizations mentioned. Most would carry messages from Taiwan leaders and in accounts of their formation, the organizations would acknowledge the help of the then Republic of China (Taiwan) Embassy.

8. Teresita Ang See, "The Chinese in the Philippines: Changing Views and Perceptions", in *The Chinese in the Philippines: Problems and Perspectives*, edited by Teresita Ang See (Manila: Kaisa Para Sa Kaunlaran, Inc., 1990), pp. 94–106.

9. Ibid. See also Teresita Ang See, "The Chinese in the Philippines: Assets or Liabilities", in ibid., pp. 107–19.

10. Teresita Ang See, "Citizenship Discussion in the Constitutional Convention", in *Philippine Chinese Profile: Essays and Studies*, edited by Charles McCarthy (Manila: Pagkakaisa Sa Pag-unlad, Inc., 1974), pp. 184–211.

11. Teresita Ang See, "The Chinese in the Philippines: Changing Views and Perceptions", in *The Chinese in the Philippines: Problems and Perspectives*. See also, Rosita Tan, "The Future of the Pinsinos is Here in the Philippines", and Victor Go "Resolve our Own Destiny," in *Crossroads — Short Essays on the Chinese Filipinos*, edited by Teresita Ang See and Lily Chua (Manila: Kaisa Para Sa Kaunlaran, Inc., 1988), pp. 127–31 and pp. 150–54.

12. Teresita Ang See, "The Chinese in the Philippines: Changing Views and Perceptions".

13. Ibid.

14. PNP Col. Reynaldo Berroya and AFP General Dictador Alqueza were accused of kidnapping Jack Chou, son of a Taiwanese businessman on 11 May 1993 in Parañaque, Metro Manila. The court convicted Col. Berroya but acquitted Gen. Alqueza. See *Tulay*, 7 August 1995, p. 4.

15. Teresita Ang See, "The Chinese in the Philippines: Changing Views and Perceptions". See also articles of Chinben See, Lily Chua, Rosita Tan and Victor Go in the fourth section of "Direction", in Teresita Ang See and Lily Chua, eds., *Crossroads,* pp. 127–68.

16. Robert Tilman, "Philippine-Chinese Youth, Today and Tomorrow," in Charles McCarthy, ed., *Philippine Chinese Profile*, p. 48.

17. Antonio S. Tan, "Five Hundred Years of Anti-Chinese Prejudices" (Paper presented at the Conference on "The Many Faces of Racism, Intolerance and Prejudices", jointly sponsored by the UNESCO and the National Historical Institute, April 1988).

18. Some of the Social Distance and Attitude Surveys include:
Allen L. Tan. "A Survey on Studies on Anti-Sinoism in the Philippines". *Asian Studies* 4, No. 2 (1968): 198–207.
Rodolfo Bulatao. "A Test of the Belief Congruence Principle in Prejudice against Chinese in the Philippines." Master's thesis, University of the Philippines 1967.
————. "Ethnic Attitudes in Five Philippine Cities". A Report Submitted to the Philippine Social Science Council Research Committee. Quezon City: Social Science Research Laboratory, University of the Philippines, 1973.

Stanley D. Eitzen. "Two Minorities: The Jews of Poland and the Chinese in the Philippines." In *Philippine Chinese Profile: Essays and Studies*, pp. 107–28.

Margaret W. Horsley. "Sangleys: The Formation of Anti-Chinese Feelings in the Philippines — A Cultural Study of Stereotypes of Prejudice." Ph.D. dissertation, Columbia University, 1950.

Chester Hunt, "Social Distance in the Philippines". *Sociology and Social Research* 40 (1956): 253–60.

George Henry Weightman. "Anti-Sinocism in the Philippines." *Asian Studies* 5, no. 1 (1967): 220–31.

———. "A Study of Prejudices in a Personalistic Society: An Analysis of an Attitude Survey of College Students — University of the Philippines." *Asian Studies* 2, no. 1 (1964): 87–101.

———. "The Philippine Chinese: Cultural History of a Marginal Trading Community". Ph.D. dissertation, Cornell University, 1960.

19. George H. Weightman and Joel V. Berreman, "Filipino Stereotypes of Racial and National Minorities", *Pacific Sociological Review* 1 (1958): 7–12.
20. Teresita Ang See, "Images of the Chinese in the Philippines", in Teresita Ang See, ed., *The Chinese in the Philippines: Problems and Perspectives*, pp. 18–44.
21. Survey conducted by the History class of Teresita Ang See, De La Salle University, 1989.
22. John T. Omohundro, *Chinese Merchant Family in Iloilo* (Quezon City: Ateneo de Manila University, 1974). See also, John T. Omohundro, "Anti-Chinese Attitudes in the Philippines — Social Distance in Iloilo City" (Results of field work conducted in Iloilo City in 1971–72 under the auspices of the Institute of Philippine Culture and the National Institute of Mental Health).
23. "Anti-Sino stages hunger strike", *Today,* 6 May 1995. In a radio interview, Jun Ducat, purportedly the head of Kalipi (*Kadugong Liping Pilipino* or Filipinos of same blood and race) said that the Philippines was for the Filipinos and not the Chinese. He pointed out that Mayor Alfredo Lim of Manila, Quezon City Representative Renato Yap, and the Cojuangcos are Filipinos of Chinese ethnicity who should be stopped from regaining their present situations. Mayor Lim called this interview "racism at its worst" and accused his chief rival, Mayor Gemiliano Lopez of initiating the racist campaign.
24. Rodolfo Bulatao, "Ethnic Attitudes".
25. At the end of 1994, the government authorities realized the shortfall in the rice harvest but as elections were to be held in May 1995 the administration did not dare to announce the rice shortage, which began to be felt by summer 1995. In June and July, newspapers headlined news on raids conducted on stores of Chinese rice traders and

government authorities were quick to blame unscrupulous traders for the rice crisis. The Kaisa Para Sa Kaunlaran, together with another non-governmental organization, Konsyensyang Pilipino, convened a forum on the rice crisis by bringing the farmers, traders, millers and consumers together. The summary of the consultations were published in *Tulay-Chinese Filipino Digest,* on 21 August, 4 September and 18 September 1995.

26. "Putting a Country in Order", interview of Gen. Jose Almonte by Margaret Thomas, *Straits Times* (Singapore), and *Business Times Weekend Edition,* 9–10 July 1994, p. EL3. See also, Budget Hearing, House of Representatives, as reported by the *Philppine News Agency,* also published in *Manila Bulletin,* and quoted by Max Soliven, in *Philippine Star* (19 September 1993), and *Asiaweek* (20 October 1993), p. 57.

27. Bernard C. Go., "The Pinsinos: Facts and Fancies", in *Philippine Chinese Profile,* p. 235. See also Joaquin Sy, "Ang Larawan ng Tsino sa Panitikang Pilipino" [The Image of the Chinese in Philippine Literature], *Tulay Literary Journal* II (February 1987): 64–87.

28. Gregorio F. Zaide, *Philippine Political and Cultural History,* Vol. II (Manila: Philippine Education Co., 1958): 63.

29. Teresita Ang See, "Images of the Chinese in the Philippines", p. 41.

30. Teresita Ang See, "The Chinese in the Philippines: Continuity and Change", in *Southeast Asian Chinese — The Socio-Cultural Dimension,* edited by Leo Suryadinata (Singapore: Times Academic Press, 1995), pp. 28–41.

31. Teresita Ang See, "The Ethnic Chinese as Manilans" (Paper delivered at the Conference on "The Ethnic Chinese as Filipinos", sponsored by the Philippine Association for Chinese Studies, the UP Asian Center and *World News,* November 1995).

32. Charles J. McCarthy, "The Chinese in the Philippines", in *Philippine Chinese Profile,* p. 1.

33. The survey covered a total of 700 respondents, which included some non-ethnic Chinese (almost all native Filipinos). For the purposes of this study, I subtracted the 190 non-*Tsinoy* respondents for accuracy.

34. Teresita Ang See, "Ethnic Chinese as Manilans".

35. Teresita Ang See, "Integration and Identity: Social Changes in the Post WWII Philippine-Chinese Community", pp. 1–17; and "Social Change: Impact on Philippine-Chinese Literature," pp. 68–83, in *Problems and Perspectives.*

36. Ibid. Teresita Ang See, "The Chinese in the Philippines: Continuity and Change," in *Southeast Asian Chinese,* pp. 28–41. See also Chinben See, "Cultural Adaptation and Integration of the Chinese Filipinos", in *Chinese Immigrants,* pp. 155–63; and Wang Gungwu, "The Study of Chinese Identities in Southeast Asia," in *Changing Identities of the Southeast Asian*

Chinese since World War II, edited by Jennifer Cushman and Wang Gungwu (Hong Kong: Hong Kong University Press, 1988), pp. 1–21.

37. A survey on Filipino youth, conducted by the advertising agency, McCann-Erickson, Philippines, January 1993.

38. Teresita Ang See, "The Chinese in the Philippines: Changing Views and Perceptions."

39. Teresita Ang See, "The Chinese in the Philippines: Integration and Identity."

40. Go Bon Juan, "The Myth of Ethnic Chinese Economic Miracle" (Paper presented at the International Conference on "Comparative Perspectives: The Chinese Overseas 1945 to 1994", sponsored by the International Society for the Study of Chinese Overseas [ISSCO], University of Hong Kong, 19–21 December 1994).

41. An account of the ethnic Chinese who participated in the EDSA people power revolution is found in Marilies Von Brevern's book, *The Turning Point*. The account is reprinted in *Tulay Journal* (literary journal of *World News*) 1, no. 1 (June 1987): 74–81. Other materials on the Chinese in the Philippine political process are presented in my article on political participation (see note 42).

42. Teresita Ang See, "Political Participation, Integration and Identity of the Chinese in the Philippines", in *The Ethnic Chinese*, pp. 139–48.

43. Teresita Ang See, "Religious Syncretism among the Chinese in the Philippines," in *Problems and Perspectives*, pp. 54-67.

44. Antonio S.Tan, *The Chinese in the Philippines 1898–1935: A Study of their National Awakening* (Quezon City: R.P. Garcia Publishing Co., 1965).

45. Teresita Ang See, "Chinese-language Education in the Philippines — Problems and Prospects" (Paper presented at the International Conference on Chinese Schools in Southeast Asia, National Pingtung Teachers College, Pingtung, Taiwan, 6–7 June 1994).

46. Teresita Ang See, "Integration and Identity".

Comments by
Renato S. Velasco on
"The Ethnic Chinese as Filipinos"
Presented by Teresita Ang See

I wish to express my gratitude to our gracious host, the Institute of Southeast Asian Studies led by a Chinese-Singaporean, Professor Chan Heng Chee, and to the organizers of this timely and interesting seminar, led also by a Chinese-Singaporean, Professor Leo Suryadinata.

I congratulate Ms Teresita Ang See for her well-documented and engaging paper. Her background as a leading Chinese-Filipino activist in the integration movement makes her piece more absorbing — if not provocative — than other previous works on the subject. Her comparative presentation of her 1988 and 1995 surveys also provide useful insights and up-to-date data on Chinese-Filipinos (Chifils or Tsinong Pinoy — "Tsinoys").

Points of Agreement
I agree with most of the arguments in Ms Ang See's paper, the most important points of which include the following:

1. The increasing identity and consciousness of the Chifils as Filipinos. This strong integration has been brought about by a good combination of push and pull factors. The push factors were the harsh or negative conditions that made them leave China, such as poverty, unemployment and unrest. The closing of PRC doors in 1949, and its avowed policy of non-interference in the Chifils' activities in the Philippines further eroded the so-called "Chineseness". The pull factors in turn were the positive conditions that helped them decide to settle and stake their future in the Philippines. These included the economic opportunities which allowed many of them to enjoy a high and comfortable standard of living; the 1975 citizenship decree which granted Filipino citizenship to most of them;

cultural pluralism and civil liberties which allowed the Chifils
to practise old beliefs and customs and freely join the various
civil society groups.

2. The deepening Filipinoness of the younger or third-generation
    Chifils. The ongoing deeper and multi-faceted integration of
    Chifils cannot be stopped. This inevitability is explained by
    the fact that they have experienced various forms of happiness,
    disappointment, pride, embarrassment, pessimism, pain, glory
    and hope as Filipinos rather than as Chinese. As revealed in
    the paper, more than 75 per cent of the Chifils are Philippine-
    born. They grew up and received their formal education in
    the country. They imbibed the Filipino language and culture
    and joined various Filipino groups and organizations. Many
    of them married Filipinos, and are starting their own families.
    They are productively engaged in different professions and
    other activities, including politics and civic action. Their
    children are studying in non-Chinese Philippine schools. They
    have more Filipino friends and associates than Chifils, and
    their command of Hokkien or Mandarin is poor if not non-
    existent.

3. There are few lingering remnants of the old stereotyped images
    of Chifils — economic animals/economic power-wielder,
    shrewd businessmen, culturally clannish, politically unreliable,
    tax evaders, abusive employers, homogeneous, monolithic, con-
    spiring bloc/network. These "perceptive myths" are, however,
    not exclusive to the Chifils. Other ethno-linguistic groups also
    suffer from these racist images: Indian-Filipinos as "foul-
    smelling and abusive usurers"; Spanish-Filipinos as "arrogant,
    lazy and cultural snobs", cultural minorities as "uncivilized,
    backward and ignorant". Overseas Filipinos are subjected
    themselves to these stereotyped linkages, such as the Japanese
    belief that many Filipinas are prostitutes; while in Singapore,
    Taiwan and Malaysia, they are domestic helpers and drivers.

4. The bases of these derogatory perceptive myths on Chifils are
    weakening and disappearing, especially their being "economic
    animals". To behave like "economic animals" in the era of
    John F. Kennedy or Mother Teresa may be derogatory, but in
    the age of Bill Gates and the World Trade Organization, it has

become quite a virtue. In the past, the Japanese were dismissed as simple transistor makers and car salesmen; now they are called management *gurus* and high-tech industry leaders. Cultural clannishness is now being perceived as a strength among the Chifils which is being seriously studied and considered as an entry point to penetrating the wide and lucrative ethnic Chinese business network. The days when Hokkien or Mandarin were considered the languages of "economic animals" or clowns are long over.

5. The periodic resuscitation of anti-Chifil images will continue because of the ingenious efforts of demagogues, politicians and "enterprising" writers. The easiest way to cover one's mistake is to put the blame on others, and the Chifils are easy targets. This simple strategy is useful in getting instant attention, fame, and more importantly, money. But the coming years will see the further erosion of this propaganda line.

6. The heterogeneity of Chifils amid the stereotyped images (Chifils in and outside Manila; citizen Chifils and non-citizen Chifils; Hokkien, or Mandarin or English-speaking Chifils; pro-PRC and pro-Taiwan Chinese). This fact which is often ignored or overlooked for some reason is also true of other ethno-linguistic groups who are perceived to be homogenous, such as the Muslims, Japanese, Europeans, and others.

Clarificatory Comments

Having said my points of agreement, I wish to raise some observations and comments. They are as follows:

1. There seems to be some over-reading of the so-called cases of anti-Chifil racism. While saying "undercurrents of racism ... are borne mostly out of isolated, unfortunate, personal experiences", the bent of the discussion of these cases seems to conjure an image of a consistent and organized anti-Chifils campaign.

   I am certain that the author is no alarmist. However, I detect a tendency or a disposition to inflate the importance of a few and isolated cases of anti-Chifil actions. The result is a neat but limp integration of unrelated, widely ignored and ridiculed cases of racism in a dramatic but unconvincing grand scheme of "new yellow peril" propaganda.

Note that Manila Mayor Alfredo Lim and Tarlac Representative Jose Yap won their re-election bids with landslide victories in the 1995 elections despite, or perhaps precisely because of, these anti-Chifil campaigns. It is significant to mention that Mayor Lim has been the mayor of the country's capital since 1992. In the 1980s, the city was run by an ethnic Indian, Ramon Bagatsing. Ms Ang See's major reference to the so-called Filipinos' "prevalent anti-Chinese belief" is 38 years old, long before the promulgation of the 1975 mass citizenship decree and the subsequent multi-sided integration of Chifils in Philippine society and culture which were documented by her own 1988 and 1995 surveys.

Presidential Security Adviser General Jose Almonte often attracts attention by issuing rhetorical and controversial statements. This usually makes him a good copy for the media but not for serious policy analysts. Not long ago when he was a doctoral student at our Department, he insisted that his dissertation proposal be "classified" and restricted to the dissertation panel "on account of national security". When the Department found that he was serious in his proposal, it also took him seriously: it opposed his proposal until he exceeded its maximum residence rule and he was dropped from the list of graduate students.

Except for the few rather insignificant materials cited in the paper, mainstream and authoritative readings on the subject are at worst simply factual or descriptive, for example, "Chinese Business Networks in Southeast Asia".

2. There is a unidimensional bent to explain the slow integration of Chifils, especially before 1975. The seclusion policy during the Spanish colonization was not limited to the Chinese but also included other cultural minorities — the Muslims in Mindanao and the Igorots in the Cordilleras. The "native" Filipinos themselves were notably slapped with individual residence certificates to facilitate the Spanish conquest by confining the "natives" to their designated *barangays*. In many ways, this colonial policy reinforced the *barrio*-based parochial

views and concerns of the natives and unwittingly advanced the interests of the Chinese. Why? Because it also positioned the Chinese traders to gain a foothold and earn profits from intra- and inter-island trade. This explains the fact that when the Philippines was opened to world trade after the termination of the Manila-Acapulco Galleon Trade in the 1820s, it was the Chinese traders who profited as brokers, agents and business partners of British, American and other foreign merchant houses. With their economic affluence, the social standing of the Chinese inevitably improved. Many of the former cultural snobs yet bankrupt members of the colonial and local élites suddenly found the "unsophisticated" and "unChristian" Chinese attractive business partners, friends, sponsors or better still husbands of their daughters. In due time, the intermarriage between the locals, mestizoes and the Chinese produced the economically-powerful, educated but politically disenfranchised middle class in the 1860s. This same class later championed the Philippine reform and independence movement against Spanish colonization and American invasion.

While admitting that the discriminatory colonial policy of "scapegoatism" was instrumental in the Chifils' sense of segregation, is it also not a fact that such policy has been abetted in some ways by acts or, at the very least, remnants of traditional exclusivism, if not cultural supremacism, of the ethnic Chinese? Note that the seventeenth century Parian (now Binondo) is still a Chinese enclave — long after the Spanish colonizers left the country in 1898. Many applaud Ms Ang See's "Citizens Action Against Crime" (CAAC) every time it lambasts the government's incapability and inaction against syndicates and criminals victimizing Chifils. But many more will praise and support the CAAC if this "citizens" movement is consistent in staging boisterous protest even in cases where the victims are not Chifils.

3. The surveys cited in the paper have some flaws and inconsistencies. First, comparison between the 1988 and 1995 surveys is limited. This is borne out by the fact that the respondents of the two surveys are not the same — the 1988 survey involved only students; while the 1995 survey involved

students and others from different groups and places. The paper should also explain further the geo-economic and sectoral characteristics of the respondents; how representative these respondents are to the entire population of Chifils, and the turn-out or percentages of completed survey questionnaires.

4. I disagree with at least two historical interpretations or misreadings in the paper. First, several reputable historical readings, including those of Renato Constantino and Miguel Bernad, which were cited in the paper, would clearly refute the assertion that the "formation of Filipino nationality" is "a twentieth century phenomenon". If this thesis is true, what was the organizing and mobilizing framework for the Filipinization of the Catholic Church's movement of the 1870s? And for the propaganda movement that campaigned for re- forms in the Philippines, the Philippine Revolution against Spain in 1896, and the establishment of the First Philippine Republic in 1898?

The more than 250 recorded revolutionary uprisings against Spain, caused by "parochial regional concerns" and "personal grievances", occurred earlier and served as the building blocks of Filipino identity and consciousness. The paper did not explain its definition of nationalism and its related but still different concepts of national unity and unification. I have yet to see, however, a nationalist movement which was started and launched without any shade of regional concerns or personal grievances. In the same vein, if an Okinawan feels that he is first an Okinawan before being a Japanese it does not mean that he is less of a Japanese compared to those from Tokyo, and that national unification in Japan has not been completed? As a yardstick of national unity, is ethnic identity always inferior to, or in conflict with national identity? The varied experiences of multi-ethnic societies in Asia and Europe offer answers and so I do not think there is a hard and fast rule on this matter.

Secondly, the author could have corrected the mis-impression/or stereotyped perceptions of other ethnic Chinese if she was aware of the abovementioned facts about Philippine history and nationhood. While I am quite touched by her answer to the question raised at a Hong Kong conference, I am, however, not intellectually convinced.

Unknown to many, including several Filipinos, the Filipinos have a rather long tradition of nationalism which pre-dates those of the Chinese and other Asians. The first successful anti-colonial war for national independence was launched by Filipinos in 1896 — fifteen years ahead of the Chinese Revolution in 1911. This historical fact made the Filipinos the first among Asians to defeat a Western colonial power in a war of independence. In the same vein, Asia's first republic was established by the Filipinos in 1898. In two years time, the country will in fact celebrate its centennial anniversary of its first republic. Like millions of Chinese brothers who died fighting against Western invasion, thousands of Filipinos perished in at least 250 revolts during the 300 years of Spanish colonization. When the Americans invaded the country in 1899, the newly established Republic asserted its independence. The war of resistance lasted for several years, resulting in the death of one million Filipinos, or 20 per cent of the population of Luzon. If China produced great patriots like Sun Yat-sen and India, Gandhi and Nehru, the Philippines has its own Jose Rizal, Andres Bonifacio and several others. This tradition of nationalism and self-sacrifice persisted during the Japanese Occupation, the martial law years, and up to the present. With or without the Chifils — but better with them — Filipinos love their country, for better or worse, then and now.

5. Finally, I wish to share a few random thoughts about the main theme of this conference on "Ethnic Chinese as Southeast Asians". I believe the Chifils — as represented by their prominent business leaders — are developing a strong sense of ASEAN regional identity and consciousness. This ASEAN psyche, as the expression of shared regional interests, vision and destiny, is engendered by the increasing trade and business linkages of Chifils with other ethnic Chinese, as well as with the local inhabitants in other ASEAN-member countries. One example is the case of the Philippines' Metro Pacific (Malaysian Chinese Robert Kuok, Chifils Andrew Gotianum, Henry Sy, George Ty and Lucio Tan) and Smart Communications

(Orlando Vea, and others), which have business tie-ups with Indonesia's huge Salim group of companies. The latter in turn has extensive joint ventures with Beri Jucker in Thailand; with Batam Industrial Park and United Industrial Corporation in Singapore; and with Kuantan Flour Mills in Malaysia.

Projecting its revolutionary impact, Keinichi Ohmae argues that robust supranational trade, led and/or participated in by the ethnic Chinese, has in fact sealed the "death" of the nation state and the "birth" of region states. As the old notion of political boundaries increasingly lose meaning, communities will be demarcated by their cultural identities. The free flow of goods and services, the facility of communication and integration of production have in turn spawned homogeneity in consumption patterns and a sharper sense of communal identity. National identity under this post-statist paradigm has become obsolete in favour of a regional or internationalist mindset.

In the same manner that Western culture and practices spread in the region under the imperatives of colonial trade, the foundations of an emerging ASEAN cultural community are firmed up by ongoing multi-faceted intra-ASEAN trade and economic co-operation. Together with the Filipinos — who led in the formation of an ASEAN Political Community — the Chifils are now playing a major role in the development of ASEANism that is strongly anchored on a vibrant and prosperous ASEAN economic community.

Chapter 6

From Overseas Chinese to Chinese Singaporeans

Chiew Seen Kong

The Overseas Chinese: A Biographical Example

The concept of overseas Chinese evokes a view of people of Chinese descent from the perspective of China, that is, these people are overseas, away from the motherland China. This concept may be true sometimes but may be false at other times. Some personal anecdotal or biographical examples will illustrate this apparent puzzle.

My parents were both born in Guangdong Province, China. However, they were married in Singapore before the Japanese Occupation. They may be described as, and they may perceive themselves to be, overseas Chinese in Singapore then.

I was born in Singapore before the Japanese Occupation. I visited my parents' home towns (Xiqiao and Foshan towns in Guangdong Province) in 1986 for the first time. Before that I had not the slightest idea what my parental hometowns or China were like, and hence I was unable to psychologically relate to or identify with these hometowns. I did not view myself as an overseas Chinese. But I did view myself culturally as a Chinese. Legally and politically, I was born a British subject and a citizen of Singapore and therefore was not an overseas Chinese.

My parents later became naturalized citizens of Singapore and were hence British subjects during British colonial times. Legally and politically, they had renounced their Chinese citizenship, and were no more overseas Chinese (citizens). But psychologically, my parents had dual identities: they viewed themselves as (a) Chinese from China and Chinese by culture, and (b) as Singapore citizens and were proud of their new political status, especially after 1949, as my father was a member of the Kuomintang (KMT).

During the Japanese Occupation, we did not identify ourselves as Japanese subjects: we hated and feared the Japanese rulers. When peace returned in 1945, we re-asserted our status as citizens of Singapore. Then came political awakening: I was psychologically moved by the nationalism and anti-colonialism movements after the end of World War II.

I received my primary and secondary education in English. I completed my Standard IX (equivalent to GCE "O"-level) education at Raffles Institution in December 1954. At that time, Britain sent two Members of Parliament (MPs) to Singapore to assess the readiness of the local British subjects to self-rule. Consequently, several political parties were formed and contested the 1959 elections. Some pressed for immediate political independence, while others wanted self-government before full independence. At this time, my Guangdong-born maid referred to Britain as my *joe ga* ("motherland" in Cantonese), and I felt offended by her assertion of identity. I told her that my *joe ga* was Singapore: I was caught by the strong winds of nationalism and anti-colonialism at that time. I was a Chinese Singaporean, not an overseas Chinese.

A mere four years later in 1963, Singapore became part of the Federation of Malaysia. But soon it was evicted from Malaysia and became politically independent in 1965. Between 1963 and 1965 I did not view myself as a Malaysian: three years were not long enough to nurture a new identity, and those three years were full of racial tension. I still thought of myself as a Chinese Singaporean during that tense period. The racial riots in Malaysia in 1969 left an imprint on Singaporeans: during the few years after 1969, intermarriage rates in Singapore declined significantly. Bad "racial" memories lingered on for a while. Under these unfavourable conditions, Chinese Singaporeans could not change their identities to Chinese Malaysians.

Thus, from teenage onwards, I had never identified myself as an *overseas* Chinese. But during teenage (when I was in Raffles Institution) I was proud to be a British subject, but anti-colonialism in the 1950s made identification with a colonial power unbearable. Nationalism and the struggle for political independence or statehood nurtured the formation of a Singaporean identity.

This narrative suggests that macro-processes of change provide the framework within which individuals view and identify themselves. Thus, some overseas Chinese of my parents' generation might also have been drawn into the whirlpool of anti-colonialism and nationalism just like their own local-born children, and became psychologically transformed into Chinese Singaporeans. Some of our first-generation political leaders no doubt underwent such a transformation. This self-image, as Chinese Singaporeans, may then become their master status, as it has become my master identity. These macro-processes of change include not only political and ideological changes but social, demographic and other momentous changes as well. The following sections of this study will document and discuss them in relation to their impact on people's identities.

Demographic Changes

Census data show that from 1921 to 1957, the proportion of the Chinese population who were born in Singapore rose steadily from 24 per cent to 68 per cent (see Table 1). Thus, when the newly formed political parties in Singapore were struggling for independence or self-government in 1959, about two-thirds of the Chinese were local born and one-third were foreign born. By 1990, 85 per cent of the citizens and permanent residents of Chinese descent were born here.

Table 2 shows that 38.7 per cent of the Chinese population in colonial Singapore in 1947 were born in China, Hong Kong

TABLE 1

Singapore-born Chinese, Singapore, 1921–90

(In per cent)

Year	1921	1931	1947	1957	1970	1980	1990
Per cent	24	35	58	68	77	80	85*

* Citizens and Permanent Residents only.

SOURCE: Chiew Seen Kong, "Citizens and Foreign Labour in Singapore" in *Crossing Borders: Transmigration in Asia Pacific*, edited by Ong Jin Hui, Chan Kwok Bun and Chew Soon Beng (Singapore: Prentice Hall, 0000), Table 28.3, p. 474.

and Taiwan (these will be referred to simply as China). Ten years later in 1957, only 25.5 per cent were born in China. The rate dropped further to 15.4 per cent in 1970, and then to 10.2 per cent in 1980 and a mere 7.1 per cent in 1990.

These demographic facts suggest that fewer and fewer Singaporean citizens of Chinese origin are likely to identify themselves as overseas Chinese.

Between 1947 and 1990, the Chinese population increased rapidly from 729,418 persons in 1947 to 2,102,795 citizens and permanent residents of Chinese descent in 1990, that is, an increase of 2.88 times (Table 2). Among the Chinese who were born in Singapore, their numbers rose from 421,406 in 1947 to 1,783,185 in 1990 (or 4.23 times). The Chinese who were born in China dropped from 282,537 in 1947 to 149,769 in 1990 (a decline of 0.53 times). They began to decrease in large numbers from 1957 onwards, that is, after mainland China turned communist (see Table 3).

These demographic facts indicate again that the concept of overseas Chinese is likely to have little relevance in the daily lives of Singaporeans of Chinese descent.

Besides Chinese born in China, there were also other Chinese who were born in Malaysia, Indonesia, and elsewhere. In the nineteenth century, the Chinese came to Singapore from China and some of them later proceeded to Malaysia and Indonesia. Singapore then served as a labour distribution centre. Thus, the Chinese moved about in the region in search of a better life. In

TABLE 2

Country of Birth of the Chinese in Singapore, 1947–90

Country of Birth	1947		1957		1970		1980		1990[+]	
	Number	%	Number	%	Number	%	Number	%	Number	%
Singapore	421,406	57.8	741,224	68.0	1,210,419	76.6	1,490,065	80.3	1,783,185	84.8
China/Hong Kong/ Taiwan	282,537	38.7	278,371	25.5	243,273	15.4	188,627	10.2	149,769	7.1
Malaysia	17,217[*]	2.4	60,181	5.5	110,643	7.0	159,985	8.6	150,774	7.2
Indonesia	7,569	1.0	7,365	0.7	11,238	0.7	13,713	0.7	13,228	0.6
Elsewhere	689	0.1	3,455	0.3	4,293	0.3	3,847	0.2	5,839	0.3
Total	729,418	100.0	1,090,596	100.0	1,579,866	100.0	1,856,237	100.0	2,102,795	100.0

* Included those born in Brunei.
+ Citizens and Permanent Residents only.

SOURCE: Chiew, op. cit., Table 28.5, p. 476; and M.V. Del Tufo, *Malaya: A Report on the 1947 Census of Population* (London: The Crown Agents, n.d.), Table 44, pp. 323–27.

TABLE 3

**Rate of Increase of Chinese by Country of Birth,
Singapore, 1957–90**

Country of Birth	1947 Number	1957–47 Number	1957/1947 Per cent	1957 Number	1970–57 Number	1970/1957 Per cent
Singapore	421,406	319,818	175.9	741,224	469,195	163.3
China/Hong Kong/Taiwan	282,537	–4,166	98.5	278,371	–35,098	87.4
Malaysia	17,217	42,964	349.5	60,181	50,462	183.9
Indonesia	7,569	–204	97.3	7,365	–3,873	152.6
Elsewhere	689	2,766	501.5	3,455	838	124.3
Total	729,418	361,178	149.5	1,090,596	489,270	144.9

Country of Birth	1970 Number	1980–70 Number	1980/1970 Per cent	1980 Number	1990–80 Number	1990/1980 Per cent
Singapore	1,210,419	279,646	123.1	1,490,065	293,120	119.7
China/Hong Kong/Taiwan	243,273	–54,646	77.5	188,627	–38,858	79.4
Malaysia	110,643	49,342	144.6	159,985	–9,211	94.2
Indonesia	11,238	2,475	122.0	13,713	–485	96.5
Elsewhere	4,293	–446	89.6	3,847	1,992	151.8
Total	1,579,866	276,371	117.5	1,856,237	246,558	113.3

Source: As for Table 2.

1947 there were 17,217 Chinese in Singapore who were born in Malaysia (and Brunei), comprising only 2.4 per cent of the community. Ten years later their numbers swelled to 60,181 (see Table 2), increasing 3.49 times (see Table 3). They increased further to 110,643 in 1970 and reached a peak of 159,985 in 1980, or 8.6 per cent of the Chinese in Singapore (see Table 2). They then dropped slightly to 150,774 in 1990, constituting 7.2 per cent of the Chinese in Singapore.

The Chinese who were born in Indonesia showed a similar pattern of change as those born in Malaysia. In 1947 there were 7,569 Chinese born in Indonesia but their number decreased slightly to 7,365 in 1957. Their proportion dropped from 1.0 per cent of all the Chinese in Singapore in 1947 to a mere 0.7 per cent in 1957. Their numerical strength then increased to 11,238 in 1970 and to 13,713 in 1980, but then dropped slightly to 13,228 in 1990 or only 0.6 per cent of the Chinese in Singapore in 1990.

These census data show that the Chinese who were born in Malaysia and Indonesia constitute only a small percentage of the Chinese in Singapore in the last four decades. They are not overseas Chinese but they may be viewed as other Southeast Asian Chinese.

Race Riots and National Integration

The 1964 race riots on Prophet Mohammed's birthday and the 1969 race riots in Kuala Lumpur showed graphically the destructive power of racial issues. The key issues of these race riots were growing economic disparity between the ethnic groups, particularly the income disparity between the Chinese and Malays, and their cultural differences. In order to avoid another race riot, the government took steps to minimize racial differences among the Chinese, Malays, Indians and other ethnic minorities.

Several measures for nation-building proposed by the All-Party Report in 1956 (a White Paper) were implemented by the government. The main objective was to integrate the various ethnic groups as much as possible. The ethnic groups had been segregated by the British colonial administration to serve their goal of divide and rule.

School Integration
Thus, the ethnic schools were integrated into English-Chinese, English-Malay and other combined schools so that Chinese pupils from the Chinese school could study with and become friends of Malay, Indian and Eurasian students in the English school, after the two schools became one integrated English-Chinese school (Chiew 1971 and 1983).

The old ethnic-oriented school textbooks were replaced by Singapore-oriented textbooks in the four official languages of Malay, English, Chinese and Tamil. In this way, students of Chinese, Malay, Indian and Eurasian origins were socialized in the same multicultural school culture. The school culture also emphasized the nurturing of a national identity, racial tolerance, and mutual cultural understanding in order to reduce cultural differences and to build a supra-ethnic, national identity. Slowly, a Singaporean identity evolved.

In a national survey in 1969, I used 23 indicators to measure, for the first time, national identity (Chiew 1971). The survey findings showed that most citizens of Chinese descent considered themselves as both Chinese and Singaporeans. When they were asked to choose between them, most of them preferred to be known as Singaporeans rather than Chinese. Other measures showed that national identity among Singaporeans of Chinese descent was high.

A slightly smaller proportion of the Chinese-educated Chinese scored high in Singaporean identity compared to the English-educated. Since bilingualism was made compulsory in schools since 1966, the proportion of Chinese-educated Chinese in the population slowly decreased as more and more Singaporeans of Chinese descent became bilingual and multicultural. Hence, the small differences in ethnic/national identity between the Chinese-educated Chinese and the English-educated in the past will eventually pale into insignificance as the number of the former slowly but steadily diminishes in the years to come.

Twenty years later in 1989, another national survey was conducted. The survey data again showed that national identity among Singaporeans of Chinese descent remained high, and even higher than previous assessments (Chiew and Tan 1990).

Disaggregated Public Housing

The Housing Development Board (HDB) was established in 1960 to provide affordable housing quickly to low-income families. Today about 86 per cent of the population live in HDB and other public (for example, middle-income HUDC) flats. Because of the official first-come, first-served policy of allocation of public housing, these public housing estates have evolved into multi-ethnic residential areas where Chinese, Malays, Indians and Eurasians of more or less the same income groups live in close physical proximity. Small-scale studies of selected housing estates (for example, Koh Yang Gek, 1993/94) showed again and again that residents of different ethnic origins do express neighbourly behaviour, but such social integration is rather superficial in nature. Deep friendships across ethnic lines are yet to form. However, friendly relations are better than ethnic suspicion and avoidance.

The 1969 and 1989 surveys mentioned earlier also showed that a higher percentage of Chinese have non-Chinese neighbours, and a higher percentage of Malays have non-Malay neighbours, and the same is true of Indian residents.

Social Integration

The 1969 and 1989 surveys also showed that higher proportions of Chinese have non-Chinese friends, and likewise higher proportions of Malays have non-Malay friends, and more Indians have non-Indian friends. They also socialize more across ethnic lines in terms of the mutual celebration of birthdays, weddings and festivals.

Chinese Singaporeans

The survey data also indicated evolutionary changes of identity, from a strong ethnic identity to a relatively strong national identity in Singapore. The first generation of Chinese immigrants initially identified themselves as overseas Chinese and had strong senti-mental attachments to their homeland in China. Their Singapore-born children, who grew up in Singapore, had their education in English schools or the current bilingual schools, and live in close proximity with other ethnic groups, know no other country and hence are unable to identify themselves with China, especially since 1949 when China became a poor, communist country. Moreover, the Chinese communists denounced many Chinese social institutions and customs as feudal and bad, and tried to replace them with Marxist-Leninist-Maoist ones, which are alien to the overseas Chinese and their Singapore-born children.

Thus, cut-off from their ancestral roots and given the various integration processes described above, the Chinese slowly became Chinese Singaporeans. A Singaporean life-style also evolved. This common life-style evolved from the close contacts among the Chinese, Malays, Indians and Eurasians in schools, in their housing estates, at their integrated places of work, in the armed forces as National Servicemen, and at recreational centres, restaurants, food courts, and so forth. This Singaporean life-style represents a fusion of the cultures and the supra-ethnic demands of urban living in a modern city.

At this point in time, there are still some noticeable cultural differences among the ethnic groups. For instance, non-Chinese do not practise the Chinese custom of ancestor worship and do not have Chinese names. Likewise, Chinese Singaporeans do not go to mosques or the Hindu temple to pray (although a few do). But Malays, Indians and Eurasians do use chopsticks and enjoy Chinese food while Chinese Singaporeans enjoy Malay, Indian and European foods and use their hands or fork and spoon to eat.

Hence, the Chinese have not yet lost their Chineseness completely even though they have stopped practising some of their customs and traditions (for example, the Seventh Moon festival). They have become Chinese Singaporeans but have not yet evolved into Singaporeans without their Chinese cultural attributes and identity.

Ethnic Identity
Cultural Attributes
There are three different perspectives on ethnic identity. The first pertains to a person's cultural attributes. One who habitually speaks a Chinese dialect or Mandarin, reads books and newspapers in Chinese, writes in Chinese, and practises various Chinese customs, is culturally a Chinese. But some are more Chinese than others. Some practise more Chinese customs and live their lives more by

Chinese or Confucian values, beliefs and norms than others. Thus, on some scale of Chineseness, Singaporeans of Chinese descent may vary in terms of their *degree* of Chineseness or extent of their possession and practise of Chinese cultural attributes. One who habitually speaks Cantonese will continue to speak Cantonese, and one who prefers to consume pork porridge or yam cake for breakfast will continue to enjoy this type of Chinese breakfast. This type of Chinese identity or Chineseness is stable and tends to be the accepted ethnic status for the individual (Wilder 1982; Smolicz 1981).

Self Image

It is conceivable that some individuals may view themselves as Chinese even though they may not have many Chinese cultural attributes. However, my parents who possessed more Chinese attributes than I are more likely to view themselves as Chinese than me as I consider my Singaporean identity as important as my Chinese identity. Generally speaking, it is hypothesized that those who score high on Chineseness are more likely to stress their Chinese identity more than those who score low on Chinese cultural attributes:

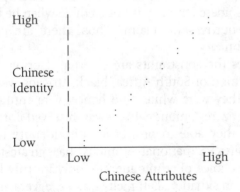

In real life, there are, of course, some exceptions. Some who have many Chinese attributes may view themselves more as Singaporeans than Chinese, while others who have few Chinese attributes prefer to view themselves as Chinese more than as Singaporeans. Such ethnic identity is a psychological state and process.

Situational Ethnicity

Situational ethnicity refers to the ethnic identity one chooses to project in a given context or situation (Clammer 1975 and 1979; and Lian 1982). It is usually instrumental in nature, that is, one chooses to call oneself a Chinese or Cantonese when doing so enhances one's benefits, such as when one is trying to strike a deal with a Hong Kong Cantonese or a Guangdong Cantonese. It is assumed here that calling oneself a Cantonese when dealing with another Cantonese would help foster a closer sentimental relation with the other Cantonese.

Suppose that a Singaporean Chinese is a *baba* Cantonese who is unable to speak proper Cantonese. Even if it is advantageous to project himself as a Cantonese, he is unable to do so. Thus, when pertinent cultural attributes are not available, the individual is not free to project his ethnic (for example, Cantonese) identity, even though he desires to do so. When a fourth generation Chinese in Thailand has lost all traces of his Chinese attributes and has become culturally a Thai, he is not able and is not free to project a Chinese identity even though it is advantageous for him to do so. He may want to assert that he *is* a Chinese but his Chinese counterparts may not accept him as one since he cannot even speak Chinese. His claim of Chinese ethnicity is not credible when he lacks Chinese attributes to buttress his claim. Thus, there are constraints to situational ethnicity.

Sometimes the constraints are external. During the apartheid days in the Union of South Africa, black Africans were not free to pretend that they were whites and hence were entitled to dine in that part of the restaurant which was reserved for whites only. Neither were they able to project a white identity in an attempt to marry whites. Situational ethnicity has greatest freedom of expression or choice of ethnic identity only in truly free societies. The literature on situational ethnicity often exaggerates the freedom of choice of ethnic identity or instability of ethnic identity and likewise plays down the social constraints.

Out-group Perception

People label each other by various cultural and/or physical criteria. One who manifests many Chinese cultural attributes is most likely to be perceived by non-Chinese to be a Chinese. However, if one has the "looks" of a Chinese but has few or even no Chinese cultural attributes except his Chinese name, non-Chinese may still identify him as a Chinese. In Singapore, in daily interactions, people often label a person at a distance as Indian by his physical traits such as a dark skin, even though they have no contact with him. Today, most people are still recognizable as Chinese, Malays, Indians, Eurasians and Europeans by their physical and cultural traits. For instance, no one will ever mistake me for an Indian, Malay, Eurasian or European. However, perceived ethnicity may or may not be correct according to people's cultural attributes, and may or may not be consistent with people's ethnic self-images. Despite the risk of wrong labelling, people often act on their perception of others. If you think that a person is a Malay, you will not treat him to a bowl of pork porridge. If a person is viewed as a member of an out-group, you may object to your daughter marrying him.

The risk of error in identification is higher if there is no interpersonal interaction. Where there is personal contact with out-group members, error in ethnic identification is lowered dramatically as interaction allows the interacting individuals to seek information to make accurate judgment of the ethnic identity of out-group members. At the point of close contact, the processes of situational ethnicity, under social constraints, come into play.

The China Factor
Chinese Singaporeans are generally aware of the momentous changes taking place in China, especially its success in economic development. Prompted by the government's encouragement to expand their economic activities in the region and in East Asia (including China), more and more Chinese Singaporeans are investing and/or working in China. As 90 per cent of Chinese Singaporeans originated from the Fujian and Guangdong provinces and the island of Hainan and are able to speak these dialects, and as these two coastal provinces and the island of Hainan have special economic zones (which are some of the most developed economic regions in China), Chinese Singaporeans tended to invest or work in these areas first. Such external developments

led to frequent projections of sub-ethnic identities as Hokkiens, Cantonese, Teochews, Hainanese, Hakkas and so forth when Chinese Singaporeans return to the hometowns of their parents or grandparents to invest or work.

Motivated by instrumental motifs, these Chinese Singaporeans began to deepen their knowledge of the Chinese language, and find out more about Chinese culture and history. Thus, in terms of Chinese cultural attributes, they become more Chinese.

In the last decade or so, Chinese Singaporeans have earned themselves a better reputation than the Taiwanese and Hong Kongers in terms of being more trustworthy business partners or associates. The relationship between the Chinese Government and the Singapore Government has been excellent. Consequently, these two factors are likely to maintain the Singaporean identity of these Chinese as this identity confers some advantages over the Taiwanese and Hong Kongers. After all, Hong Kong will be returned to China and will be governed by the mainland. Politically, Beijing is the ultimate "boss" while Hong Kongers are their "provincial" citizens; likewise, likely the Taiwanese. But Singapore is a friendly, rich, sovereign state and Singaporeans are not the "little brothers" of the mainland Chinese but are perceived as the smarter, more knowledgeable "overseas Chinese" to the people on the mainland. Hence, the "Singaporean" identity is likely to be maintained.

It must be stressed that those Chinese Singaporeans who invest or work in China come from the small managerial or professional "class", and not from the rest of the population such as bus drivers, salesgirls, or typists. As Singapore's multinational corporations (MNCs) grow in number and size, more and more of this small top segment of Singapore society will venture overseas, including to China. To these Singapore citizens, the world seems borderless (but not borderless to the typists, hawkers or school teachers) as they live here for a few months or years and then perhaps in another country wherever their business takes them. Some of them are likely to emigrate and put down roots where the reward is high. There is some chance therefore that Singapore will lose some of its already small number of talented Chinese Singaporeans to China or Hong Kong (after 1997) if in the next decade or two China's economy takes off and corporations (local or foreign) in

China pay competitive salaries and other benefits. Thus, China's projected economic growth into a giant or super economy in the next two or three decades is likely to cause a brain drain from Singapore. As more and more Chinese Singaporeans deepen their knowledge of the Chinese language and culture, and as more and more of them work in China, some may marry their Guangdong, Fujian, Shanghai or Beijing colleagues and settle down in China. This process implies a reversal in the flow of Singaporeans of Chinese descent to China, from the nineteenth century Chinese migration to Singapore. In the nineteenth century, the flow was one of quantity but the future reversed flow is likely to be one of quality.

Conclusion
The first generation of Chinese immigrants from China may be conceptualized as overseas Chinese. But this concept would be inappropriate to describe the ethnic identity of their children or grandchildren who were born and brought up in Singapore, especially when their early years coincided with two major events: nationalism and independence from British rule in Singapore and the turning of China to communism in 1949, and thereafter. These macro domestic and external changes provided the macro framework within which the first generation of Chinese immigrants and their local-born children developed their ethnic and national identities. In a multi-ethnic society, the presence of non-Chinese cultural groups and the process of out-group perception and identification invariably lead to self-identification as Chinese in the cultural and sometimes also physical sense. But macro processes of change, such as educational transformation, residential integration, social integration and so forth, slowly but surely reduce the cultural distinctiveness and foster the evolution of a Singaporean life-style or culture embraced in varying degrees by all. Nation-building processes, planned and unplanned, slowly foster a national identity. But ethnic or cultural attributes and practices change slowly and hence ethnic identity co-exists with national identity at this point in time. A dual identity as Chinese Singaporeans thus emerges. As China develops and becomes an economic power in the near future these Chinese Singaporeans who invest or work in

China will find their Singaporean identity an asset which they would like to preserve. However, economic opportunities in China are likely to encourage Chinese Singaporeans to learn more about Chinese culture and history and thus maintain, if not strengthen, their Chinese cultural identity and to continue to project their Chinese (and Singaporean) identity in China. China is expected to become the biggest economy in the world by the second or third decade of the twenty-first century. As China approaches this target, Singapore may lose some of its talented Chinese Singaporeans to China when corporations (local and foreign) in China are able to pay competitive salaries and other benefits to them. China's development in the next few decades is thus likely to arrest the evolution of Chinese Singaporeans into Singaporeans here, especially among its professional and managerial class.

References

Chiew Seen Kong. "Singaporean National Identity". M.Soc.Sci. thesis, University of Singapore, 1971.

————. "Ethnicity and National Integration: The Evolution of a Multi-ethnic Society". In *Singapore: Development Policies and Trends*, edited by Peter S.J. Chen. Singapore: Oxford University Press, 1983.

————. "Citizens and Foreign Labour in Singapore". In *Crossing Borders: Transmigration in Asia Pacific*, edited by Ong Jin Hui, Chan Kwok Bun and Chew Soon Beng. Singapore: Prentice Hall, 1995.

Chiew Seen Kong and Tan Ern Ser. "The Singaporean: Ethnicity, National Identity and Citizenship". Singapore: Institute of Policy Studies, 1990.

Clammer, John. "Overseas Chinese Assimilation and Resinification: A Malaysian Case Study". *Southeast Asian Journal of Social Science* 3, no. 2 (1975).

————. *The Ambiguity of Identity: Ethnicity Maintenance and Change Amongst the Straits Chinese Community of Malaysia and Singapore*. Occasional Paper, No. 54. Singapore: Institute of Southeast Asian Studies, 1979.

Koh Yang Gek. "Corridors to Harmony: Inter- and Intra-ethnic Interaction in a HDB Housing Estate". Honours Academic Exercise, Dept. of Sociology, National University of Singapore, 1993/94.

Lian Kwen Fee. "Identity in Minority Group Relations". *Ethnic and Racial Studies* 5 (1982): 42–52.

Smolicz, Jerzy. "Core Values and Cultural Identity". *Ethnic and Racial Studies* 4, no. 1 (January 1981): 75–90.

Tufo, M.V. Del. *Malaya. A Report on the 1947 Census of Population*. London: The Crown Agents, n.d.

Wilder, W.D. "Psychosocial Dimensions of Ethnicity". *Southeast Asian Journal of Social Science* 10, no. 1 (1982): 103–15.

Comments by
A. Mani on
"From Overseas Chinese to Chinese Singaporeans"
Presented by Chiew Seen Kong

Dr Chiew Seen Kong has used the biographical approach, where he refers to his own life experiences, to discuss the shift from being migrants to becoming citizens of Singapore. This approach has made the discussion of the process of becoming citizens extremely interesting.

In the biographical approach, he has covered a number of dimensions. Among these is the comparison across generations, of how migrants become citizens. Then he discusses the socialization of citizens, achieved through shared and localized education. The third dimension is the historical conditions which help to shape one's sense of ethnic identity and national loyalties.

First generation migrants from China had viewed Singapore as a foreign land. They were overseas Chinese, whose sentiments were close to their country of birth. Even though many were not successful in accumulating enough money within a period of time to return home, they were psychologically attracted to events that took place in their homeland.

The second generation Chinese underwent different life experiences. As they were born in Singapore, they were British subjects, and thought differently according to their socializing experiences. Those who went to English medium schools, like the author, retained their cultural affinity of being Chinese but otherwise felt Singapore was their home, while appreciating their parents' affinity to China.

Those who, unlike the author, went to Chinese schools were closer to Chinese culture, but probably saw their life chances worsening as Malaya progressed towards independence. Probably in asserting their rights they were viewed as extremist Chinese who were not so loyal to the local government.

Both groups, however, lived in a plural society where a Chinese way of life in the context of Singapore was shared only amongst them, more than with any other ethnic group in Singapore. The progression towards becoming more Malayan in the 1950s and early 1960s would have made most of them feel that they had to give up "something Chinese". This "something" would have meant differently to different groups, be they be clans, dialect groups, business associations, or even the Chinese Chamber of Commerce.

The generation of ethnic Chinese in Singapore in the 1950s and the 1960s would also have experienced larger community processes of pulling together various groups of Chinese to form a larger identity, like the establishment of Nanyang University. They might also have felt the processes of creating a nation state from the late 1950s to mid-1970s as a desinification attempt, to make Singaporean Chinese give less emphasis to Chinese language and culture.

This period can be described as one during which the government was able to effectively break down not only the intra-ethnic cleavages in Singapore but also inter-ethnic barriers to communication and interaction.

Ethnic Chinese born in post-war Singapore would generally have attended schools organized by the government of the day and they would have been socialized into the ethos of that period.

The third aspect is the historical conditions that have shaped the meaning of ethnicity for Chinese Singaporeans. World War II and the Japanese occupation of Singapore probably made all of them more Chinese. A similar process could be said for Indians. Similarly, the historical conditions up to the time Singapore joined Malaysia, then being in Malaysia, and then suddenly thrust with independence in 1965, when for the first time the ethnic Chinese formed the majority in a state within Southeast Asia could have brought euphoria to some and apprehension to many. It is remarkable that this dominance of the Chinese in a country far away from China has been managed rationally to create a better Singapore for all.

Ethnicity is one of the many identities that people can have in nation states. The history of political realities in Malaysia and Singapore has emphasized the maintenance of ethnic identity together with national integration. Thus, while migrants have become citizens, they have also merged from being Cantonese, Hakka, and so on, to become the Chinese. This may not be similar to other Southeast Asian countries, especially Indonesia and Thailand, where the ethnic Chinese identity has not been publicly encouraged. In Singapore, everyone has to have an ethnic label, however much they may object to it. Singaporeans have been given the generic labels of being either Malays, Chinese, Indians, or others, with nothing in-between. Any anomalous identities are ethnically labelled after one's paternal identities. Despite these observations, for a variety of reasons, as discussed in Dr Chiew Seen Kong's paper, large segments of the first generation migrants and their descendants have retained their cultural identities. These cultural identities themselves have undergone mutations that may be different from present-day conditions in the natal areas of the first generation migrants. To many visitors from India to Singapore and Malaysia, for example, it is a surprise to realize that Thaipusam and Theemithi are the dominant festivals of Hinduism, whereas in India they are merely localized religious festivals.

Even though demographically, Singaporeans are enumerated according to racial groups, the statistics hide the process of integration and assimilation that has proceeded in Singapore. Dr Chiew Seen Kong has taken this into account by shifting the discussion from "racial categories" as implied by demography to a discussion of ethnic identities. Both internal and external factors have aided the process of ethnic Chinese Singaporean identity. Besides the internal process already mentioned in the paper, the author could have reviewed the attempts by Singapore's political leadership since 1977 to have "Speak Mandarin" campaigns, to emphasize "Confucianism", to force the use of *hanyu pinyin* names for ethnic Chinese, to implement the Special Assistance Plan schools, to make the top 10 per cent of ethnic Chinese students after their Primary Six learn Mandarin at the first language level, and finally to encourage a Chinese Cultural Month which had not been done before. Is it not possible that in the post-1980s period, there is an assertion of state-supported Chinese Singaporean identity *vis-à-vis* other ethnic identities in Singapore? For instance, after 1987, other ethnic identities in Singapore have become constitutionally classified as "minority" ethnic identities to be accommodated by the dominant ethnic Chinese Singaporean identity. Do these developments mean that Singapore is now a predominantly ethnic Chinese society located in Southeast Asia?

Can an argument be made that political élites in Singapore since the 1980s embarked on a resinification process of the ethnic Chinese in Singapore? This process can have implications for other ethnic groups in Singapore. It could also be viewed as a reversal of the process of desinification pursued from the 1950s to the 1970s with the eventual closure of Nanyang University, reorganization of the Chinese newspapers, and the de-emphasis of Chinese grassroots organizations such as clan associations.

The author raises the question whether "economic opportunities in China may arrest the expected process of evolution from Chinese Singaporeans to simply Singaporeans". This raises numerous questions for Singapore in Southeast Asia as well as for Singaporeans to ponder whether economic benefits alone should decide their social goals as a people located in Southeast Asia.

Chapter 7

From Siamese-Chinese to Chinese-Thai: Political Conditions and Identity Shifts among the Chinese in Thailand*

Supang Chantavanich

"Siamese-Chinese" or Jin-Sayam (in Thai), or Sian Hua (暹华 in Chinese) was the name that the overseas Chinese in Thailand called themselves. It might be Sheow Hut-seng, a Hokkien scholar who was editor of the *Siamese-Chinese Magazine* (*Hua Sian Sin Po* 华暹新报), who introduced the term. King Wachirawut of Siam, using a pen-name, criticized the term as one connoting a new Thai breed whom one could not guess when they would consider themselves as Thai and when as expatriate. The dubious name thus represented a group of undesirable people who overtly showed that they were watching the way the wind was blowing. According

* I would like to express my thanks to Dr. Suwadee Tanaprasitsatana and Kullada Kesboonchoo who provided me with some useful documents; and to Aaron Stern and Colleen Mitchell for their editorial comments.

to King Wachirawut, these Siamese-Chinese could become Thai only when they proved their allegiance to Thailand, not China.[1]

Why did King Wachirawut express so strongly and overtly his feeling against the overseas Chinese, as he did in his two pamphlets, *The Jews of the Orient* (1914), and *The Clogs on Our Wheels* (1915)? Why did he introduce the nationalist concept against the Chinese? Why did Phibulsongkhram, the Thai Prime Minister in 1938, revive the nationalist movement against the Chinese in Thailand? How did such movements affect the self-identity of the Chinese? What is the Chinese situation after World War II? Do they remain overseas Chinese or have they assumed a Thai identity? This chapter will try to address these questions.

The assimilation of the overseas Chinese in Thailand was a long process which lasted for over a century. In this process, the integration was sometimes smooth and successful but it was also difficult and confrontational at other times. The Thai stances on nationalism were significant political conditions which acceler-ated the assimilation of the overseas Chinese. This chapter will examine these political conditions, namely, Thai official national-ism and its impact on the identity of the overseas Chinese. It will also analyse the Chinese nationalist movement as a resisting force against assimilation. Finally, it will describe the naturalization phenomenon among the overseas Chinese and their gradual change of identity.

The first Thai nationalist movement lasted about twelve years (1913–25). The second movement also lasted about twelve years (1938–50), but there was a gap of thirteen years between the two movements, which did not happen without a reason. The two movements were the reaction of the Thai State to the Chinese nationalist movement which spread among the overseas Chinese in Thailand. The two nationalist ideologies interacted with each other and finally had an impact on the Sino-Siamese identity.

First Wave of Thai Nationalism in 1910
King Wachirawut did not introduce the Thai nationalist ideology to the overseas Chinese without good reason. Earlier in 1908, the Chinese in Bangkok had held a strike, refusing to sell consumer goods or to work. The cause of this strike was the Thai Government's

decision to increase the amount of tax per head on Chinese aliens from 4.25 baht to 6 baht (which was the rate for Thais). In the past, the Chinese in Thailand had paid a lower tax as they made up the majority of the labour force.[2] When the decree on the tax increase was announced, the Chinese who could not read nor understand the Thai language very well reacted demonstratively. They distributed a letter inviting compatriots to join the strike. For three days, most Thai people in Bangkok could not find rice or food for their daily consumption. They then realized that they depended a lot on the Chinese merchants. To many Thais, the strike also demonstrated that "the Chinese valued the small amount of tax increase over allegiance, obedience and justice".[3] As a result they did not consider the Sino-Siamese to be their friends any longer.

The strike took place three months before the death of King Chulalongkorn. When Wachirawut succeeded his father to the throne, he did not forget the event. As a young king educated in England — where imperialism was strong at the time — Wachirawut was inspired by the ideology of a modern nation state and nationalism.[4] The fall of the Ching dynasty in 1911 was another factor. He had good reason to be afraid of the republican Sino-Siamese whose ideology could be a threat to the Thai monarchy. A historian described Wachirawut's nationalism as follows:

> Wachirawut... [modelled] himself on the self-naturalizing dynasts of Europe. Although and because he was educated in late Victorian England, he dramatized himself as his country's 'first nationalist'. The target of this nationalism... was the Chinese whom his father had so recently and blithely imported. The style of his anti-Chinese stance is suggested by the titles of two of his most famous pamphlets: The Jews of the Orients (1914) and The Clogs on Our Wheels (1915).
>
> Here is fine example of the character of official nationalism, an anticipatory strategy adopted by dominant groups who are threatened with marginalization or exclusion from an emerging nationally imagined community. (It goes without saying that Wachirawut also began moving all the policy levers of official nationalism: compulsory state-controlled primary education, state-organized propaganda, official rewriting of history, militarism here

more visible show than the real thing – and endless affirmations of the identity of dynasty and nationality).[5]

Thai official nationalism as introduced by King Wachirawut considers the three pillars of the Thai state — the monarch, the nation and religion — as the traditional symbols with which the Thais can identify themselves. The King's nationalist ideology was to maintain the position of the monarch as the pillar of loyalty, to develop the concept of nation, which was new to most people, and to enhance the role of traditional religion. The monarch was put at the core of the nationalist concept, giving the analogy that the state was like an organic body and the King was the brain. The King represented the nation's dignity and therefore should receive all honour appropriate to the nation. Government officials should devote themselves to their duty and to the king. Unity within the nation was a key condition of solidarity. Buddhism was used as a tool to keep people's morality and as a code of conduct.

King Wachirawut's nationalism had a clear logic behind it and should not be labelled as "romantic", as Skinner, an expert on the Chinese in Thailand, once called it.[6] A vigorous call for democracy and a republican regime had been made in 1912 in the Thai court. An aborted *coup d'etat* led by young government officials occurred two years after Wachirawut's ascension to the throne. After the coup, he established the Wild Tiger Corps (Sua Pa), a paramilitary organization to serve as the King's new security force and as means to disseminate the official ideology to government officials. The aborted coup, the Chinese strike, the heated debate between the King (under his pen-name in the newspaper) and Sheow Hut-seng (the Chinese scholar), and the visit of Dr. Sun Yat-sen in 1908 to campaign for the revolution in China all led to the King's decision to introduce official nationalism.

Concrete measures were taken by the King not only in the form of the two books attacking the Sino-Siamese. Historical data also reveals that the King promulgated the following laws and announcements:

1913 First Nationality Law, which indicated that local-born Chinese were of Thai nationality.

1913 Last Name Law

1914   Association Law, which controlled the activities of all
        associations and clubs, especially the Chinese associations
        in order to make them non-political.
1921   Primary School Act
1925   Announcement to close Sheow Hut-seng's printing house.

However, since most legal measures were not strictly enforced
at the time, the Sino-Siamese were not directly affected by this
nationalism. Most still kept their strong ties and participated in
the Chinese nationalism propagated by Dr Sun Yat-sen. The Chinese
nationalism played a significant role in preserving the Chinese
qualities of the Sino-Siamese.

Chinese Nationalism and the Tung Meng Hui Movement

Sun Yat-sen's visit and address to the Chinese community in
Chinatown in 1908 were the beginnings of Chinese nationalism
in Thailand. In that same year, after the visit, Sheow Hut-seng
formed the Tung Meng Hui movement, or the Chinese Revolution
Alliance, to support the democratic revolution in China. Although
there was a group of pro-Ching royalist Chinese in Thailand, they
were smaller in number and less rigorous in their ideology compared to the Tung Meng Hui supporters. Another group of non-
aligned Chinese formed themselves into the Chinese Chamber
of Commerce (CCC) led by Koh Hui-chiya in 1910. The CCC
members pledged loyalty to King Wachirawut and expressed their
regret about the Chinese strike in 1908.[7] (However, two decades
later, the CCC became engaged in the Chinese nationalist movement.) Wachirawut himself was not happy with Sun Yat-sen's visit
and criticized the latter in his writings.[8]

When China became a republic in 1911, the Tung Meng Hui
nationalists in Thailand became more confident. They formed
themselves into the Sino-Siamese Consolidation Club in 1914.
The club openly supported the Kuomintang. In response, King
Wachirawut promulgated the Association Law in 1914.

Another factor which strengthened the Chinese nationalist
movement in Thailand was the weakening of the language boundary
among the five dialect groups, that is, the Teochew, Hokkien,
Cantonese, Hakka, and Hainanese. In the late nineteenth century,

the five groups had been very conscious about their sub-ethnic status. Competitions and disputes were common among them and each group had its own secret society to protect its members. The founding of Tien Hua hospital in 1906 and the CCC in 1910 were significant events because they illustrated the inclinations of the groups. The Tien Hua hospital was founded by funds donated by Chinese traders to offer medical treatment to Chinese people from all dialect groups. A representative from each group would take turns directing the hospital. Simultaneously, the CCC executive committee consisted of representatives from all dialect groups.[9] With such solidarity, the Chinese from all the five groups participated in the Chinese nationalist movement in Thailand, although their levels of participation differed.

There were two factions within the nationalist movement, the pro-democracy and the pro-communist. However, the factions which split according to the Kuomintang and the Communist parties in China were not so evident during this period.

The business élite who formed the Sino-Siam Consolidation Club (the group which engaged in political activities) exhibited a new trend of national identity by changing their names — that is, by adding a Thai last name to their existing names, according to the Family Name Act 1913. Some examples were Sheow Hud-seng Sibun-reung, Tiensieng Kannasut, Chua Penpakkul, Tan Hong-hi Tantivejakul. On the other hand, business leaders who joined the CCC (which was non-politically oriented initially) such as Koh Hui-chiya and Tan Lib-buay still kept their Chinese names. Suehiro hypothesized that the élite who used Thai last names were people born in Thailand but with Chinese ancestors. They were instilled with Thai nationalism and required to have a Thai last name according to the Nationality Act and the Family Name Act.[9] Another interpretation is that this group of business élite (with Sheow Hut-seng as leader) had experienced King Wachirawut's nationalist measures and had learned how to demonstrate their loyalty to Thailand, by adopting Thai family names. However, all of them maintained their Chinese names for dealing with other Chinese businessmen. This attempt to keep a dual identity among the Chinese was consistently found when confronted by political conditions later.

The Anti-Japanese Movement: Second Wave of Chinese Nationalism

The first period of Chinese nationalism in 1910 accelerated the consolidation of the five dialect groups and revealed various factions based on political ideologies. The Japan-China war intensified Chinese nationalism because of the appearance of a concrete, external enemy. All factions united against the Japanese. The merging of the Communist Party and the Kuomintang (KMT) to fight for China enabled the various factions to unite to form a new nationalist movement.

The decade of the 1930s was the peak of the second wave of Chinese nationalism and political upheaval. In 1925, the anti-Japanese movement had started with a strike led by Puy-yin School children and Chinese workers. Later in 1928, after the attack at Shandong Cape where more than 5,000 Chinese were killed by the Japanese, the Sino-Siamese boycotted Japanese goods and Japanese trade. The boycott lasted many months. The Chinese leaders used the secret societies to force and threaten Chinese businessmen who traded with Japanese traders. Murasima described the anti-Japanese strike as follows:

> From June to September 1928, the boycott worked effectively. All buying and selling of Japanese goods stopped totally.... The boycotters used the secret societies to threaten traders... Chinese businessmen who traded with Japanese traders were forced to pay a fine to the boycott gang... Some were threatened for life...
>
> ...On August 6, 1928, Ang Khu-eng, the son of Ang Sia-leng Pharmacy owner was shot dead... The Siamese government put all the boycott gang to investigation... Some of them were deported... In April 1929, the anti-Japanese strike calmed down.[10]

The anti-Japanese movement was aggravated by the death of Sun Yat-sen. After his death, the nationalists were divided again into the pro-Chiang Kai-shek group and the pro-Wang Chao-ming group. Tan Siew-meng, the son of Tan Lib-buay who founded the CCC with his friends, was the leader of the Pro-Chiang clique while Hia Kwang-Iam, another business leader, led the pro-Wang clique. Tan Siew-meng was elected the Chairman of the CCC and also appointed Trade Attache for the Chiang government in Thailand. The two leaders co-operated throughout in the anti-Japanese movement and raised funds for remittance to China. The amount of remittances sent to China during August 1937 to February 1938 reached 705,086 baht (US$28,203).[11]

While the Japan-China war continued in China, the boycott of the Sino-Siamese continued in Thailand in 1937. Some Chinese traders who refused to join the boycott because of the attractive profits to be derived from such trading were targets of the movement. The nationalists treated the traders harshly through the secret societies. The secret societies would send a letter ordering the traders to pay a fine for being disobedient. A group of seven or eight gangs assassinated sixty-one traders. Hia Kwang-Iam was among them.

Hia Kwang-Iam's death in 1932 could be considered as the apex and the point when the second wave of Chinese nationalism began to decline. As an ardent nationalist, Hia had devoted his energy, time and resources to supporting the movement. One hypothesis is that his death was a revenge killing by a Chinese family whose father was killed by the secret society. Some suspected that Hia commanded the secret society. Another explanation was that the Japanese ordered a Chinese to kill him since he was very active in the anti-Japanese boycott. The important point is that he was assassinated by a compatriot while he was active in the movement. This incident had a great impact on the nationalist movement. Many of his followers began asking themselves many questions: Who are we? What are we doing? The defeat of the Chinese army in 1938–39 might also have weakened the morale of the nationalists in Thailand. Meanwhile, the number of Chinese traders who decided to trade with the Japanese merchants increased. They felt the boycott was a foolish way to save the nation.[13] All these factors brought about the decline of Chinese nationalism in Thailand. The Sino-Siamese began to realize that Thailand might be the place to live their lives and this helped to tone down their nationalist ideology. Nonetheless, they continued to keep their dubious national identity.

Constitutional Monarchy and Phibulsongkhram's Nationalism

The second half of the Chinese nationalist picture can be seen in the emergence of the second wave of Thai nationalism under

Phibulsongkhram. In 1927, during the reign of King Prachadhipok (successor to King Wachirawut), the Thai Government promulgated the Immigration Act. Although King Prachadhipok did not promote nationalism to the same degree as his father, the number of Chinese immigrants during his reign increased so much that the government felt compelled to enforce the Act. During 1927–28, an estimated 154,600 immigrants arrived in Thailand.[14] At the dawn of constitutional monarchy, Thailand had no immediate anti-Chinese policy and the Chinese nationalist movement enjoyed full liberty.

When Phibulsongkhram became Prime Minister of Thailand in 1938, the Chinese nationalist movement and the fear of communism were the two factors that convinced him of the need for stronger Thai nationalism. It is important to note that Phibulsongkhram's nationalism differed from Wachirawut's. It was a chauvinistic nationalism expressed in an aggressive, expansionistic and militaristic manner. Phibulsongkhram's aim was to protect social cohesion and public order. Certainly, the Chinese nationalist movement was considered a threat to Thai social cohesion and public order. However, Phibulsongkhram's nationalism was not against the ethnic Chinese but against the allegiance which the ethnic Chinese had for China. He and other leaders always emphasized that they themselves had some Chinese blood and therefore their protest was not against the Chinese *per se* but because they were nationalistic towards China and not loyal to Thailand. Such persons could bring communism to the country.

Like Wachirawut, Phibulsongkhram's nationalism had a clear rationale. There was a revival of Chinese nationalism. Chinese newspapers, divided into factions, were very popular. Chinese schools increased in number from 48 schools in 1925 to 271 in 1933.[15] They were also active in the nationalist movement: teachers were activists and funds were raised among students to support the Kuomintang army in China; and the Chinese national flag was hoisted on various occasions.[16] Secret societies also expanded their memberships, especially among the students and labourers. These circumstances alerted Phibulsongkhram to the danger of Chinese nationalism towards Thailand. He decided to close the Chinese schools and newspapers in 1939, the same year that Hia was killed. Phibulsongkhram also took over the remittance business because it was the way that the nationalist Chinese supported the KMT army. In 1940, the Phibulsongkhram government deported a group of Chinese activists who were members of secret societies. On the other hand, the government opened the door to those who expressed their loyalty to Thailand and agreed to be naturalized in 1939. During 1939–40, there were 104 naturalizations. Most of those naturalized were among the business élite who had resided in Thailand for more than twenty years and were literate in the Thai language.[17]

Phibulsongkhram also introduced economic nationalism in addition to his political measures. He wanted to take back economic power from the Chinese businessmen. Between 1938 and 1939 he used naturalized Chinese businessmen like Ma Liab-kun (Ma Bulkul) and Ung Chak-meng (Amporn Bulpak) to run state-owned companies, such as the Thai Rice Company, the Thai Commercial Company, and the Thai Crop Trade Company.[18] In addition, a group of Thai merchants formed the Siamese Chamber of Commerce (SCC) in 1933 to promote business by Thai traders. The establishment of the SCC was in accordance with the 1932 constitutional policy to strengthen the Thais' role in the economy.[19] Later, in 1941, Phibulsongkhram enacted a law to reserve certain occupations for Thai people. In 1949, he implemented a major cut in the quota for Chinese immigrants from 10,000 persons per year to 200 persons per year.[20]

Phibulsongkhram believed that the Chinese schools and Chinese secret societies strongly linked the Sino-Siamese to China. He therefore announced in a Cabinet meeting on 1 November 1939, that: "Anything can be done; just to disappear Chinese schools and the *ang-yi*."[21] Four restrictive measures were consequently implemented: 1) the closure of Chinese schools; 2) the closure of Chinese newspapers; 3) the closure of Chinese secret societies; and 4) the seizure of control over Chinese remittances.

Regarding the schools, Phibulsongkhram reintroduced the Primary School Act 1921 and the Private School Act 1919 to control all Chinese schools which were considered as private schools. Chinese language courses were reduced to 7 hours per week and the language of instruction for other courses had to be in Thai. Teachers had to have Thai educational qualifications. The Chinese community protested strongly against these policies (which started in 1933–36), but the protest was in vain. As a result, Chinese schools, where more than 8,000 Chinese pupils were studying, had to close voluntarily or were closed by the government because they did not comply with the Private School Act.

These Chinese schools had earlier shifted from teaching in the various dialects to Mandarin in 1930. The decision was the result of discussions among the élite from different dialect groups who agreed that Mandarin would be the most useful and consolidating language for their children.[22] Unlike most Chinese schools in Southeast Asia, which taught only a single dialect depending upon the ethnicity of the dominant dialect group residing in that country, Chinese schools in Thailand amalgamated the five dialect groups by teaching Mandarin. The members of each dialect group thus shifted their identity from Teochew, Hokkien, Cantonese, Hakka and Hainanese to a Chinese national identity. And when the Chinese schools had to teach in Thai, the identity of the Chinese in Thailand again shifted to that of the Chinese Thai.[23] In this way, education played an important role in shifting the Chinese identity towards Thailand.

Chinese newspapers in Thailand were also highly politicized. The leading business élite normally owned a newspaper each, with each promoting a particular Chinese nationalist political ideology. Thus, most newspapers aroused nationalistic feelings and anti-Japanese sentiments. The Chinese businessmen who traded with the Japanese were forced to announce their apologies to the Chinese community in those newspapers.[24] During 1937–38, daily sales of Chinese newspapers reached 20,000 copies. Phibulsongkhram used the Printing Act of 1927 to close some of these newspapers. Later, in 1939, he closed all the Chinese newspapers, alleging that they were destroying state order and good relationship with other countries. Only one newspaper (*Tong Guan*) continued to publish by changing its theme from political to social news. In 1941, this newspaper was taken over by the Japanese.[25] From that point onwards, the Chinese community turned away from the Chinese newspapers and they gradually began to lose their Chinese identity.

Like Chinese secret societies elsewhere, the *ang-yi* in Thailand were guilds, a type of informal occupational association. Most of the members were workers in saw mills, rice mills or construction. Skinner indicated that in 1910, almost all Chinese railway workers were members of secret societies.[26] These occupational groupings were considered to be an overseas Chinese culture. When these people left China; they had no family nor kin. They therefore needed protection, especially in their work, and thus turned to secret societies which were based on the idea that brotherhood could offer protection to workers employed in the same occupation. The leaders, who acted as heads of a big family, could negotiate with employers and corrupt officials.[27] For example, during the anti-Japanese period, the secret society *sae-khang* had 3,000 members. In 1938, Phibulsongkhram ordered police raids into the opium dens where society members usually gathered. He deported 3,156 Chinese, many of whom were members of the *ang-yi*. His action convinced the Chinese in Thailand that they should withdraw from those associations and stop their secret activities. The ties with their homeland through membership of the *ang-yi* were cut and resulted in a shift of their Chinese identity away from their homeland.

During the anti-Japanese movement, Chinese remittances were not familial or kinship affairs. They became a nationwide activity because money was sent back to support the KMT to save the country from the Japanese invasion. Many Chinese organizations in Thailand campaigned for such contributions. Although the Thai Government forbade cash donations, the Chinese continued to accept donations in kind (especially rice). The Overseas Chinese Bank and other Chinese banks were very active in facilitating the money transfers. In 1939, in a police raid on those banks, it was found out that an amount of US$2,400,000 was sent to China during November 1938 – April 1939. The bank managers were arrested and later deported. After this discovery, the Bank of Thailand took control over remittances. This affected the transfer of money to relatives in China, and the Chinese in Thailand had to send remittances secretly. With the victory of the Communist Party in China in 1949, most connections and remittances from Thailand to China were totally cut off. Hence, the Chinese identification with their homeland through remittances was stopped step by step.

Chinese Nationalism and Chinese Identity

The communist victory over Chiang Kai-shek in 1949 had a strong impact on the nationalist Chinese in Thailand. After this event, some Chinese decided to naturalize. During 1942–44, a group of 167 Chinese in Thailand were naturalized under the Naturalization Act of 1912 and Phibulsongkhram's newly set measures. Such measures were not easy to fulfill. The Committee for the Consideration of the Chinese in Siam set the following requirements for naturalization.[28]

1. the person must be 20 years of age;
2. the person must work with the government or have performed something good for the government;
3. the person must declare his properties, especially real estate;
4. the person cannot be a worker;
5. the person's spouse and children must also be naturalized;
6. the person should send his/her children to Thai schools; and
7. the person must be able to read and write Thai.

It was also stated that the applicant had to stop his allegiance to China and have a strong intention to become Thai. All such measures were publicized in the local Chinese newspapers.

Although the number of naturalized Chinese was small compared to the total number of Chinese in Thailand at that time, this naturalization was important because it was the first time that the Thai Government permitted the Chinese to obtain Thai nationality. Moreover, Thailand did not usually grant Thai nationality to nationals of a country with whom Thailand had no diplomatic relations, which was the case with China at that time. Such permission offered the chance for the Chinese in Thailand to choose their identity. Wang Gungwu observed that the Chinese overseas in Southeast Asia were mostly loyal to their homeland. However, this group of migrants had a complex set of identities. There were two major types of identity: one was a politically-focused identity while the other was a culturally-focused one. The political identity covered the Chinese nationalist identity, the local national identity and the ethnic (racial) Chinese identity which emphasized their legal and political rights in the receiving country. The cultural identity, which focused on the glorious history of China, was the historical, and ethnic (cultural) identity which emphasized the distinctiveness of Chinese culture. In reality, the overseas Chinese possessed a multiple identity which changed over time, as Wang Gungwu has observed:

> ...The Chinese sense of their own identity could be changed by changing events. The new indigenous élite seemed to have understood this and had good reason to expect the Chinese to change again when circumstances further changed. Thus, for several decades to 1950, Chinese historical identity seemed to have been partially superseded by Chinese nationalist identity. But, even when this nationalist identity was at its peak in the 1930s and 1940s, not all Chinese changed in favour of Chinese nationalism. Some had sought to identify with local indigenous nationalist movements.... the point to note is that consciously changing their identity was an option which some younger Chinese were already exploring.[29]

With regard to the Chinese in Thailand, such observation fits well with reality. Wachirawut's official nationalism and Phibul-songkhram's nationalism were both causes and consequences of the Chinese community's economic power, a power shown clearly when the Chinese consolidated in the strike against the increase in Thai taxes. Sun Yat-sen's visit to Thailand also magnified fears of Chinese nationalism among the Thai authorities. Thus, Thailand's first nationalism was a consequence of Chinese nationalism. This first period of nationalism might not have aroused many feelings about a Chinese identity among the Chinese in Thailand. But it signalled to the Sino-Siamese that a demonstration of total allegiance to China would irritate the Thai élite. It also shifted the Sino-Siamese's historical-cultural identity towards a more Chinese nationalist oriented one.

The disruption of the Thai nationalist stance during the reign of King Prachadipok allowed Chinese nationalism and the Chinese nationalist identity to nurture their intensified ideologies. All over Southeast Asia, the KMT movement spread rapidly among the overseas Chinese. Simultaneously, the number of Chinese immigrants to Siam reached its peak in 1927–28 when 154,600 people arrived. The Japan-China war aroused more emotional contagion and the increasing number of immigrants made the Chinese aware of their massive political force. Consequently, the Sino-Siamese, with the invention of Japan as their common enemy, consolidated and built among themselves an "imagined community" where nationalism was the core ideology. This imagined community was quite similar to Benedict Anderson's description, that is, an imagined political community both inherently limited and sovereign.[30] Such a community is built upon the use of a common language and the printing technology which give rise to a shared ideology and nationalism. The overseas Chinese community in Thailand was an imagined community in the sense that it was built upon the transformation of the five dialects into the Mandarin language and the popular printed newspapers that brought all Sino-Siamese into a common sense of nationalism and a shared ideology, that is, Chinese nationalism and KMT ideology. And in 1930, all Chinese schools in Thailand started to teach in Mandarin. Mandarin was then used in business and politics. It was also the means of arousing patriotic feeling among the overseas Chinese. Concurrently, the nine Chinese newspapers printed in Thailand were very active in discussing political issues and disseminating them to the Chinese who were in the same imagined community, although many of them did not reside in Sampheng or Chinatown in Bangkok. Such an imagined community was larger then the physical boundary, but it was inherently limited — that is, limited to only the ethnic Chinese. However, the sovereignty of this community was dubious and its existence was always changing like the Chinese identity.

There is inadequate information to discuss in more depth the sovereignty of the imagined community of the Chinese in Thailand. Nonetheless, the flag hoisting event, which will be discussed later, may be related to this sovereignty. For the moment, what we can conclude is that the imagined community of the Chinese in Thailand was constructed with the support of the common Mandarin language and the printed Chinese newspapers. The nationalist ideology of the community determined the Chinese identity of its members.

Three characteristics of an imagined community are its boundary, its sovereignty and its communal brotherhood. The next section examines the characteristics of the Chinese community in Thailand and the way they conditioned the Chinese identity.

The Chinese conglomerates in Thailand were mostly located in the Sampheng, Yaowarat, Rachawong, Plabplachai, and Bang Rag areas of Bangkok. But as the Chinese had settled in every part of the country, the Chinese community was not confined to Chinatown. The boundary of the community was based on "Chineseness" and the Chinese nationalist ideology. It was a collective behaviour of people who although they did not live in the same physical space shared the same ideological and cultural space. Those people believed to a certain extent that they had sovereignty over their "ideological territory". An example of such a belief was the flag hoisting phenomenon.

Leading Chinese organizations such as the CCC, the Sino-Siamese Consolidation Club and the Chinese schools always asked the Chinese people in Thailand to hoist the Chinese and the Thai flags at various important occasions — for example, hoisting the Chinese flag at half-mast to commemorate the death of Sun Yat-sen (1925); decorating areas with the Thai flag on the King's birthday (1928); hoisting the Chinese flag to celebrate the news that the Chinese army had defeated the Japanese at Shanghai (which was not true) (1932); and decorating schools with Chinese flags on Chinese National Day (1934). More often, people hoisted the Chinese flag. The Chinese in Thailand affirmed their Chinese-ness and sovereignty of their community through the act of hoisting the Chinese flag. Flag-raising emphasized the estrangement between them and the indigenous people. On the Thai side, the government considered such flag hoisting as an overt challenge to state authority. Thus, the imagined community of the Chinese existed on the dichotomy of sovereignty and confirmation of Chinese identity on one hand and the conflict with the Thai state on the other land.

The *ang-yi*, or triads, were the most concrete form of brotherhood ideology of the imagined community. Although the relationship in those secret associations had a vertical direction, with big brother (*Tua-hia*) at the top of the hierarchy; the relationship at the bottom was more horizontal, linking mostly labourers in the same occupation together. This horizontal relationship resembled the fraternity principle of an imagined community.

Thus, the overseas Chinese in Thailand constructed an imagined community which, led by the nationalist ideology, had a specific task, that is, to push its members to support the KMT. This Chinese imagined community was the cause of Phibulsongkhram's reintroduction of Thai nationalism in 1938.

The identity of the Chinese during the nationalist movement was politically oriented. This identity bound all Chinese together against the Japanese. Without the China-Japan war, Chinese nationalist identity would not have been so intense and politicized. The harsh regulations that Phibulsongkhram implemented had affected the configuration of the identity of the Chinese. In his study of the politics of the Sino-Siamese, Murasima[31] classified the Sino Siamese into three categories. The first group of Chinese were those who had absorbed a Thai identity. They cultivated a Thai national identity through the process of naturalization and co-operation with the Thai state in developing the Thai economy. The second group, at the other extreme, rebelled to maintain their Chinese national identity. Their reward was deportation. With only 167 naturalized Chinese and 3,256 deportees, we can guess the trend of the majority which constituted the third group. This last group was more flexible. They acted according to four conditions: 1) the Thai government's strict measures towards the Chinese; 2) ties with the homeland in China; 3) the protection of business interests; and 4) the changing political circumstances in both Thailand and China. They down-played overt Chineseness. And, as Wang Gungwu described, "consciously changing their identity was an option which some younger Chinese were already exploring." This is supported by Ruth McVey's remark: "[D]irect pressures, acculturation to the model set by the ruling elite, and the business need for close relationships with the state all make for down-playing overt Chineseness, and the line between what is Chinese and what is indigenous is becoming increasingly uncertain."[32]

The uncertain identity among the third group of overseas Chinese was obvious. In their actions, they co-operated with the

Thai government as the first group did. They tried to prove their allegiance to Thailand. For example, they donated money to buy weapons for the Thai Army on Constitution Day. They also donated money to support the rally in the Thai-French dispute over Indochina and to build hospitals and academic buildings. Nonetheless, they continued secretly to support the KMT. When Japanese troops landed in Thailand in 1941, these Chinese, mostly businessmen, co-operated with the Thai Government and the Japanese army. Yet, they assisted the anti-Japanese movement secretly. During the period of watching which way the wind blew, the Chinese developed a three-tiered kind of identity: 1) a secret Chinese nationalist identity; 2) an overt Thai nationalist identity; and 3) a Chinese ethnic and cultural identity.

The Post-War Identity Shift
Phibulsongkhram's decision to bring Thailand to join Japan in the Axis in World War II was very significant to the Chinese in Thailand. The nationalist Chinese had demonstrated a strong reaction against the Japanese in Thailand during the Japan-China war. When Thailand joined the "Greater East Asia Co-Prosperity Sphere", the Chinese had to camouflage their hostility against the Japanese in order to adapt to the Thai political policy. In such conditions, the third group of overseas Chinese down-played their supporting role to the KMT. When the war came to an end with the victory of the Alliance, the overseas Chinese had to admit that they could not continue to keep the Chinese nationalist ideology.

The defeat of the Republican government by the Communist Party in China in 1949 was the turning point of the Chinese national identity in Thailand. Since Thailand decided not to have diplomatic relations with the People's Republic of China and even considered the communist regime as a threat to the nation, the Chinese in Thailand knew that they could not continue overtly to keep their Chinese national identity and express their allegiance to China. The radical societal changes at the beginning of the communist regime in China also alerted the overseas Chinese that their homeland was no more a safe place to return.

With the closure of Chinese schools in Thailand, Thai schools provided the Chinese children with a new programme of socialization and more Chinese youth were assimilated into Thai society; their parents constituted another contributive factor. During the post-war period, many Chinese youth had parents who were born in China but there were some who were born in Thailand. It was found that the Chinese youth whose parents were born in China were less likely to assimilate than those whose parents were born in Thailand.[33] The reason is that the first generation parents were more Chinese-oriented and maintained the traditions of their homeland. Their memory of China reinforced their Chinese identity. On the other hand, the local-born parents had less personal attachments to China and less Chinese orientation in their family. As a result, the latter group were more likely to be assimilated. The languages spoken in the family confirm this. Children with Chinese-born parents spoke more Chinese with their parents and their siblings while children with local-born parents spoke more Thai.

The results of assimilation for the Chinese in Thailand, especially the younger generation, were the new opportunities available to them in society in general. As Guskin describes:

> ... As a result of his new ethnic identity, attitudes and behavior, the assimilated Chinese student can choose, as freely as his Thai peers, the occupation and educational level he desires. For, if a Chinese person talks like a Thai, behaves like a Thai, has a Thai name, and identifies as a Thai, Thai society will quite readily accept him and behave towards him as if he were a Thai. This is even more true if the assimilated Chinese person was born in Thailand.[34]

Consequently, the Chinese, especially the youth, continued to assimilate in larger numbers due to two major factors: family orientation and the assimilation pressures from Thai politics and Thai schooling. Simultaneously, the number of new Chinese immigrants also declined substantially after the 1930s. The arrivals which reached 154,600 in 1927–28, started to decline in 1931. As shown in Table 1, Chinese immigration during 1931–35 decreased to 46,400 persons. Later, it declined to 38,200 and 21,300 during 1936–40 and 1941–45 respectively. Only after World War II and before the victory of the Communist Party in

TABLE 1

Chinese Immigration, 1921–50

(in thousand persons)

| Period | Annual Average | | | Total Addition |
	Arrivals	Departure	Net	
1921–25	95.0	61.0	34.0	169.9
1926–30	116.5	70.8	45.7	228.6
1931–35	46.4	40.2	6.3	31.4
1936–40	38.2	23.7	14.5	72.5
1941–45	21.3	20.9	0.4	2.2
1946–50	45.2	14.9	30.2	151.2
Total				665.8

Source: Sompop, cited in Pasuk Phongpaichit and Chris Baker, *Thailand: Economy and Politics* (Kuala Lumpur: Oxford University Press, 1995), p. 178.

1949 did the last batch of immigrants reach 45,200 persons. In 1952, the Thai Government announced that the Chinese quota had been completely filled,[35] and no new immigrant could come. The local Chinese community, therefore, stopped expanding in size.

Naturalization and Citizenship

It was believed that the overseas Chinese in Thailand were primarily more concerned with making a living and took a passive interest in the formal political life of the country. The Thai Government policy towards them was quite complex. Whereas in education and economic activities there was a clear and steady policy, in the case of citizenship and nationality, the government occasionally changed its policy. Thailand started its citizenship policy as a liberal one, then changed to a more restrictive one, then became more benevolent again. For the Chinese, the first nationality law which became effective in 1913 ruled that all Chinese born on Thai soil were Thai citizens. However, the Nationality Act in 1952 rescinded this and stated that only persons with at least one Thai parent could be granted citizenship. Thus, the children born in

Thailand of Chinese alien parents stayed as aliens. The Nationality Act of 1956 again changed the policy and accepted any persons born within the Kingdom as its citizens.[36]

The Chinese aliens who wished to become Thai had to go through the naturalization procedures, which again followed the same government policy on nationality. As a result, naturalization was relatively liberal at the beginning, then restrictive, and later more liberal again. The Thai Government did not always encourage the naturalization of the Chinese, neither did some of the Chinese want to become Thai citizens. The reason for the former was that the government still considered the huge number of Chinese (if they were naturalized but not assimilated) as a threat to national security. As for the Chinese, they preferred to keep their Chinese nationality as they still identified themselves as Chinese. In addition, becoming Thai would mean that they had to do military service (for all male citizens). Therefore, only during the war years when by acquiring Thai nationality they could escape the restrictions imposed on aliens did some Chinese want to become citizens. Statistics of Chinese applications for Thai citizenship and naturalization in Table 2 illustrate the low number of applications. However, in 1943 the number of applicants increased drastically because of wartime restrictions. After this, applications became low again, but the number of persons granted citizenship by naturalization were even lower. Only 4,652 Chinese persons were naturalized in twenty-four years (1935–58). Later, the number of Chinese who became Thai citizens increased because of two factors: the Nationality Act of 1956 and the drop in the number of new immigrants. The Nationality Act 1956 granted citizenship to Chinese children who were born in Thailand, resulting in the second generation Chinese becoming Thai automatically. In addition, no new arrivals could officially come to Thailand after 1949. As a result, the number of Chinese aliens stopped increasing.

Table 3 shows that the number of Chinese aliens in Thailand decreased during 1939–47. In 1929, official records showed 185,080 cases of aliens. In 1939 and 1947, the number dropped to 78,788 and 47,480 persons which proved that almost all Chinese had become Thai citizens. A population census later showed that there were 409,508 Chinese aliens in Thailand in 1960 and 311,093

TABLE 2

Chinese Applications for Thai Citizenship and Naturalization

Year	Number of Applications for Citizenship	Number of Persons Naturalized
1935	22	22
1936	33	33
1937	83	80
1938	109	109
1939	192	170
1940	131	124
1941	646	589
1942	134	100
1943	6,086	2,761
1944	789	175
1945	47	11
1946	6	4
1947	13	10
1948	43	11*
1949	104	—*
1950	118	3*
1951	97	1
1952	20	13
1953	54	38
1954	47	30
1955	92	61
1956	118	96
1957	196	163
1958	104	48
Total	9,302	4,652

* No naturalization was permitted between November 1948 and April 1950.

SOURCE: R. Coughlin, *Double Identity: The Chinese in Modern Thailand* (Hong Kong: Hong Kong University Press, 1960), p. 176.

in 1970. Most of the new arrivals after 1975 were businessmen who stayed in the country as aliens. It should be noted that a new influx of illegal immigrants from Southern China came to Thailand for employment in the 1990s.

TABLE 3

Number of Chinese Aliens in Thailand

Year	Number
1929	185,080
1939	78,788
1947	47,480
1960	409,508
1970	311,093

SOURCE: Data from 1929–47 came from Coughlin, op. cit., p. 24. Data from 1960–70 came from Thailand national population census and housing of 1960 and 1970.

Contemporary Ethnic Chinese in Thailand

Finally, most of the Siamese-Chinese of the mid-twentieth century have all become Thai citizens, and the appropriate term for them should be "Thais of Chinese descent" or "Chinese-Thais or Sino-Thais". These ethnic Chinese live comfortably in Thai society because they can keep their ethnic Chinese identity while at the same time use their national identity as Thai. This dual identity is accepted as long as the Chinese prove their allegiance to Thailand and express their nationalist ideology by supporting the three traditional and everlasting symbols of Thai nationalism: nation, religion and king. It is possible to be a Thai and an ethnic Chinese at the same time as the Thais define national identity in political, cultural and ideological terms, while ethnicity, in terms of descent and traditional practices, does not come into conflict with Thai national identity. Unlike conditions in some Southeast Asian countries, the ethnic Chinese in Thailand are free to observe their ancestral and traditional customs even in public. But they also absorb the Thai culture in their everyday life.

The ethnic Chinese businessmen have constituted the majority of the entrepreneurial class in Thai society. Beginning with their trading activities in the South China Sea among the Chinese conglomerates, these ethnic Chinese expanded their business to cover trade in rice, pepper, sugar and forest products. Later, they were involved in banking and finance, manufacturing, agro-business and real estate. There were at least sixty-five family groups holding assets worth US\$ 6 billion in Thailand in the decade of the 1970s.[37] Most of these families were ethnic Chinese family corporations. They accumulated their capital through business among the local dialect group or ethnic Chinese network, the corporate culture of *kongsi* in the family, intermarriage among business families, and other political factors.[38] Finally, they consolidated themselves into business associations whose roles in Thai politics emerged gradually. Many political leaders today are descendants of Chinese parents or grandparents, for example, Chamlong Sri Muang (former leader of the Palang Dharma Party), Chuan Leekpai (leader of the Democrat Party and former Prime Minister) and Banharn Silpa-Archa (Prime Minister in 1996). But all of them strongly identify themselves as Thai, not as Chinese. They do not deny having Chinese ancestors (as many Thais do) or a Chinese name. However, it is evident that they do not consider themselves as ethnic Chinese. Among those ethnic Chinese who are active in politics and those active in business, the latter group can more easily admit that they are ethnic Chinese. The election laws of 1951 and 1956 denied voting and candidacy rights to citizens with alien parents who had not attended a Thai secondary school.[39] Consequently, the Chinese factor can still be sensitive for Thai politicians of Chinese descent.

Conclusion

The origin, spread and impact of the Thai and Chinese nationalist movements in Thailand during 1908–41 have been discussed above. The two nationalist movements resulted in the configuration of the Siamese-Chinese identity. At the beginning, Chinese nationalist identity was dominant owing to the growth of KMT nationalism and the anti-Japanese movement. However, the Sino-Siamese were aware of the Thai government's concern with regard to such an identity. They consequently adapted by down-playing their Chinese-ness and switching to a more cultural and ethnically-oriented identity. This changing identity is complex in nature, consisting of political, racial, ethnic and cultural aspects.[40] The composition depended on the pressures from the Thai side and their efforts to keep a balance from their own side. What finally emerged was an

overt Thai nationalist identity with a secret Chinese national identity.
However, after 1949 political circumstances in China and Thai
foreign policy forced them to mitigate their Chinese nationalist
identity and to demonstrate only their Chinese cultural identity
and Thai nationalist identity in order to survive.

The post-war period saw the Chinese in Thailand more
assimilated because of Thai schooling and generational factors.
The communist regime in China also accelerated the identity shift
of the Chinese towards Thailand since they were not certain about
the future of their homeland. When Thai society became more
open and receptive after the Nationality Act of 1956 which accepted
any person born within the Kingdom as a citizen, more Chinese
became Thais. The contemporary Chinese in Thailand can thus
be called Chinese Thais because they keep their Thai national
identity and only identify themselves as Chinese in terms of descent.
The ethnic Thai and ethnic Chinese are now so mixed that Nai
Busya, a well-known Thai poet in the reign of Wachirawut,
described in his "Niras Sampheng" (A Visit to the Chinatown) the
mix of the Thai and Chinese as follows:

> Small road is crowded by Jek [Chinese] and Thai,
> Unavoidably mingling, clashing with one another.
> Jek mix with Thai beyond recognition,
> Who is who?
> One can't help but wonder.
> Modern times deviantly mess up the place.
> Jin [Chinese] cut off their pigtails and become Thai undetectably.
> What an unconventional abnormality,
> People surprisingly reverse their ethnicity.[41]

There is not enough data to examine the shifts of identity
among the overseas Chinese in Thailand with different socio-
economic backgrounds. Nonetheless, there seems to have been a
tendency for the non-Teochew dialect groups to adapt themselves
more easily compared with the Teochews. Most of the naturalized
Chinese were not Teochews when naturalization began. At the
same time, those who rebelled against the Thai government and
were deported were also not Teochew. Some of them were
Hainanese workers. Another observation is that ethnic identity by

speech groups was not so significant among the second generation of Chinese immigrants, because they attended schools where the language of instruction was Mandarin, not dialect. This identity shift had an impact on the running of businesses since it enlarged the dialect group hub of trade to the Chinese race hub. It affirmed the Chinese identity but not the speech group identity of the second generation Chinese in Thailand.

Notes

1. The description is summarized from the article "Mixed Thai! Undesirable People", in *Ten Opinions of Asawaphahu* (2458, pp. 81–87), cited in Sirirat Phoomkerd, "Asawaphahu and His Use of Literary Work to Disseminate Political Ideology" (M.A. thesis in History, Faculty of Arts, Chulalongkorn University, 2538), pp. 97–98.
2. W. Skinner, *Chinese Society in Thailand: An Analytical History*, Thai translation (Cornell University Press, 1957), p. 164.
3. Ibid., p. 163–65.
4. For more details on King Wachirawut's nationalism, see Walter F. Vella, *Chaiyo! King Vajiravudh and the Development of Thai Nationalism* (Honolulu: East West Center, 1995), p. xiv, 6, 67–68. See also Kullada Kesboonchoo, "Official Nationalism Under King Vajiravudh" (Paper presented at the International Conference on Thai Studies, Canberra, 3–6 July 1987).
5. B. Anderson, *Imagined Community: Reflections on the Origin and Spread of Nationalism* (London: Verso Editions, 1983), pp. 94–95.
6. Skinner, op. cit., p. 158.
7. Ibid., p. 172.
8. King Wachirawut expressed his disagreement with Sun Yat-sen's concept in his articles, "The New Huangti" and "The Future of China", in *Nine Opinions of Asawaphahu*, during 1915–16, as follows: "Dr. Sun Yat-sen finally accepted that... his dream for democracy was unachievable. After the suppression of the Ching, he continued to dream...". King Wachirawut also showed his displeasure with Sun Yat-sen's visit to Thailand. He said, "I am not a Chinese subject, therefore, I should not have to suffer from hearing the Chinese disputing with each other in my own house. In addition, if they decide to get into quarrels; for what reason should they raise funds from Chinese in Thailand to support them?", cited in Sirirat Phoomkerd, op. cit., pp. 103–5.
9. A. Suehiro, "An Analysis of the Registered Limited Companies in the Pre-War Period 1901–33", *Kikan Keizei Kenkyu* (Osaka City University, 14 June, 1991), pp. 27–71.

10. E. Murasima (author and translator), Worasak Mahatranobol (translator and editor), *Sino-Siamese Politics: Political Movements of the Overseas Chinese in Thailand during 1924–1941* (Chinese Studies Center, Institute of Asian Studies, Chulalongkorn University, 1996), pp. 14–15.

11. Murasima, op. cit., p. 49.

12. Ibid., pp. 132–42.

13. Ibid., pp. 142–43.

14. Skinner, op. cit, p. 177.

15. Ibid., p. 231.

16. Murasima, op. cit., p. 30.

17. Ibid., pp. 186–87.

18. Suehiro, op. cit., p. 16.

19. Murasima, op. cit., p. 187.

20. Skinner, op. cit., p. 181.

21. Murasima, op. cit., p. 180.

22. Skinner, op. cit., p. 236.

23. I have described elsewhere in more detail the process of socialization in Chinese schools where children were acculturated into Thai practices and at the same time were taught to preserve their ethnic Chinese identity. See S. Chantavanich and Somkiat Sikharaksakul, "Preservation of Ethnic Identity and Acculturation: A Case Study of a Hainanese School in Bangkok", *Southeast Asian Journal of Social Science* 23, no. 1 (1995): 78–87.

24. See Vipha Uttamachan et al., *Role and Status of Chinese Newspapers in Thailand* (Institute of Asian Studies, Chulalongkorn University, 2528) pp. 19–20.

25. Murasima, op. cit., p. 134.

26. Skinner, op. cit., p. 141.

27. See Wang Gung-wu, "The Culture of Chinese Merchants", in *China and the Chinese Overseas* (Singapore: Times Academic Press, 1991), p. 191.

28. Murasima, op. cit., p. 179. See also R. Coughlin, *Double Identity: The Chinese in Modern Thailand* (Hong Kong University Press, 1960), pp. 170–77.

29. Wang Gung-wu, "The Study of Chinese Identities in Southeast Asia", in *China and the Chinese Overseas*, pp. 206–7.

30. Anderson, op. cit., pp. 14–16.

31. Murasima, op. cit., pp. 186–88.

32. Ruth McVey, "The Materialization of the Southeast Asian Entrepreneur", in *Southeast Asian Capitalists*, edited by Ruth McVey (Cornell Modern Indonesia Project, Cornell University, 1992), p. 20.

33. Alan E. Guskin, *Changing Identity: The Assimilation of the Chinese in Thailand* (Ph.D. dissertation, University of Michigan, 1968), pp. 94–95.

34. Ibid., pp. 122–23.

35. Coughlin, op. cit., p. 29.

36. Ibid., p. 29.
37. Krirkiat Phipatseritham and Kunio Yoshirara, *Business Groups in Thailand*. Research Notes and Discussion Paper, No. 41 (Singapore: Institute of Southeast Asian Studies, 1982).
38. Supang Chantavanich, "From Gongsi to Business Corporatism: Socio-Cultural and Political Conditions of Ethnic Chinese Big Business Families' Success", in *Entrepreneurship and Socio-economic Transformation in Thailand and Southeast Asia*, edited by A. Pongsapich et al. (Chulalongkorn University Social Research Institute and French Institute of Scientific Research for Development in Cooperation, 1993), pp. 297–305.
39. Coughlin, op. cit., pp. 177–78.
40. Nai Busya, *Niras Sampheng*, cited by Kasian Tejapira, "Pigtail: A Prehistory of Chineseness in Siam", *SOJOURN* 7, no. 1 (1992): 114.
41. With regard to the multi-faceted identity changes of the Chinese, Richard Coughlin analysed Chinese citizenship and political interests in Thailand and confirmed that naturalization was useful for the Chinese businessmen because it entitled them to a Thai passport and therefore travel without restriction (p. 176). Finally, the overseas Chinese had altered his way of life, culturally and socially, to such an extent that much of his behaviour was no longer compatible with the patterns of people still living in China (p. 189). See Coughlin, op. cit. Guskin also analysed the changing identity of the Chinese in Thailand during a later period (the 1960s) when the second-generation Chinese were more assimilated into Thai society through Thai schooling. See details in Guskin, op. cit., pp. 61–92.

Comments* by

Anusorn Limmanee on

**"From Siamese-Chinese to Chinese Thai:
Political Conditions and Identity Shifts
among the Chinese in Thailand"**

Presented by Supang Chantavanich

In her paper, Professor Supang Chantavanich seems to focus on
the reactions of the Thai state against the Chinese nationalist
movement as the main and direct political conditions which
influenced the identity shifts of the Sino-Siamese between 1910
and 1941. The reactions were evidently expressed twice as the
two Thai nationalist movements, the first one from 1913 to 1925
and the second between 1938 and 1950. The shifts of identity
were self-adjustments of the Sino-Siamese for their political survival
and resulted mostly from the conflict between Thai and Chinese
nationalism. As a consequence, the identity of the Sino-Siamese
has become less politically but still culturally and ethnically
oriented. Thai nationalism was, therefore, the only political force
which caused the identity shift, while other political conditions
seemingly influenced the rise of the ideology. In other words,
those political conditions, except Thai nationalism, had likely just
indirect effects on the changes of the Sino-Chinese identity during
the period.

According to the paper, the first wave of Thai nationalism was
initiated by King Wachirawut as a response of the state to the then
actual and potential threats — for example, the 1908 Chinese
strike and the visit of Dr Sun Yat-sen, the fall of the Ching dynasty
and the abortive coup of 1911. A series of legal measures were
imposed with the Sino-Siamese as their main targets, although
their enforcement was noticeably not strong enough to weaken

---

* These comments are based on an earlier version of Supang's paper which
only covers the pre-war period.

the Chinese nationalist movement in Thailand. However, this anti-Chinese policy triggered an adjustment of identity among some Chinese business leaders by adopting Thai family names.

In the second wave, the implementation of the nationalist policy by Phibulsongkram's government led to the harsh suppression of Chinese secret societies and the strict control over Chinese schools and newspapers for fear of the Chinese roles in the nationalist and communist movements. Economically, measures were also taken to lessen the Chinese domination over the Thai economy. The policy, together with the communist victory over Chiang Kai-chek, forced some Sino-Siamese to change their national identity through naturalization.

In the paper, as in some other works on nationalism in Thailand, the term "nationalism" is not clearly defined. Since the meaning of nationalism is quite broad and multi-dimensional, this tends to lessen the usefulness of the concept for historical analysis (see Barmé 1993, p. 7). It is also questionable whether there was or were any other form(s) of nationalism before and during the period. In addition, the two waves of nationalism, as described in the paper, seem to suggest that the Thai nationalist movement was unsuccessful. With regard to the identity shifts among the Sino-Siamese, in fact even without the two nationalist movements the identity of the overseas Chinese in Thailand has gradually changed. The assimilation of the overseas Chinese into Thai society through, for example, marriage, education, and working in the public bureaucracy, has long been known to dilute the Chinese identity. Thus, the identity shifts described in this paper are special cases because they were pressured by the state.

In my view, the two waves of Thai nationalism were just particular forms of nationalism which the two Thai leaders applied to achieve some ideological goal and to avert certain political problems. They took place under specific political and economic conditions both on the local and global scale and cannot be separated from the ideological conflicts among various groups, particularly between the liberal and conservative groups in Thai society. Before discussing these points, I would like to begin with a quick look at the nature of nationalism in order to understand what nationalism means in this paper.

Historically, nationalism grew side by side with the rise of the nation state and spread to peripheral societies in the early twentieth century. Its traditional goal is nation-building through either unification or achievement of independence. However, nationalism is, in itself, a political doctrine without ideological unity and can be expressed in various and sometimes opposite ideologies. Regarding its form, nationalism may take a liberal, or conservative or chauvinistic form. In the liberal form, nationalism, apart from its opposition against every kind of foreign domination and oppression, also wants to establish a representative and constitutional government in society as well as a peaceful and friendly international order. On the contrary, conservative nationalism, usually developed in established nation states, places strong emphasis on the promise of social cohesion and public order embodied in the sentiment of national patriotism. The defence of traditional institutions and the traditional way of life is an important tenet of this form of nationalism. As for chauvinistic nationalism, it is the aggressive, expansionistic and militaristic form which expresses itself in intense patriotism and belief in ethnic superiority. Each form is generated by such factors as the leaders' ideology, social structure, historical developments and geographical location. At different times nationalism in a society can take different dominant forms which influence the activities of the movement or policies of the state. In addition, the movement may change from an élite movement to a mass movement and from a united to a divided one and vice versa. Despite its many forms, what every kind of nationalism has in common is the belief that the national interest is more important than individuals, and the government is an indispensable agency for the expression of these interests (see Heywood 1992, chap. 5; Kohn 1968, pp. 63–65; Watkins 1964, p. 40). In the periphery, this political doctrine was developed as a political reaction against Western imperialism. Through its colonization, imperialism brought into peripheral societies not only various aspects of modernization but also some political ideologies and doctrines which shaped directly or indirectly their nationalism.

By its form, Thai nationalism in the two periods described was conservative and more or less chauvinistic, promoted by the political leaders of the Thai state. Thus, the term "nationalism", as used in the paper, means a conservative and chauvinistic form of official nationalism. To differentiate it from other nationalist activities in Thailand before, during, or after the two waves of nationalism, as pointed out by the paper, it should be clearly defined as the two waves of conservative and chauvinistic nationalism. They were conservative owing to their aim to defend some traditional institutions, for example, the monarch, the nation and religion in King Wachirawut's nationalism (Kullada 1987) or to protect social cohesion and public order as in Phibulsongkhram's nationalist policy (Likhit 1987, p. 251). However, Phibulsongkhram's nationalism was evidently much more chauvinistic than that of King Wachirawuth. This is why the second wave of nationalism was more anti-Chinese and had a stronger impact on the identity shift among the Sino-Chinese than the first wave. The Pan-Thai policy of Phibulsongkhram's regime certainly speaks for itself. As social movements, the two waves of nationalism in Thailand, unlike the Chinese nationalist movement in the same period, were less mass-based and more élite-dependent, though some groups of Thai people were mobilized to support them through, for example, the Wild Tiger Corps in the first wave, and the Yuwachon military movement in the second wave.

Nationalism in Asia generally developed after World War I and became a powerful driving force of political developments in this area. It inspired, at first, élites and intellectuals and, later on, the masses to pursue the goal of national liberation and modernization. During this period, as shown by the paper, the nationalist movements both in Thailand and China came into existence. Nevertheless, the formation of a nationalist movement in Thailand can be traced back to the late nineteenth century, particularly in the period of King Chulalongkorn (Kullada 1984). The concept of nation or *chat* or *chat baan muang* was widely discussed and applied by the élite to implant Thai patriotism among the educated public from the 1880s. A good example of the nationalism of this period is found in the petition submitted by a group of princely officials to King Chulalongkorn suggesting the need for radical reform to maintain the political independence of Siam (Barmé 1993, pp. 16–17). The growth of this movement was instrumental in the administrative reform and the rise of an absolutist nation state. Since no freeman had existed in Thai society until the dissolution of the corvée system and slavery in 1905 (Likhit 1987, pp. 207–8), in the beginning nationalism in Thailand was formed as an élite movement led by the young King and composed of the King, his brothers and relatives and some leading civil servants. To escape Western colonization and to consolidate royal power, this élite gave its first priority to modernization and nation-building. As a consequence, the nationalist movement was, at first, relatively liberal in its form. Although before and during this period a huge number of Chinese immigrants flooded into Thailand, no anti-Chinese policy was imposed by the state. A basic reason was that they were the biggest sources of labour and entrepreneurs necessary for the rapidly expanding economy (Keyes 1989, p. 47).

The modernization itself, however, generated a new generation of nationalist intellectuals and middle class in Thai society. Exposed to better education, communication and information, these intellectuals of Thai and Chinese descent began to develop their own notion of nationalism. Once the reform seemed to end up with the establishment of an absolutist state and a new bureaucracy without political reform, the people began to criticize the existing political regime and to ask for constitutional democracy. In the early twentieth century, a journalist named Tianwan, for example, proposed in his newspaper that parliamentary democracy should be introduced into Thai society (Likhit 1987, pp. 234–35). This was certainly in opposition to King Chulalongkorn's view that the Thai people were not yet ready to rule themselves. From then, the conservative form of official nationalism started to take root.

Amid the rise of republican nationalism and the fall of many kingdoms in Asia, King Wachirawut ascended the throne in 1911. In 1912 he was faced with a coup attempt by some military officers who wanted to replace the absolute monarchy with constitutional democracy. Threatened by the tide of revolutionary change and the increasing challenge from the middle class in addition to the conflict between himself and the royal élite, he developed a more conservative form of nationalism called for by the intellectuals (see Wyatt 1984, chap. 8). As a main and easy target of the King's nationalist campaign, the Sino-Chinese were frequently harassed by him. In his view, they dominated the Thai economy and some of them, like Sheow Hut-seng, were critical intellectuals who ideologically opposed him. But the King's weak base of power, variety of interest and relatively short reign did not enable him to enforce the anti-Chinese policy strictly.

This does not mean that the conservative and somewhat chauvinist form of nationalism in Thailand disappeared with the death of King Wachirawut in 1925. Certainly, from 1925 to 1938 it had not been the official ideology but was still kept or expanded chauvinistically by such élite as Prince Boworadet or Luang Wichit Wathakan and even minor officials like Chamrat Sarawisut (Terewil 1991). The rise to power of the People's Party in 1932 with economic nationalism as its official ideology paved the way for the return of the conservative form of nationalism, though at first its nationalism seemed politically liberal. After the victory of Phibulsongkhram in the intra-party struggle for state power, official nationalism became more conservative and chauvinistic. Phibulsongkhram's attempt to consolidate his power, and his desire to make Thailand a great power in Southeast Asia were likely the basic reasons behind his nationalist campaign. It was carried out amid a closer relationship between Thailand and Japan and the growth of the anti-Japanese movement among the overseas Chinese as well as the spread of Chinese-dominated communist activities in Thailand. Under these conditions, the Sino-Chinese were unavoidably the main targets of the nationalist policies. This led to a substantial shift of identity among the Sino-Chinese. However, the widespread and voluntary change of identity among them actually occurred after World War II when their ties with mainland China were severed by the triumph of the Communist Party.

It is clear that although some political conditions did have some relevance to the identity shifts among the Sino-Chinese between 1910 and 1941, they did not have any direct effect on the changes. They just influenced the rise of the conservative and chauvinistic form of Thai nationalism. Since nationalism was found to be the only political condition which directly caused the shifts, it deserves to replace the "political conditions" in the title of the paper. In addition, to do justice to the term "nationalism" more elaboration is needed.

References

Barmé, Scott. *Luang Wichit Wathakan and the Creation of a Thai Identity*. Singapore: Institute of Southeast Asian Studies, 1993.

Heywood, Andrew. *Political Ideologies*. London: Macmillan, 1992.

Keyes, Charles F. *Thailand: Buddhist Kingdom as Modern Nation State*. Bangkok: Duang Kamol, 1989.

Kohn, Hans. "Nationalism". In *International Encyclopedia of the Social Sciences*, edited by David L. Sills, pp. 63–70. New York: Macmillan and Free Press, 1968.

Kullada Kesboonchoo. "Official Nationalism under King Chulalongkorn". Paper presented at the International Conference on Thai Studies, Bangkok, 22–24 August 1984.

————. "Official Nationalism under King Vajiravudh". In *Proceedings of the International Conference on Thai Studies*, Vol. 3, Part I, pp. 107–20. Canberra: Australian National University, 1987.

Likhit Dhiravegin. *Evolution of Thai Politics and Government* (in Thai). Bangkok: Chulalongkorn University Press, 1987.

Terweil, B.J. "Thai Nationalism and Identity: Popular Themes of the 1930s". In *National Identity and its Defenders*, edited by Craig J. Reynolds, pp. 133–55. Chiangmai: Silkworm Books, 1991.

Watkins, Federick M. *The Age of Ideology: Political Thought, 1750 to the Present*. New Delhi: Prentice-Hall, 1964.

Wyatt, David K. *Thailand: A Short History*. Chiangmai: Silkworm Books, 1984.

Chapter 8

Ethnic Chinese in Vietnam and Their Identity

Tran Khanh

Introduction

In the last decade, the open-door policy and economic reforms of Vietnam, as well as the improved economic and diplomatic relations of Vietnam with the Southeast Asian countries where many ethnic Chinese reside have led to the resumption of the roles played by the ethnic Chinese in Vietnam's economy. The ethnic Chinese community once again became influential in the development of the domestic trade, and the restoration and diversification of business links between Vietnam and the region. It seems that changes in Vietnam in the last decade have also contributed to the ethnic Chinese being better integrated with the larger Vietnamese community.

This chapter is an attempt to grapple with some aspects relating to the policies of Vietnam and China towards the ethnic Chinese, and their impact on the integration of the ethnic Chinese in Vietnamese society. It will also consider the overseas connection of the Vietnamese Chinese and its bearing on the economic and cultural activities of their country. Finally, some concluding remarks will be made on the position, role, and identity of the ethnic Chinese in Vietnam in the past, present, and future.

Nation-State in the Policies of Vietnam Towards Ethnic Chinese and their Position in Vietnamese Society

In the great family of the Vietnamese nation, there are altogether fifty-five small and large ethnic groups, of which the Viet (known as the King) form 87 per cent of the total Vietnamese population. The ethnic Chinese (known as the Hoa) who constitute 1.4 per cent (or more than one million out of the 75 million population) is the third largest ethnic group in the country.[1]

The Viet are the descendants of the two Viet tribes, Lac Viet and Au Viet. In ancient times, these two Viet clans belonged to the same racial and cultural groups. Together with the Bach Viet (Hundred Yues tribes), they lived south of the Yangtze River.

Towards the third century B.C., the Lac Viet and Au Viet gathered together and founded the Au Lac Kingdom, the first ancient state in Vietnam. Early in the second century B.C. (year 111), the Au Lac Kingdom was conquered by the Han dynasty which integrated this Kingdom into its empire. After more than ten centuries of Chinese colonization, this Vietnamese territory became one of the many places for refugees, convicts, officers and garrisons coming from northern China. Most of them consisted of men.[2]

During the one thousand years of Chinese domination, the Han feudal lords implemented a policy of systematic assimilation between the Han-Tang and Viet peoples. History records the fact that many Han peoples came to live in and subsequently dominated North Vietnam with each succeeding generation. They married Viet women and their children later became the local people, like other Viet. Many of them joined the indigenous population in its struggle for Vietnam's independence and sovereignty.[3]

It should be noted that during the one thousand years of Chinese political domination, the Han administrators and the Chinese troops garrisoned in North Vietnam controlled only the districts and populated centres. Thus, the Chinese character and Confucianism only penetrated the noble families and the Buddhist priests in the Han occupied areas. Real power still remained in the hands of the Viet leaders of the different clans. The communal villages of the Viet people remained almost intact with the traditional way of life and culture of the people practising wet rice cultivation.[4]

The struggle for the survival of the Viet people against the Hans enhanced the community spirit of the Viet people. They felt that they were brothers and sisters with common ancestors and did their utmost to safeguard their culture and race. In order to maintain their national community, the Viet people nurtured a strong will to gain back control over the country. Since then, the Viet have developed a strong sense of national sovereignty. The year 939 was a turning point in the history of the Viet nation-state. In that year the Viet, under the leadership of Ngo Quyen, rose up to expel the Southern Han troops from the whole territory known as Northern Vietnam today, thus ushering in the era of national independence for Vietnam.

From the tenth century onwards, the community spirit and national sovereignty developed into that of a nation-state. The concept of the Vietnamese nation-state at that time was synonymous with the motherland or homeland where they lived and earned their livelihood. In the course of time, they felt that they shared a common history of struggle for building and defending the country and a common cultural heritage. For that reason, the spirit of building and defending the motherland became a yardstick for measuring the Vietnamese identity.

It should be emphasized that motherland or homeland constitutes the essence of Vietnam's culture. This concept is not found in the orthodox Confucian doctrine. Confucius did not mention the concept of motherland or homeland. What he mentioned was the concept of people "under Heaven" together with the concept of the behaviour of men "under Heaven". The people "under Heaven", according to Confucianism, is a form of cultural community, not a country or homeland. Thus, human being is a component part of the whole world and the people at large (under Heaven) live in it; he is not a component part of the motherland or nation. In Confucianism, "dutifulness" means the obligation of children towards their parents, while "loyalty" implies the faithfulness of subjects to the king or leader. But in Vietnam, "dutifulness" is divided into small and great ones. "Small dutifulness" is the respect for and obedience to one's parents while "great dutifulness" is the devotion to one's motherland and people. "Loyalty" means faithfulness to the country, and to the rights and interests of the nation-state.[5] Thus, for the Vietnamese, the concept of nation-state is closely connected with the notion of motherland or homeland.

Successive invasions against the independent nation of Vietnam by various Chinese feudal dynasties from the tenth century onwards further enhanced the spirit of national sovereignty and unity among the Vietnamese. Nguyen Trai, a national liberation hero and a man of culture, who lived in the fifteenth century, characterized the Vietnamese nation-state as follows:

1. The nation is a form of community having a particular culture, a specific history of struggle for building and defending the country;
2. The nation possesses its own territory and border undeniably;
3. The nation boasts its own customs, habits and regulations;
4. The nation enjoys full sovereignty and is not dependent upon any foreign country.[6]

The concept of the nation-state that Nguyen Trai had described has found the clearest expression in Vietnam's modern history.

As the perception of the Vietnamese nation-state is closely connected with the concept of motherland or homeland, anyone who claims to be a Vietnamese, or has a Vietnamese identity, must first and foremost have a culture of, and loyalty to, his or her motherland. These notions have governed the policies of the Vietnamese state towards the Chinese settlers.

In order to build a nation-state with its own national characteristics and to cope with the schemes of annexation of Vietnam by different Chinese feudal dynasties, the feudal rulers of Vietnam imposed a policy of assimilation on the Chinese migrants.

During the reign of Ly's (1009–1225) and the subsequent Tran dynasty (1226–1400), the use of ethnic Chinese scholars and other political fugitives from China in leading administrative positions was advocated. But this applied only to those Chinese who chose to settle permanently in Vietnam.[7]

Under the later Le dynasty (1428–1592) and during the rules of the Trinh lords in the North until 1777, the assimilation and surveillance of the ethnic Chinese community were intensified. The Chinese who permanently resided in Vietnam had to abide by Vietnamese laws, conform with Vietnamese customs and traditions and dress in the Vietnamese way. The migrant Chinese were not free to travel within Vietnam and were only permitted to settle in a special zone. The Chinese merchants were also heavily taxed and they were not allowed to distribute Chinese books and other literature in Vietnam.[8] The more stringent Vietnamese attitude towards the Chinese community was due to the fact that the Le's reign came about as a result of having defeated the occupied force of the Ming dynasty in China. The Chinese army had earlier entered Vietnam on the pretext of helping the then Tran dynasty to quell a rebellion. However, they stayed on for twenty years (1407–27).

By the second half of the seventeenth century, Chinese settlements in Vietnam had reached a critical stage. Prior to this, Chinese migration had been gradual and the migrants would tend to assimilate over the years. From this time onwards, however, Chinese immigrants were permitted to reside in major economic and trading centres of Vietnam, especially in the south. The massive and continuous Chinese migrations resulted in the emergence of Chinatowns in the big cities and major trading centres, such as Pho Hien (in centre of the Red River Delta), Thang Long (Hanoi), Hoi An (in the central part of Vietnam), Gia Dinh and Cho Lon (part of Ho Chi Minh City today), and Ha Tien (in the extreme south-west of Vietnam). It was at this time that the Chinese also began to congregate on the basis of their dialect group. The large Chinese settlement in Vietnam since the seventeenth century was the result of Vietnamese policies. The Nguyen lords in the South (1592–1777), and later the Imperial Court at Hue (1802–1945) allowed Chinese immigrants to settle permanently in Vietnam and to prosper in their business. The Chinese who chose to settle permanently in Vietnam had the same civil rights as the Vietnamese, but they were exempted from military service and corvée. Chinese merchants were usually involved in the collection of taxes. They could buy houses, acquire land and set up their social, religious and economic organizations.[9]

In order to control the Chinese community, the Nguyen dynasty introduced a law on the status of the ethnic Chinese. Under the reign of Emperor Minh Mang (1820–1831), the Chinese residents were divided into two groups: the Minh Huong people and Thanh (Qing) people. The Minh Huong, like the *peranakan* of Indonesia, had ancestors who migrated from China in the sixteenth or seventeenth centuries. Most of them were of mixed Sino-Vietnamese parentage. Until 1829 their children were considered to be Chinese, but later they were regarded as Vietnamese and were granted political rights. During Emperor Minh Mang's reign they were also allowed to take civil service examinations, but they were not permitted to participate in the election of Chinese *bang*. The Minh Huong and their children were prohibited to leave for China and were also required to dress like Vietnamese.

The Thanh people, like the *totok* Chinese of Indonesia, came to Vietnam in the eighteenth or nineteenth centuries (during the Qing dynasty in China). These people continued to use Chinese dialects as their main languages of communication, followed Chinese customs and retained links with China. Most of them did not intermarry with the indigenous people. They were regarded as foreign citizens and were not entitled to hold office in the Vietnamese government services but they were granted rights to reside in Vietnam.[10]

The preferential treatment for Chinese immigrants and naturalization exercise under Nguyen rules during the seventeenth and nineteenth centuries helped the ethnic Chinese to expand their business activities, and encouraged their integration into Vietnamese society. Most of the Chinese descendants considered Vietnam as their homeland and many, such as Trinh Hoai Duc, Phan Thanh Gian, and so forth, became high-ranking mandarins during the Nguyen dynasty.[11]

The establishment of the French colony in Nam ky (Cochinchina) in 1867 and protectorates in Bac Ky (Tonkin) and Trung Ky (Annam) in 1884 drastically altered the evolution of the

Chinese community in Vietnam in general, and the legal status of the ethnic Chinese in particular. The Chinese community came under French attention, not only in the form of different attempts at taxation, but also in the control of Chinese immigration to Vietnam.

Like the Nguyen dynasty, the French colonial administration practised a "divide and rule" policy towards various ethnic groups. The Chinese residents in Vietnam were divided into those of Chinese descent, known as the Minh Huong and Chinese sojourners (later known as *Huaqiao*). Until 1885, the Minh Huong were regarded as Vietnamese. Later, the French offered them the right to choose to be Chinese nationals or belong to a new category known as French Asian citizens.[12] According to a French official source, in Cochinchina (Namky) in 1921 there were about 46,500 Minh Huong who formed 42 per cent of the total Chinese population in that area. In 1950 the number of Minh Huong had increased to 75,000 persons, constituting about 10 per cent of total Chinese population in Cochinchina.[13] This big drop in the proportion of Minh Huong gives an indication of the size of the influx of Chinese immigrants during this period. In addition, the Chinese who migrated from China during 1920–40 brought their families. From that time on, Chinese men had more opportunities to marry their country women.

Another Chinese group was the *Huaqiao*. These people were considered Chinese nationals or foreigners and were required to join one of the *bang* associations according to their dialect group if they wanted to live in Vietnam.[14] In order to get more financial benefits from the Chinese, the French granted the *Huaqiao* the privilege of not paying personal taxes. Meanwhile, other foreigners such as the British and Indians had to pay this tax.[15] Thus, the "divide and rule" policy of the French by promoting a separate status for the Chinese residents in Vietnam, together with the use of Chinese *bang*, tended to make the Chinese socially isolated from the Vietnamese.

Starting from the French colonial period, the Chinese were mainly engaged in commerce and a few were in processing industries such as the milling of rice. They refrained from investing heavily in other industries because the French excluded local and other foreigners (Chinese) from the industrial sector. It was not until the Nanjing Agreement between France and China on 16 March 1930 that the Chinese in Vietnam obtained their right to participate in foreign trade and industrial activities. Later, the Chongqing Agreement of 26 February 1946 gave the Chinese the right to be involved in mining, buy and develop land, and put up buildings.[16] This led to the domination of the Chinese in Vietnam's domestic trade.

After the French left in 1954, Vietnam was temporarily divided into two political systems. In the South, Ngo Dinh Diem became Chief-of-State and proclaimed the Republic of Vietnam (ROV). The Ngo Dinh Diem authority further attempted to assimilate or, more precisely, to turn the overseas Chinese into Vietnamese citizens and to break their economic power. A Nationality Decree No. 10 promulgated on 7 December 1955 in the South revived what had been the practice before French rule: all children born of mixed Chinese-Vietnamese parents were considered Vietnamese citizens. In 1956, President Ngo Dinh Diem (1956–63) declared that all overseas Chinese born in Vietnam were Vietnamese citizens, irrespective of their parents' or their own wishes. All other Chinese were aliens and needed to apply for residential permit, which had to be renewed periodically. Subsequently, Decree No. 52 was issued on 29 August 1956 which required all Vietnamese citizens to adopt a Vietnamese name within six months or pay a heavy fine. Decree No. 53, which was issued on 6 September 1956, listed eleven types of trade which aliens could not engage in; at that time, all of these trades were heavily dominated by the ethnic Chinese. The aliens who were involved in these trades had six months to liquidate or to transfer their businesses to Vietnamese citizens.[17] Given these laws, a great majority of the ethnic Chinese in the ROV adopted Vietnamese nationality out of necessity. Many simply became Vietnamese citizens or passed their businesses to sons or daughters who were born in Vietnam. There was no strong resistance from the Chinese community.[18] Thus, the Ngo Dinh Diem laws in general did not operate too punitively against the ethnic Chinese businesses. The message to the ethnic Chinese, however, was clear: the ROV wanted them to assimilate as quickly as possible.

At the same time, the Ngo Dinh Diem government took steps to control the Chinese education system by requiring the Vietnamese language to be used in all Chinese schools and all principals had to be Vietnamese. There was further evidence of this assimilation policy of the Diem regime: the banning of the Association of Patriotic Overseas Chinese in 1956, and *bang* associations in 1960.[19] Notwithstanding this, the Chinese *bangs* and Chinese independent schools were not only maintained but were further developed by the ethnic Chinese until the communist victory in 1975.

Owing to the escalation of the war, the Nguyen Van Thieu regime (1964–75) in the South did not pay much attention to the assimilation of the ethnic Chinese. At that time, the Chinese efforts were focused on business undertakings and the maintenance and development of their culture. They became more successful in business. Their disproportionately high involvement in business in the South was one of the main reasons which set the ethnic Chinese apart from the Vietnamese, giving rise to resentment among the indigenous Vietnamese. This situation was similar to those experienced by other countries in Southeast Asia during 1950–60.

The Democratic Republic of Vietnam (DRV) in the North (1945–75), and thereafter the Socialist Republic of Vietnam (the whole country since 1976) approached the issue of the ethnic Chinese from the standpoint of class solidarity. Since the formation of the Indochina Communist Party (in 1930), the Vietnamese communists had considered the Chinese workers and labourers as allies of the Vietnamese revolution. Many Chinese immigrants were recruited into the Vietnamese revolutionary army and were granted political rights.[20]

After the restoration of peace in Vietnam in 1954, the Hanoi government, like the regime in Saigon, had to sort out the confused situation of the nationality of the ethnic Chinese left behind by the French. In 1955, the Vietnamese Workers Party (VWP; since 1976 it has been renamed the Vietnamese Communist Party or VCP), and the Chinese Communist Party came to an official agreement under which the ethnic Chinese in North Vietnam were placed under the leadership of the VWP and were gradually to become Vietnamese citizens. In February 1957, Hanoi and

Beijing agreed that the Ngai, a minority group found in Quang Ninh province, would be considered Vietnamese citizens even though they were sinicized in language and culture. As for most of the ethnic Chinese living in the DRV, they were to become Vietnamese citizens by the end of the 1950s and would be treated as citizens of the DRV.[21]

After the liberation of the South in 1975, and the reunification of the country in 1976 as the Socialist Republic of Vietnam (SRV), the government continued to regard the ethnic Chinese as part of the great family of the Vietnamese nation-state, and a large number of them as an integral part of the Vietnamese revolution. However, the socialist transformation of the private capitalist industry and trade in the newly liberated South and tense relations between Vietnam and China during 1977–79 affected negatively the integration of the ethnic Chinese into Vietnamese society. At that time, hundreds of thousands of ethnic Chinese rejected Vietnamese nationality. They considered themselves as Chinese citizens, or as overseas Chinese, notwithstanding that they were already Vietnamese citizens since the late 1950s. These ethnic Chinese had the intention to leave Vietnam. According to one estimate, from the fall of Saigon on 30 April 1975 to the end of September 1979, about 230,000 ethnic Chinese left Vietnam for China and another 220,000 left for Southeast Asia by boat.[22] The rejection of Vietnamese nationality by the ethnic Chinese, together with their exodus, gave rise to the Vietnamese government's suspicion on their loyalty towards the Vietnamese nation-state. For that reason, the Vietnamese authorities at that time did not prevent the exodus of these ethnic Chinese.

Since the early 1980s, the Vietnamese government has gradually reintegrated the ethnic Chinese into the mainstream of Vietnamese society. By 1982, the Vietnamese Communist Party had officially reversed its policy towards the ethnic Chinese. Directive 10, which was passed on 17 November 1982 by the secretariat of the Party Central Committee, stipulated that the ethnic Chinese living in Vietnam would be considered as Vietnamese. They had the same rights and obligations as other Vietnamese citizens. It also emphasized, however, that cadres and students of the ethnic Chinese would be allowed to participate in or study for certain professions only. They had the duty to serve in the army, but could not become officers.[23] Thus, the Vietnamese government began to acknowledge that the ethnic Chinese should no longer be considered as reactionaries, but they were still suspected as a "fifth column". The suspicion of the Vietnamese government towards the ethnic Chinese was also manifested in Act 14 which was issued on 13 September 1983 by the Politburo of the Vietnamese Communist Party. The Act reads in part: "to forbid ethnic Chinese participation in commerce, transport, printing, cultural business, information and operating of schools".[24] Obviously, this Act has hindered ethnic Chinese investment endeavours, and it has also delayed the reintegration of the ethnic Chinese into Vietnamese society.

The new period of reintegration of the ethnic Chinese into Vietnamese society began in 1986, when the Vietnamese Communist Party formally introduced a programme of reforms known as *doi moi*. Prior to the sixth Communist Party Congress in December 1986, specifically on the question of the ethnic Chinese community, Directive 256 was issued in October 1986 by the Chairman of the Ministerial Council to implement the suspended Directive 10.[25] The most important force reactivating ethnic Chinese education was the decrees of the local authorities (cities and provinces) on the implementation of Directive 256. For example, the Decree of the Municipal People Committee of Ho Chi Minh City, which was issued on 20 February 1987 with regard to the implementation and realization of the Directive 256, reaffirmed that the ethnic Chinese had the same rights and obligations as other Vietnamese citizens. Their children had rights to participate in or study for all professions at all national education levels. The primary and secondary schools with high concentrations of ethnic Chinese students were allowed to resume teaching in the Chinese language, but the teachers had to follow a curriculum prepared by the Ministry of Education.[26] The ethnic Chinese have also been allowed to set up a body called the Association to Sponsor Chinese Language Teaching.[27] In 1988, the Ministry of Education of Vietnam also issued a series of decrees concerning ethnic Chinese education. The decrees once again confirmed what were noted in Directive 256.[28]

Vietnam's efforts to reintegrate the ethnic Chinese into Vietnamese society were manifested in the commitments made at the seventh Congress of the Communist Party of Vietnam in 1991. The commitment stated that the Vietnamese government guarantees all civil rights and civic duties of the ethnic Chinese community, to respect their culture and religion and to create conditions for them to work confidently, so that they can contribute to the building of Vietnam and cultivate friendly relations between the people of Vietnam and China.[29]

In short, *doi moi* and its endorsement of a multisector economy in Vietnam since 1986 have given propitious opportunities for restoring the civic consciousness and duties of the ethnic Chinese. They have also been fully involved in the economic restructuring of Vietnam. Some of their industries, such as in garment, shoes, textiles, plastics and foodstuff processing, have regained their previous status as major players in Vietnam's light industries. In political life, the ethnic Chinese are no longer regarded as some kind of "fifth column" working in favour of China's interests. They have the same rights and obligations as other Vietnamese citizens. In culture and education, the ethnic Chinese have been allowed to resume teaching, broadcasting, and printing in the Chinese language. However, their activities in this area are still much less than before 1975.

The China Factor and the Integration of the Ethnic Chinese in Vietnam

After a long period of subjugation to the Chinese empire, it was not until the tenth century that Vietnam regained its independence. During this time, the inhabitants living in the southern part of the Yangtze River as well as the Viet and the Chinese who were living in the lands forming North Vietnam today were considered to be subjects of the Chinese Empire.

From the tenth century to the latter half of the nineteenth century, the Chinese immigrants and settlers became the objects of assimilation by the Vietnamese authorities. Because of the relative similarities in terms of culture, style of living, religion, socio-political and administrative structures between Vietnam and China, the ethnic Chinese could live in comfort in Vietnam and integrate themselves well into Vietnamese society. The natural assimilation of the Chinese settlers continued throughout Vietnam's feudal history.

But owing to their permanent readiness and high vigilance to cope with the threat of invasion at any time by the Chinese Empire, the feudal Vietnamese dynasties had to impose compulsory assimilation on the Chinese immigrants. The main aim was to have strict control over the latter in the event of any attack against Vietnam. It was also to prevent the Chinese immigrants and settlers from establishing political relations with China. The Vietnamese feudal dynasties at the same time, however, considered the Chinese immigrants and settlers to be a bridge linking the two countries in the development of their relationships.

Until the second half of the nineteenth century, the successive Chinese dynasties seemed to pay no heed to the fate of their subjects living in foreign countries.[30] In order to survive and develop in foreign lands, the overseas Chinese had to adjust themselves to the conditions of their host country. They engaged mainly in trading activities and formed traditional social organizations, such as *bang*, clan, religious and other associations. In the early days, these organizations were often independent of the jurisdiction of the host country. Nevertheless, they neither attempted to seek the protection of Chinese law nor requested official recognition from China.[31]

From the second half of the nineteenth century, the Chinese authorities began to officially recognize and protect the rights and interests of the overseas Chinese. They intended to seek political and financial support from the overseas Chinese in order to counter the possibility of intervention and aggression by the European powers and Japan. At the same time, they wished to expand their influence over the countries where the overseas Chinese were living to attract capital investments from them to rebuild China.

The overseas Chinese in Vietnam during the French colonial period came under the protection of the Manchu dynasty and later, the Kuomintang (KMT) government. In the years 1885–86, the French government and the Manchu administration signed a number of treaties of friendship and trade in Tianjin in which there was a provision recognizing the trading rights of the overseas

Chinese in Vietnam. The Nanjing Agreement of 1930 and the Chonqing Agreement of 1949 between the French and the Kuomintang governments gave the *Huaqiao* more rights to engage in economic and social activities in Vietnam.

The Geneva Agreement in July 1954 led to the temporary partition of Vietnam at the seventeenth parallel into two parts. In the southern part, the anti-communist force set up the Republic of Vietnam (ROV). The Kuomintang government in Taiwan (Republic of China, or ROC) and the ROV were close strategic friends in the U.S.-led alliance against communism in Asia. This was the reason that Taiwan was able to wield influence over the Chinese community in South Vietnam. In order to extend its influence, the Taiwan representatives in Saigon participated in the organization and leadership of the ethnic Chinese associations. This explains why, although the Chinese *bang* associations were abolished by ROV law in 1960, in reality they remained until the communist victory in 1975. This also explains why other social organizations, such as regional and clan associations, became more important among the ethnic Chinese in the South during 1960–75.

The education of the ethnic Chinese in southern Vietnam before 1975 was also strongly influenced by the Kuomintang. School textbooks and teaching aids were supplied by the Overseas Chinese Affairs Committee in Taipei.[32] Moreover, Taiwan also provided ethnic Chinese firms with technology, financial support and skilled manpower. The connection helped some small and medium-sized ethnic Chinese enterprises in the south to upgrade themselves into large-scale enterprises with modern equipment and advanced management.[33]

During 1956–57, the Ngo Dinh Diem government in the South tried to gain control of ethnic Chinese economic activities and forced them to adopt Vietnamese citizenship. The Taiwan authorities protested against the action of Ngo Dinh Diem. On 7 May 1957, Taiwan declared that the ethnic Chinese in Vietnam who did not want to take up Vietnamese citizenship would be given help to resettle in Taiwan.[34] However, the actions of Taiwan did not affect the Chinese situation in South Vietnam. Instead, the ethnic Chinese eventually chose to become Vietnamese citizens.

The economic domination of the ethnic Chinese community was not broken. On the contrary, by becoming Vietnamese citizens, they were able to expand their businesses.[35]

Like the Taiwanese administration, the government of the People's Republic of China (PRC) in its foreign policy also considered the overseas Chinese to be an important force. It put up a resolute struggle to secure its position and gain influence over the overseas Chinese communities. However, the PRC has followed the path of socialist development and has approached the issue of the ethnic Chinese from the standpoint of class solidarity.

Up to the late 1970s, the relationship between Beijing and the Chinese abroad was based on both politics and class. The ethnic Chinese were then used as a tool by Beijing for the spread of Maoism. Since 1977, however, Beijing has greatly changed its attitude towards the ethnic Chinese who are now not only regarded as a bridge to expand the PRC's influence abroad, but also constitute an economic force capable of helping mainland China modernize.

In Vietnam, since the late 1940s, the Chinese Communist Party has established close relations with the communist organizations of Vietnam, of which there was one comprising the overseas Chinese. Many cadres of the People's Liberation Army of China went to Vietnam in the years 1946–54 in order to help the Vietnamese Communist Party to organize different unions of overseas Chinese to fight against French imperialism and colonialism.[36] For that reason, since the 1940s, the political organizations of the overseas Chinese in Vietnam (especially in Northern Vietnam) have been ruled by the Chinese Communist Party.

After the re-establishment of peace in Vietnam in 1954, the PRC had more chances to extend their influence over the ethnic Chinese in North Vietnam. During 1954–58 the Democratic Republic of Vietnam (DRV) allowed the Chinese Affairs Commission in Beijing to organize Chinese education for the ethnic Chinese in the DRV. The school administrators were despatched from China to head Chinese primary and secondary schools in Hanoi and Haiphong. At the same time, the Hanoi Teacher Training Institute was set up by China to train ethnic Chinese teachers for Chinese primary and secondary schools in the DRV.

Since late 1958, the PRC had initiated new policies (known as "3 good" policy, such as nationality, no-interference, resettlement), encouraging the overseas Chinese to integrate themselves into Vietnamese society. At that time, the Chinese Embassy in Hanoi was informed that the right of running Chinese schools in Vietnam was being transferred to the DRV. Since then, the Hanoi government has begun to take over the administration of the Chinese schools in the DRV. By 1962, administrators and teachers sent by China had all been gradually withdrawn. By the mid-1960s, the Chinese language in the Chinese schools in Vietnam was downgraded to the level of a foreign language. Although the Chinese education system was Vietnamized, the Chinese Embassy in Hanoi still maintained their links with the ethnic Chinese in the DRV through ethnic Chinese mass organizations, such as the Hoa Lien (United Hoa) Association and the General Association of Hoa in Vietnam.[37] However, the Cultural Revolution in China during the 1960s weakened the linkages between Beijing and the ethnic Chinese in Vietnam.

After 1975, especially during 1976–79 the ethnic Chinese society in Vietnam in general, and their consciousness of Vietnam as their homeland in particular, were sharply shaken. In 1976, when the socialist government of a united Vietnam carried out a registration campaign for foreign residents, hundreds of thousands of ethnic Chinese identified themselves as citizens of China. In 1977–78, there was an outflow of hundreds of thousands of ethnic Chinese from North Vietnam to China by land, and from South Vietnam to the countries of Southeast Asia by sea. One of the factors which created this disturbance among ethnic Chinese in Vietnam at that time was the impact of mainland China.

With a view to gain influence and control over the ethnic Chinese community in South Vietnam, the Beijing-led "Progressive Chinese" group[38] set up several new political organizations in Saigon-Cholon: they were the Chinese Resident's Peace Association, the *Huaqiao* Association for Saving the Country from Danger, the Overseas Chinese Marxist-Leninist Youth Union, and so on. The aims of these organizations were to mobilize capitalists and intellectuals to pool money and expertise to help the land of their ancestors. When Saigon was liberalized on 30 April 1975, this group tried to seize the Taiwan Embassy, the offices of the Newspaper *Vien Dong* (Far East), the Nghee An School, the Teochew Hospital and the Taiwan tourist agency. It also mobilized the ethnic Chinese in Cholon to display the Chinese national flag and the portrait of Mao Zedong. In 1976–78 the Beijing agencies intensely incited the ethnic Chinese to leave Vietnam for China.[39]

With the incitement from Beijing, the cutting off of aid, the withdrawal of experts and specialists from Vietnam, the support given to the Pol-Pot administration in Cambodia to attack Vietnam's south-western provinces, the concentration of troops near the Vietnam-China border and the 1978 despatch of war vessels to Vietnamese territorial waters caused much perplexity and anxiety among the ethnic Chinese, especially those who lived in Vietnam's northern provinces. As a result, hundreds of thousands of ethnic Chinese fled Vietnam for China. On the other hand, the campaign for the socialist transformation of "capitalist" industry and trade, which was launched in March 1978 by Vietnam, also caused hundreds of thousands of ethnic Chinese to flee Vietnam for foreign countries by boat. In addition, the war of aggression by China against Vietnam in the spring of 1979, together with Vietnam's economic decline also caused the departure of the ethnic Chinese.

The reintegration of the ethnic Chinese in Vietnam took place in the early 1980s, especially from the second half of the decade. In recent years, thousands of ethnic Chinese who had formerly left Vietnam for one reason or another, have expressed their wish to return to Vietnam to remake their living.[40] This trend may have been motivated by the new policy of economic renovation, implemented during the past decade. Moreover, normalization of relations between Vietnam and China, which started in the late 1980s, has also contributed to the process of reintegration of the ethnic Chinese into the Vietnamese population.

Before 1975, the ethnic Chinese in South Vietnam had business and kinship ties with other Chinese, especially those in Taiwan, Hong Kong, Singapore, Thailand and Cambodia. Although Vietnam was largely closed for a decade after 1975, many Vietnamese Chinese managed to maintain close contact with them. The mass exodus of ethnic Chinese from Vietnam during 1978–79 expanded their ties with the Chinese in other regions (such as North America, and

Australia). Vietnam's statistics show that at the end of 1987, 55 per cent of the ethnic Chinese households in Ho Chi Minh City had relatives living in twenty countries in the world, excluding China. It is estimated that at the beginning of the 1990s, about two-thirds of the ethnic Chinese in this city have relatives abroad.[41]

At the present time, there are more than 2 million overseas Vietnamese, of whom about 35 to 40 per cent are of ethnic Chinese origin.[42] Among them, about 50 to 60 per cent live in North America, especially in the United States of America.[43] According to the 1991 census of Australia, more than 30 per cent of the Vietnamese-born community in Australia have Chinese ancestry.[44] Within the last fifteen to twenty years, a large number of Vietnamese refugees, including ethnic Chinese, have made it good in their new countries. Many of them have become wealthy businessmen and are capable of providing their relatives in Vietnam with capital to explore business opportunities, made possible by the more relaxed and liberal economic policy of *doi moi*.

Apart from these investments by returnees, who are ex-citizens, foreign investments coming into Vietnam are also being led by people of the Chinese race. Currently, the East and Southeast Asian capital-rich economies are major investors in Vietnam, and three of them — Taiwan, Hong Kong and Singapore — are predominantly Chinese. As a whole, investments from the ASEAN countries where the Chinese form a minority, are derived mainly from their wealthy ethnic Chinese tycoons.

Since the Sino-Vietnamese border was informally reopened in February 1989, especially after Sino-Vietnamese diplomatic relations were normalized in October 1991, border trade between the two countries has rapidly developed. In the pre-1989 period, import-export turnover of commodities through the Vietnam-China border had stood at only several million U.S. dollars, but in 1991 it attained US$247 million, and reached about US$900 million in 1995.[45] The hustle and bustle of the border market between Vietnam and China in the past five to seven years has created busy commercial centres along the common border. On the Vietnam side, the border trade activities have brought back prosperity to these border areas. Before 1989, such areas as Dong Dang, Tam Thanh and the town of Lang Son in Lang Son province; the town of Mong Cai in Quang Ninh province; and the town of Lao Cai in Lao Cai province remained severely devastated by the Vietnam-China border war of 1979. Since then, however, these towns have become thriving urban business centres in Vietnam. Many traders and companies from China, Hong Kong, Macao and Taiwan are operating in those towns. For example, the Mong Cai market in the town of Mong Cai had up to 300 large stalls and stands by the end of 1993, of which over 100 were rented to Chinese traders from Guangxi.[46]

With the good conditions created by Vietnam's open-door policy and its improved diplomatic relations with China, the ethnic Chinese in Vietnam and those formerly repatriated to China for political reasons during the 1978–79 period, have now plenty of opportunities to pay visits to one another and pool their resources into joint ventures for making profits. China itself has undergone economic reforms in recent years, and Southern China has been widely recognized as one of the most promising growth areas with vast economic potential. This has given rise to a people-to-people relationship between China and Vietnam. It has also contributed to the extension of economic activities of the ethnic Chinese in Vietnam.

Vietnam's official membership in ASEAN since July 1995 and its participation in AFTA (ASEAN Free Trade Area) since January 1996 have had a great influence on Vietnam's socio-economic developments in general, and on the ethnic Chinese community in particular. At this juncture, the ethnic Chinese in Vietnam have had more opportunities to restore and develop their business networks with other ethnic Chinese trading communities in the world, especially those in Asia. This will not only create more economic competitive strength for the ethnic Chinese in Vietnam, but will also give an impetus to their cultural development, especially the development of the Chinese language in the community.

In short, the business and kinship relations of the ethnic Chinese in Vietnam with their counterparts outside Vietnam are one of the factors affecting the integration of the ethnic Chinese in Vietnam. These relations once maintained and developed will create a stronger economic competitiveness for the ethnic Chinese and consolidate their cultural character. The setting up of a series of Chinese language teaching centres in towns and cities inhabited by the ethnic Chinese in Vietnam is a typical example. In recent years, there has been an emergence of a Chinese language learning movement in Ho Chi Minh City and in many towns of the Mekong River Delta where a large number of the ethnic Chinese live. Though the curricula of these Chinese language centres in different localities are diverse in content, they nevertheless bear the character of foreign language teaching. The teaching materials used by these centres are mainly based on those published by Taiwan or the PRC. The Chinese language teaching centres have a big enrolment of ethnic Chinese children. Moreover, the Chinese language is also taught in the families of the ethnic Chinese, and this is particularly common in Ho Chi Minh City. Because more time is spent in learning Chinese and English, many ethnic Chinese students in public schools have neglected the learning of the Vietnamese language and other subjects. Hence, many ethnic Chinese children do not read and write Vietnamese well.[47] The teaching of school subjects in the Chinese language is clearly a matter of importance to the ethnic Chinese in Vietnam. This meets the requirements of the market and the aspirations of the ethnic Chinese themselves. However, the promotion of the Chinese language among the ethnic Chinese is one of the main factors helping to preserve the Chinese identity. This attention to learning Chinese and neglect of the Vietnamese language among the ethnic Chinese community may create a line of demarcation between the ethnic Chinese and the host Vietnamese community, thereby slowing down the process of integration of ethnic Chinese into Vietnamese society.

Concluding Remarks

The integration experiences of the ethnic Chinese in Vietnam during the different historical periods reveal some significant trends and implications.

First, owing to Vietnamese history, language, religion, culture, social and administrative structures and political institutions and the more than two thousand years of contact with China, including almost one thousand years of Chinese political domination, the Chinese migrants were easily integrated into the mainstream of

Vietnamese society. However, the Chinese migrants were sometimes the targets of discrimination by the Vietnamese authorities. Compulsory assimilation was imposed on the Chinese migrants, mainly through the requirement for the defence of national sovereignty and security, against intervention from China. Thus, the ethnic, cultural and religious differences between the Vietnamese and ethnic Chinese were not the main reasons for Vietnamese hostility towards the ethnic Chinese.

Secondly, in order to survive and develop in Vietnam, the ethnic Chinese had to adjust themselves to the conditions of Vietnamese society. They engaged in trading activities and established their social organizations such as *bang*, clan and religious or occupational associations. Chinatowns and their traditional organizations were the nucleus for maintaining their Chinese identity.

Thirdly, the "divide and rule" policy of the authorities in Vietnam by promoting a separate status for Chinese residents according to parentage and birthplace, together with the use of the Chinese *bang* as an administrative unit, also contributed to the social isolation of the Chinese from the Vietnamese.

Fourthly, the socialist transformation of private capitalist industry and trade in South Vietnam during 1977–79 was one of the reasons for the ethnic Chinese to identify themselves as Chinese citizens, or as overseas Chinese, despite the fact that they were already Vietnamese citizens during the late 1950s. The main reason for rejecting Vietnamese citizenship was pragmatic: by claiming to be Chinese or Taiwanese citizens, they probably hoped that as foreign nationals they would be in a better position under the new rules and be allowed to leave Vietnam easily.

Fifthly, the tense relationship between China and Vietnam together with the incited racial policy of China during 1978–79 contributed to the Chinese departure from Vietnam. The rejection of Vietnamese nationality by the ethnic Chinese together with the exodus of hundreds of thousands of ethnic Chinese from Vietnam, especially from the North, to China in 1978, gave rise to the suspicion by the Vietnamese government on the loyalty of the ethnic Chinese towards Vietnam. For that reason, Hanoi at that time did not prevent the exodus of the ethnic Chinese, and also carried out some measures to restrict ethnic Chinese involvement in political and social activities. These factors hindered the integration of the ethnic Chinese into Vietnamese society.

Sixthly, during the 1980s, especially the latter half, there was reintegration of the ethnic Chinese into Vietnamese society. In recent years, many ethnic Chinese who had formerly left Vietnam, have expressed their wish to return to Vietnam. This trend was due mainly to Vietnam's renovation policy. In the economic area, the ethnic Chinese have returned to most of the activities which they were involved in prior to 1975. They are no longer regarded as the "fifth column" working for China's interests, and their civil rights and duties are now guaranteed. Their cultural and educational rights have also been restored. However, their activities in the socio-cultural area are still at a much reduced level compared to the mid-1960s in the North and before 1975 in South Vietnam.

Seventhly, the normalized economic and diplomatic relations between Vietnam and China, the increased economic co-operation between Vietnam and the East and Southeast Asian nations where many people of Chinese descent live, and the geographical and cultural closeness of Vietnam and China, may create more opportunities for the "China factor" to penetrate Vietnamese society. At present, the Vietnamese Chinese community constitutes an influential socio-economic entity which is playing an important role in the economic development of Vietnam. A long-term effect of the above-mentioned economic and political trends and the close traditional ties between the ethnic Chinese themselves may see the community in Vietnam regain its economic pre-eminence. If a sizeable portion of Vietnam's economy is in the hands of an ethnic Chinese minority, it may give rise to Vietnamese resentment as the indigenous Vietnamese would want an equitable share of the national economy. This was the reason that had set the ethnic Chinese apart from the Vietnamese, and may again result in a discriminatory policy towards the ethnic Chinese. This will, of course, have an impact on the identity of the ethnic Chinese. If Vietnam becomes more thriving and democratic, more ethnic Chinese would devote their loyalty to Vietnam, but if "Greater China" becomes one of the most powerful economic and political entities in the world, more ethnic Chinese would revert to the status of an overseas Chinese identity.

Notes

1. The 1989 census of Vietnam found the number of individuals who identified themselves as ethnic Chinese (known as the Hoa) to be 962,000. See Tran Khanh, *The Ethnic Chinese and Economic Development in Vietnam* (Singapore: Institute of Southeast Asian Studies, 1993), pp. 26–27.

2. See Dao Duy Anh. *Dat nuoc Vietnam qua cac doi* [Vietnam in various dynasties], Parts I–VII (Hue: NXB Thuan Hoa, 1994); and, *Kitai i Saseiv drevnosti i Sretnic vekok* [China and neighbouring countries in ancient and middle times] (Moscova: Nauka, 1970), pp. 63–66.

3. Nguyen Van Huy, *Nguoi hoa tai Vietnam* [The Hoa in Vietnam] (Costa Mesa: Nha xuat ban NBC, 1993), pp. 276–79.

4. See Nguyen Tai Thu, ed., *Lich su tu tuong Vietnam* [History of Vietnamese Ideology], Volume 1 (Hanoi: NXB Khoa hoc xa hoi, 1993), part 1 and 2.

5. Phan ngoc, *Van hoa Vietnam va cach tiep can moi* [Vietnamese culture: The new approach] (Hanoi: NXB Van Hoa – thong tin, 1994), pp. 106–7, and 117–18.

6. See Nguyen Tai Thu, ed., *Lich su tu tuong Vietnam* [History of Vietnamese Ideology], Volume 1 (Hanoi: NXB Khoa hoc xa hoi, 1993), parts 2 and 3.

7. Fujiwara Ruchiro, *Chinh sach doi voi dan Trung Hoa di cu cua cac trieu dai Vietnam* [Policies of the Vietnamese dynasties towards Chinese migrants] (Saigon: Vietnam khao co tap san, 1974), pp. 142–44; and Nguyen Van Huy, op. cit., pp. 22–24.

8. Tran Khanh, op. cit., p. 17.

9. By 1814, during the reign of Emperor Gia Long (1802–20), the Chinese *bang* were legally recognized and authorized to operate publicly. From the later nineteenth century, each *bang* had its own financial investment organization, its own chamber of commerce, schools, clinics, etc. At the beginning of the twentieth century, they organized a Chinese Regional Grouping administration to represent all the *bang*. See Tran Khanh, op. cit., pp. 17–20, 34–36.

10. Dao Trinh Nhat, *The luc khach tru va van de li dan vao Nam ky* [The Position of the Chinese Sojourners and Problems of Emigration into Cochinchina] (Hanoi: Butky Trung Hoa, 1929), p. 4.

11. See Nguyen Van Huy, op. cit., pp. 279–302.

12. In 1933, a new law was passed by the French permitting Minh Huong born in Cochinchina, in the cities of Haiphong, Hanoi and Danang, as well as their children after that date to become a new category of

French Asian citizens. Those who were born before that date were considered Chinese nationals or foreigners. See Tsai Maw Kuey, *Les Chinois au Sud – Vietnam* (Paris: Bibliotheque National, 1968), pp. 199–200.

13. Tran Khanh, op. cit., p. 28.
14. In 1886, the Chinese *bang* or "congregations" were legally recognized by the French and these were used as administrative services and were given the power to regulate certain matters within their respective communities. The prerogatives of *bang* were to settle disputes, handle matters of immigration, act as guarantee for newcomers, levy taxes, keep family registration up-to-date and carry out public welfare projects. See Nguyen Van Huy, op. cit., p. 57; and Tran Khanh, op. cit., p. 34.
15. Nguyen Van Huy, op. cit., p. 57.
16. See Tran Khanh, op. cit., Chapter II.
17. Tsai Maw Kuey, op. cit., pp. 199–200; and Tran Khanh, op. cit., pp. 28–29.
18. In South Vietnam in 1955 there were approximately 621,000 ethnic Chinese who were Chinese nationals. Three years later that number decreased to 3,000. By 1961 this number had dwindled to 2,000. This remaining small number consisted mainly of those carrying the Chinese nationality conferred by Taiwan. In November 1963, a new nationality law of the Republic of Vietnam was passed allowing Chinese aliens to choose Vietnamese or retain their Taiwanese citizenship. See Kotova T.M., "Kitaiskaia obsina Vietnama – politicheskie orugie v rukac Peking" [Chinese community in Vietnam – political instrument of Peking], *Far Eastern Issues*, No. 4 (1978), p. 105. See also Wu Yuan-Li and Wu Chun hsi, *Economic Development in Southeast Asia: The Chinese Dimension* (California: Hoove Institute Press, 1980), p. 119.
19. Nguyen Van Huy, op. cit., pp. 76–80; Chang Pao-ming, *Beijing, Hanoi and the Overseas Chinese* (California: Institute of East Asian Studies, University of California, 1982), p. 12; and Ramses Amer, *The Ethnic Chinese in Vietnam and Sino-Vietnamese Relations* (Kuala Lumpur: Forum, 1991), p. 20.
20. *The Hoa in Vietnam. Dossiers*, Vol. 1 (Hanoi: Foreign Language Publishing House, 1978), pp. 23–24.
21. Ibid., pp. 19–20.
22. Ramses Amer, op. cit., p. 106.
23. "Nguoi Hoa o Vietnam va chinh sach cua Dang ta" [The ethnic Chinese in Vietnam and our Party's policies] (Hanoi: National Central Committee for Mobilization of the Hoa in Vietnam, 11 January 1989), pp. 23–25.
24. Ibid., p. 25.
25. See Mac Duong, *Xa hoi nguoi Hoa o Thanh pho Ho Chi Minh sau 1975* [The Hoa society in Ho Chi Minh City after 1975] (Hanoi: Social Science Publishing House, 1994), pp. 174–79.

26. Ibid., pp. 189–98.

27. Phan Van Bien, "Ve tinh hinh giao duc tieng Hoa hien nay trong cong dong nguoi Hoa o Thanh pho Ho Chi Minh" [On the situation of Chinese language education among ethnic Chinese community in Ho Chi Minh City at present time], *Language Education and Development of Culture of Ethnic Minority Groups in Southern Vietnam* (Hanoi: Social Science Publishing House, 1993), pp. 186–87.

28. See Murray Hiebert, "Cautious re-emergence by ethnic Chinese: Market test", *Far Eastern Economic Review*, 1 August 1991, pp. 24–25.

29. Ramses Amer, "The Chinese minority in Vietnam since 1975: Impact of economic and political changes", *Ilmu Masyarakat*, no. 22 (1992), p. 28.

30. During the sixteenth to eighteenth centuries, the overseas Chinese in the Philippines and Indonesia were suppressed by Western colonialists. In Vietnam during the reign of Tay Son (1792), there was a massacre of the Chinese in Cho Lon.

31. See Wang Gungwu, *China and Chinese Overseas* (Singapore: Times Academic Press, 1991), chapters 6 and 7; and *Dai Trung Hoa va nguoi Hoa o nuoc ngoai* [Greater China and Chinese abroad] (Thong tan xa Vietnam. Tai lieu tham khao so 10 va 11, 1994), pp. 33–49.

32. E.S. Ungar, "The struggle over the Chinese community in Vietnam, 1946–1986", *Pacific Affairs* 60, no. 4 (Winter 1987–1988): 605.

33. Tran Khanh, op. cit., pp. 67–70 and 106.

34. The small number of ethnic Chinese were allowed to leave Vietnam because the Republic of Vietnam and the Republic of China did not reach an agreement on how to carry out the operation. Relations between the two states were soured as a result. See Ramses Amer. *The Ethnic Chinese in Vietnam*, pp. 20–21.

35. Tran Khanh, op. cit., pp. 29, 53–73.

36. The United Hoa association for the struggle against imperialism and colonialism was set up in 1950 by the Viet Minh. The Association of Patriotic Overseas Chinese was founded by the Chinese Communist Party in 1948.

37. E.S. Ungar, op. cit., pp. 603–604.

38. Vietnam's dossiers published in 1979, note that some Chinese from the People's Republic of China who had worked in North Vietnam before 1967 were afterwards sent to Cambodia during the Lon Nol era, and were ordered to go to Saigon in April 1975 after the fall of Phnom Penh. These agents were sent to organize "Young Red Guards", targeting ethnic Chinese children, students and teachers. See *Su thuc ve quan he Vietnam – Trung Quoc trong 30 nam qua* [The facts about Vietnam-Chinese relationship in the last 30 years] (Hanoi: Bo Ngoai giao, 1979), pp. 80–81.

39. Ibid., pp. 82–84; and E.S. Unger, op. cit., p. 607.

40. Mac Duong, op. cit., p. 30.
41. "Phat huytiem nang cua nguoi Hoa trong chien luoc phat trien kinh te – xa hoi cua Thanh pho Ho Chi Minh 1991–2000" [To utilize ethnic Chinese resources in the strategy for the socio-economic development of Ho Chi Minh City in 1991–2000] (Consultative material for the Mobilization of the Hoa in Ho Chi Minh City, 1992), p. 9.
42. The number of ethnic Chinese who left Vietnam illegally during 1978–79 and the ODP (Orderly Departure Program) during 1979–91 was estimated to be 700,000 persons. The number of ethnic Chinese who left Vietnam illegally during 1975–77 and the 1980s may be between 50,000 and 100,000 persons. Thus, the total number of ethnic Chinese who left Vietnam from 1975 to 1990 was between 750,000 and 800,000 persons, constituting about 35 to 40 per cent of the total Vietnamese-born Chinese community abroad. See Ramses Amer, *China, Vietnam and the Chinese Minority in Vietnam*, Discussion Paper No. 22 (Center for East and Southeast Asian Studies. University of Copenhagen, November 1993), p. 32.
43. Nguyen Van Huy, op. cit., p. 153.
44. Mandy Thomas, "The Vietnamese in Australia: A Demographic and Socio-economic Profile from the 1991 Census" (Department of Anthropology, Australian National University), p. 5.
45. Tran Anh Phuong, "Bien mau Viet – Trung va nhung tac dong kinh te xa hoi" [Vietnam-China border trade and its socio-economic impact]. *Kinh te chau A – Thai Binh Duong* 2, no. 3 (1994): 28; *Vietnam dau tu nuoc ngoai* [Vietnam Investment Review] 138 (28 November 1995): 7.
46. Tran Anh Phuong, op. cit., pp. 27–29.
47. See Pham Van Bien, op. cit., pp. 186–92.

Comments by
Ta Huu Phuong on
"Ethnic Chinese in Vietnam and Their Identity"
Presented by Tran Khanh

Dr Tran Khanh's paper is interesting, comprehensive and well-researched. It traces the historical development of Sino-Vietnamese relations and the socio-economic activities of the ethnic Chinese in Vietnam. The paper also gives a historical account of the policies implemented by the Vietnamese authorities on the Chinese community in Vietnam and discusses the implications of these policies.

After reading Dr Khanh's paper and listening to Professor Leo Suryadinata's presentation of his paper on "Ethnic Chinese in Southeast Asia: Overseas Chinese, Chinese overseas or Southeast Asians?" I could not help but note that the various Vietnamese policies on the ethnic Chinese fit very well into Leo's framework of assimilationist and accommodationist policies.

Over the years these two strategies were used by the Vietnamese authorities on two main aspects of activities, namely, socio-economic life and education.

In addition, I note that, invariably, "selective restrictions" were also imposed from time to time. I will show this by going through the different periods of Vietnamese history. Let me start off with the Le dynasty.

1. The Le dynasty (1428–1592) and the Trinh lords (1592–1777) practised an *assimilationist* policy: ethnic Chinese must conform to Vietnamese customs and traditions including dressing. Examples of selective restrictions are: the ethnic Chinese were allowed to live in special zones only; they were not free to travel within Vietnam; the merchants were heavily taxed; and people were not allowed to distribute Chinese books and literature.

2. The Nguyen dynasty in the south (1592–1777), and later
    the Imperial Court of Hue (1802–1945), implemented an
    accommodationist policy approach. The ethnic Chinese were
    allowed to buy land and houses, to set up social, religious
    and business associations. In general, they had the same civil
    rights as the Vietnamese, but were exempted from military
    service.

    Here we must highlight the important contributions of the
    ethnic Chinese to the socio-economic development of Vietnam,
    such as Trinh Hoai Duc and Phan Thanh Gian.
3. After independence in 1954, both North and South Vietnam
    adopted an *accommodationist* policy. The government of the
    Republic of Vietnam in the south allowed the ethnic Chinese
    to have the same civil rights as the Vietnamese and considered
    all Chinese born in Vietnam as citizens. However, the ethnic
    Chinese were required to learn Vietnamese in the schools and
    to change their names to Vietnamese ones.

    In the north the government of the Democratic Republic
    of Vietnam granted political rights to the ethnic Chinese and
    considered them as allies of the regime.
4. During the period after reunification in 1975, the Vietnamese
    government first adopted an *assimilationist* strategy and later
    switched to an *accommodationist* mode.

Khanh attributed the adoption of the assimilationist policy
during the decade 1975–85 to the tense relations between China
and Vietnam (1977–79) and the change from a capitalist system
to a socialist regime in South Vietnam.

Since early 1986, the introduction of *doi moi* (renovation) saw
a reversal to the accommodationist policy. The ethnic Chinese
have the same rights and obligations as the Vietnamese. They are
allowed to participate in all professions and to teach the Chinese
language within the curriculum given by the government.

An interesting point to note is that, in many instances, the
switch between these two strategies, known in strategic management literature as the push-pull approach, sometimes by the same
authorities was practised by various administrations over the past
generations.

It would be worthwhile to find out whether the switch was due to external influences (for example, the state of the relationship with China and neighbouring countries) or to internal influences (such as the self-realization by the Vietnamese leadership that the contribution of every citizen of the land is to be appreciated).

Appendix

Women and Chinese Identity: An Exchange at the Closing Session of the Workshop

Towards the end of the workshop, four participants — Mely Tan, Wang Gungwu, Leo Suryadinata and Tan Chee Beng — discussed the role of indigenous/*peranakan* women who married Chinese men. The discussion is presented below.

Mely Tan

I am wondering why we have not really looked at the role of women in this whole process. Why have we ignored the role of 50 per cent of the ethnic Chinese that we have been talking about? In Asian culture, both parents, especially the mother, are the socializers of the younger generation. To my knowledge, in our culture in this region, mothers are usually given the task of educating the young. Now, we seem to have completely forgotten how the women educate their children in this whole process. That is why I asked Dr Chiew Seen Kong about his sisters who went to Chinese language schools, while all his brothers went to English schools.

I was serious about this question but he took it lightly, saying that there is a problem but did not pursue the point. If I leave this conference without saying anything about this, I will feel sorry. All my friends who went to China to attend the Beijing United Nations conference on women will also feel sorry. What did we do in this workshop? We talked about the continuation of cultural change and ignored completely the role of 50 per cent of the people — the women. Well, there is no time to remedy this situation but I think in future conferences, we should really consider this issue. Thank you.

Wang Gungwu

I am absolutely delighted that Mely has raised this question. But the answer may well be unpalatable to the ethnic Chinese — that is, of all the communities in Southeast Asia, the Chinese are probably the most male chauvinistic in their cultural tradition. In fact, Southeast Asians are much more bilateral in the descent line. It is probably a reflection of how unintegrated the ethnic Chinese are to Southeast Asian culture that they are still so patriarchal. In a sense, this is a test because of all the cultures that I know, Chinese culture is the most strictly patriarchal. Of course, it has been in a way reinforced by the fact that from the very beginning, it was mostly men who came to Southeast Asia and they married local women. If you look at the background of the *baba/peranakan* family you will see that the males were able to dominate and preserve a Chinese identity. The very fact that we see the survival of these *baba/peranakan* families is a sign of the "maleness" of the Chinese tradition itself. When you consider that the mothers were Southeast Asians, most of their children should have become Southeast Asians very quickly, if the children followed their mother tongue and their mother's culture; in a bilateral cultural situation, this would have been very normal. In many ways, I think that is what happened in the Philippines, where the indigenous bilateral line was strong enough. Moreover, with the support of the Catholic Church, the Chinese males had to identify locally and could not dictate the adherence to Chinese culture to the same extent as the *baba/peranakan* did in Indonesia and Malaysia.

I always find it fascinating that in the Philippines, the assimilation of the next generation of ethnic Chinese did not follow the male line as much as in the Malaysian and Indonesian world. I think the reason is that in the Philippines the bilateral line descent tradition is very strong. I mean, you can see even among the indigenous Filipinos themselves, the tensions between the patrilocal and matrilocal lines. Islam brought a male chauvinistic line to Malaysia and Indonesia, and so with the male chauvinistic Chinese culture plus the male chauvinistic Islamic culture, we get this *baba/peranakan* kind of community. In Vietnam, Thailand or Myanmar, the women were also stronger in their bilateral descent relationship and therefore it was just as likely for the product of a mixed marriage to follow the mother and not necessarily accept the culture of the Chinese father. That may be one of the reasons why we do not really hear of the equivalent of a *baba/peranakan* culture in Myanmar, Thailand or Vietnam. They could either go one way or the other but not in between; only in Malaysia and Indonesia do we have this *baba/peranakan* community.

This relates very much to the question of why in the Philippines it is the other way around. When we look at the mestizo, few of them really maintain a Chinese ethnic identity. There is no *baba/peranakan* kind of situation in the Chinese mestizo. Although people may say they still have Chinese links, they are really Filipinos. The fact that their grandfathers were Chinese is irrelevant because they were brought up mainly by the mother, or the female line, with the backing of the Catholic Church, thus ensuring that they were much more Filipino. So I agree with Mely that the role of the women should be examined more closely if we have another opportunity to do so, by tracing the product of intermarriages where the role of the women have made a difference to the degree of assimilation and integration. I think that is a very important point.

Leo Suryadinata

Professor Wang has raised an interesting point on the role of women in the retention of Chinese identity. I remember William Skinner did a study in the early 1950s, arguing that the marriage custom of the *peranakan* in West Java followed the indigenous pattern. It was "matriarchal" as the wedding was held and the marriage was consummated in the bride's home rather than in the bridegroom's house.

We do not know their precise identity. It is possible that some of them became more indigenous but others remained Chinese, depending on the cultural background of the men. In the twentieth century, many *peranakan* women married *totok* men. The male chauvinist culture was revived and dominated the *peranakan* society again. Perhaps, the preservation of the Chinese ethnic identity among the *peranakan* Chinese is also a result of the Dutch "ethnic separation" policy in Java. I don't know. I think more study should be conducted on this issue.

Tan Chee Beng

Can I add to that? Yes, this is an interesting issue. I do agree with Professor Wang that the male ideology is quite strong even among the *baba*. Among the *baba* of Malacca, Singapore, and Penang, there was this phenomenon of matrilocal marriage. This is actually an expression of male ideology involving the class factor. The *baba* were more established, and *peranakan* women (*nyonya*) were very "precious". When a Chinese immigrant wanted to marry a *nyonya* from an established family, her father might say to the future son-in-law, "Well, you have to come in to my family". This is what I mean by the class factor. So this matrilocal marriage became established. But there is another factor which Leo raised, which is important. With the influx of the Chinese migrants, the *baba* eventually had to conform to the rules of the non-*baba* Chinese. Thus, the *baba* today do not practise matrilocal marriage any longer.

In the case of the *nyonya*, I think they played an important role in the socialization of identity, in perpetuating the *baba* or *nyonya* kind of culture, in the forms of cuisine, dress, and language, of course. And the *nyonya* played an important role in making the local-born Chinese speak Malay within a generation. But if we study the subject of cooking, its development really reflects the traditional male ideology, in that women were expected to stay at home to cultivate feminine skills like cooking, so as to be marriageable and to serve men at home.

Leo Suryadinata
The role of women and ethnic identity is very interesting but we do not have time to examine it in detail. I hope this topic will be further explored.

Index

Abdul Rahman, Tengku 76
Abim 97
Ahmat, Adam 108
Aidil Fitri (Idul Fitri) 97
Ali, Bachtiar Dr 59
Alien Certificate of Registration
   (ACR) 177
Almonte, General Jose 172
Ambonese 44
ang pao 44
Angara, Edgardo, Senator 190
Anusorn Limmanee 260
Anwar, Dato Seri Ibrahim 97
APEC 58
Aquino, Corazon (Cory Aquino)
   13, 188, 190
Aquino, Ninoy, Senator 188
Association of Southeast Asian
   Nations (ASEAN) 116, 209,
   210
Atmadjaja, Usman 59
Au Lac Kingdom 268

Baba 19, 26, 30, 83, 297, 298
Bachtiar, Harsja W. 34
Bakom-PKB 56, 58, 59, 60, 67
Baladraf, Qomariah (Tan Giok
   Sien) 56
Balinese 44, 55, 46
Banharn Silpa-archa 12, 255
bangsa Malaysia (Malay nation)
   80, 81, 82, 98, 99, 113, 114
bangsa Melayu 82
Barisan Nasional 96
Barmar (Burman) 121
Berjaya Group 78, 103
Bernad, Miguel A. 162
Berroya, Colonel Reynaldo 166
Bicolanos 160
Binondo 172
Bouer, Otto 35
Boworadet, Prince 265
Buddhism 12
Budiyatna, Muhammad 56
Bukit China (Malaysia) 94

bumiputra 6
Burma Citizenship Act of 1948
136
Burma Citizenship Law (1982)
133, 135, 136
Burma Road 118
Burma, the term 147

Cai Ceng 36
Centre for Strategic and
International Studies (CSIS) 35
Chamlong Sri Muang 255
Chan, Heng Chee 203
Cheng Ho, tomb of 97
Chiew Seen Kong 230
Chifils (Chinese-Filipinos) 203–16
Chinese Chamber of Commerce
(Malaysia) 97
Chinese Chamber of Commerce
(CCC, Thailand) 236, 237, 247
Chinese Chamber of Commerce
(in Yangon) 140–41
Chinese Chamber of Commerce
(Singapore) 229
Chinese Communist Party (CCP)
77, 249
Chinese Consultative Committee
(CCC) 104
Chinese diaspora 28, 159
Chinese mestizos 179
Chinese New Year (Lunar New
Year) 97, 102
Chinese Unity Movement 110
Cho Lon 271
Chongqing Agreement 274
Christianity 12
Chuan Leekpai 12, 255,
Chulalongkorn, King 234, 263, 264
Citizens Action Against Crime
(CAAC, Philippines) 207
Cold War 1, 15

communism 14
Confucianism 269, 230
Coppel, Charles 35
Coseteng, Nikki 190
Cushman, Jennifer 39

Dahana, A. 66
Dalian Economic Zone 78
Deklarasi Jimbaran (Bali) 53
Democratic Action Party (DAP),
89, 94, 95, 105
Democratic Republic of Vietnam
(DRV) 276, 281
Deng Xiaoping 15, 190
Dewan Pertimbangan Agung
(DPA) 34
doi moi 14, 278, 294
Dong Jiao Zhong (Malaysia) 93, 100
double identity 31
Ducat, Jun 171
Dutch 44

East Asian Economic Caucus
(EAEC) 77
Ekran 103
Enterprise Nationalization Law
(Burma) 126
Ethnic Chinese
and concepts of nation 4–7
and Southeast Asian
citizenship 7–9
as Southeast Asians 15–19
definition of 2–4; 25–28
governments' policies towards
11–15
identity and women 296–300
numbers of (Southeast Asian) 21
Overseas Chinese and 3
Family Name Act (Thailand) 237
Federation of Filipino-Chinese
Chambers of Commerce 163

Filipinos of Chinese descent 197
Furnivall, J.S. 156

Gandhi 209
General Association of Chinese
    Schools (Philippines) 163
Gerakan 94, 95
Gerakan 30 September (G-30-S)
    35, 69
Go Bon Juan 187
Go Tik Swan, Hardjono 55
Golkar 67
Gondomono 49, 57
Gotianum, Andrew 209
Grand Family Association
    (Philippines) 163
"Greater China" 3 159, 161
Greif, Stuart, 45, 57, 68
Guanyin (Goddess of Mercy) 145

Habibie, J.B. 53
Haiwai huaren 26
Hakka 46, 48, 57
Hamka, Buya 56
Hasan, Mohamad (Bob) 53
Hoa Lien Association (Vietnam)
    282
Hong Leong 103
Housing and Development Board
    (HDB) 219
Hua Sian Sin Po 232
Huaqiao 2, 3, 181, 273
Huaren 2, 3, 28, 29
Huayi 2, 4
Huayü 29
Hussein Onn, Dato 92

Ilocanos 160, 170
Immigrant Certificate of Registration
    (ACR), Philippines 177
Indians 18

Indochina Communist Party 275
Indonesia
    citizenship and identity of the
        Chinese in 33–45
    empirical studies of the
        Chinese in 45–50
    future of the Chinese in 50–54
    Islam and the Chinese in 69
Islam and Confucianism 97, 110
Islamic Administration Enactment
    Act 91
Jahja, Junus 56, 69
Jakarta 37
Javanese 6, 47
Jiang Zemin 77, 190
jos soli 164
jus sanguinis 7–8, 164

Kaisa Para Sa Kaunlaran 196
Kalipi 171
Kamunting Corporation 103
Kennedy, John F. 204
Khin Maung Kyi 147
Khoo Kay Peng 103
Kua Kia Soong 105
Kuala Lumpur Stock Exchange
    (KLSE) 78
Kuok, Robert 103, 104, 209
Kuomintang (KMT) 118, 129,
    130, 279, 280, 212, 238, 241,
    245, 246, 248, 249, 256
kungfu 51
Kusumah, Indradi 56, 59

Labour Party 88
Le dynasty 271
Lembaga Pertahanan Nasional
    (Lemhanas, National Resilience
    Institute) 35, 58
Lemhanas, *see* Lembaga
    Pertahanan Nasional

Lee, Joseph (of the CASH group) 103, 104
Lee Kam Hing 108, 111, 113, 114
Lee Lam Thye 105
Lee Loy Seng 103
Leoni Fatimah (Pak Kiem Lioe) 56
Li Peng 36
Liem Sioe Liong 104
Lim, Alfredo (Manila Mayor) 171, 190, 206
Lim Gaik Tong 79
Lim Goh Tong 103
Lim Kim Hong 79
Ling Beng Siew, Tan Sri 103
Lion Corporation 103
Lippo Group 104
Loh Boon Siew 103
Luang Wichit Wathakan 265
Lunar New Year (Chinese New Year or Imlek) 43, 68, 97

Mackie, Jamie 35
Mahathir, Dato Seri Mohamad 77, 78, 80, 81, 91, 92, 96, 97, 98, 99, 100, 110, 111
Makati 172
Malay Chamber of Commerce 97
Malayan Communist Party (MCP) 75, 76, 77
Malayan Indian Congress (MIC) 85
Malayan People's Anti-Japanese Army (MPAJA) 76
Malaysia
    Chinese response to Malay nation 91–96
    development of new nation in 111–14
    economic relations between China and 77–79
    Malay and Chinese relations in 82–89; 96–99
    Malay character of the state in 89–91
    new society of 80–82
    overall picture of the Chinese in 108–11
    recent Chinese position in 96–106
Malaysian Business Council Meeting 113
Malaysian Chinese Association (MCA) 84, 85, 86, 88, 89, 90, 91, 92, 94, 100, 101, 102, 109, 110
Manchu dynasty 279
Mani, A. 228
Mao Zedong 190, 283
Marcos, Ferdinand, President 7, 163, 188, 190
Masagung (Tjio Wie Thay) 56
McCann Erickson 183
Medan, Anton (Tan Hok Liang) 56
Menadonese 44
Merdeka University 93
mestizo 4, 7
Minangkabau 44
Minh Huong 272, 273
Minh Mang 272
Multi-Purpose Holdings (MPHB) 92, 93, 110
Mursjid, Saadilah 53
Mya Than 147
Myanmar (Burma)
    Burma and 147
    Chinese and nation-building in 121–22
    Chinese and their identity in 138–43
    Chinese economic position in 122–28; 149–55

Chinese immigration to 148
Chinese legal status in 133–38
Chinese political position in
   128–30
Chinese problem 156
Chinese social position in
   130–33
ethnic Chinese in 117–21

Naisbitts, John 38
Nanjing agreement 274, 280
Nanyang University 93
nationalization and indigenization
   policy (Burma) 125
Ne Win, General 8
Ne Win, U, 136
Nehru 209
New Development Policy (NDP)
   113
New Economic Policy (NEP) 67,
   90, 102, 112, 113
New Era College (Kajang) 100
New Order 54
Ngo Dinh Diem 274, 275, 280
Ngo Quyen 269
Nguyen dynasty 271–73
Nguyen Trai 270
Nguyen Van Thieu 275
Nio Cwang Chung 56
Niras Sampheng 256
Noer, Rosita 59
non-governmental organizations
   (NGOs) 105
non-*pribumi* 58, 68
nyonya 299

Ohmae, Keinichi 210
Omohundro, John 170
Onn, Jaafar Dato 83
Overseas Chinese Affairs
   Committee 280

Overseas Chinese Marxist-Leninist
   Youth Union 282

Palang Dharma Party 255
Pancasila 34, 48, 53
Pangestu, Prayogo 53
panthay 115, 119
Parti Gerakan Rakyat Malaysia
   (Gerakan) 89, 101
Parti Islam Se Malaysia (PAS) 91,
   100, 104, 105
Parti Semangat '46 (New Semangat
   Party) 98, 100
pauk phaws 143
peranakan 4, 42, 44, 45, 46, 48,
   49, 50, 51, 52, 57, 59, 67,
   83, 297, 298, 299
Pernas 93
People's Action Party (PAP) 89
People's Party (of Thailand) 265
People's Progressive Party (PPP)
   88, 89
People's Republic of China 1, 10,
   11, 15, 17, 33, 36, 37, 45,
   116, 129, 163, 164, 177, 195,
   203, 281, 282
Permodalan Nasional Berhad
   (PNB) 92
Petronas 78, 102
Phan Thanh Gian 272
Phibulsongkhram (Prime Minister)
   239, 240, 241, 242, 243, 263,
   265
Phileo Allied Group 103
Philippine Citizenship 164
Philippines
   acceptance of the Chinese in
      the 194–96
   Chinese and Filipino
      nationalism in the 209
   Chinese and nationhood in the
      161–66

Chinese diversity in the 174–81
Chinese integration in the
181–94
Chinese legal status in the
168–74
identity of the Chinese in the
196–98
pro-Taiwan and pro-China
Chinese in the 167–68
Pol Pot 283
Prachadhipok, King 240, 245
Pribadi, Henry 53
pribumi 6, 46, 58, 59, 67, 68, 70,
71
Promet 103
Purcell, Victor 118, 122, 125,
129, 142
putong hua 29
Pyi Thu Hluttaw 135

qiaoling (community leader,
Philippines) 174–75
Quek Leng Chan 103

Ramadhan 43, 56
Ramos, Fidel V. 172
Razak, Tun 76
Razaleigh, Tengku Hamzah 93, 98
Renan, Ernest 34, 35
Republic of China (ROC, Taiwan)
177, 178, 195
Republic of Vietnam (ROV) 274,
280
Riots in Semarang 45
Riots in Solo 45
Rizal, Jose 209
Ryadi, Mochtar 57

Saleh, Ismail 36, 37
Salim Group 104, 210
Salim, Sudono 57

Sam Poo Kong temple 46
Samals 160
Sarawak United People's Party
(SUPP) 95, 100
Satria Utara Enterprise 102
Seagrave, Sterling 38, 159
See, Teresita Ang 18, 203
Seenivasagam 74
Sheow Hut-seng 235, 236, 237
Siamese Chamber of Commerce
241
Silalahi, Harry Tjan 34, 56, 59,
67
Sim Song Thian (Alifuddin El
Islami) 56
Simons, Lewis M. 159
Sin, Jaime Cardinal 13
Sindhunata, K. 56, 58
Singapore
Chinese demographic change
in 213–17
China factor in 223
race riots in 217
school and social integration in
218–19
various identities of the
Chinese in 228–31
Singh, Dr Dillon 59
Singh, Kapal 74
sinkeh 26
Sino-Bamar 142
Sino-Indonesian Treaty on Dual
Nationality 33
Sino-Thai 13
Smolicz, Jerzy 221
Soeharto, President 36, 41, 52, 53
Soekamdani 59
Soekarno 34, 35, 45, 67
Soerjadjaja, William 59
Soviet Union 14
Speak Mandarin Campaign 230

State Law and Order Restoration
Council (SLORC) 128
Straits Chinese 83
Subagio, Natalia 59
Sudarsono, Juwono 58–59
Sudwikatmono 53
Suehiro 237
Sumatran 6
Sun Yat Sen, Dr 190, 209, 235,
236, 245, 247, 261
Sundanese 44
Supang Chantavanich 232, 260
Suryadinata, Leo 1, 25, 203, 296
Sutomo, Jos 56
Sy, Henry 209

Ta Huu Phuong 293
Tagalog 6, 18, 170
Tan Chee Beng 25, 32, 296
Tan Cheng Lock 83
Tan Kah Kee 16
Tan, Lucio 209
Tan, Mely G. 33, 66, 296
Tausugs 160
tayoke ni 130
tayoke phyu 130
Teh Soon Seng 103
Tengku Abdul Rahman (TAR)
College 102
Teresa, Mother 204
Thai Nationality Act (of 1956) 252
Thailand
Chinese and local citizenship
in 251–54
Chinese and local nationalism in
233–36; 239–44, 260–65
Chinese nationalism in 236–39
post-war Chinese identity in
249–51
pre-war Chinese identity in
244–49

Thean Hou Temple 94, 95
"Third China" 159
Tilman, Robert 168, 183
Ting Pik Khiing 103
Tiong Hiew King 103
Tjan Tjoe Siem 55
Tjan Tjoe Som 55, 69
Torajanese 46
totok 42, 44, 48, 50, 57, 67
Tran dynasty 270–71
Treaty of Amity and Co-operation
116
Trinh Hoai Duc 272, 294
Tsinong Pinoy 177, 203
Tsinoys 177, 192, 203
Tulay 192
Tung Meng Hui 236
T'ung yeh kung hui 125
Ty, George 209

Union of Myanmar 116–17
United Malayan Banking
Corporation (UMBC) 93, 95
United Malays National
Organization (UMNO) 84, 85,
89, 90, 91, 92, 95, 96, 98,
99, 100, 101, 109, 112
United Nations 165
United States of America (USA)
52, 284
Universiti Kebangsaan Malaysia
(UKM) 112
Urban Development Authority
(UDA) 92

Velasco, Renato S. 203
Vietnam
China and the integration of
the Chinese in 278–86
Chinese and local nationalism
in 267–78

ethnic Chinese policy of
   293–95
general survey of Chinese
   position in 286–89
Vietnamese Communist Party
   277–78
Vietnamese Workers Party 275

Wachirawut, King 232–33, 234,
   235, 240, 260–63, 264, 265
Wan Adil Wan Ibrahim 78
Wan Sidek Hj Wan Abdul Rahim
   78
Wanandi, Jusuf 59
Wang Gungwu 39, 40, 41, 111,
   113, 116, 245, 248, 296, 297,
   298, 299
Warganegara Asing (WNA) 34,
   45, 47, 48, 49
Warganegara Indonesia (WNI) 49,
   54

Wawasan 2020 (Vision 2020) 80,
   113
Weightman, George H. 169
West Kalimantan 37
Westmont Holdings 103
Wijayakusuma, Haji Muhammad
   Hembing 56
Wild Tiger Corp. 235, 263
Wilder, W.D. 221
Wing On/Sincere 16
Wong Kam Fu 56
World Hokkien Conference 87

Yayasan Abdul Karim Oei 69
"yellow peril" 27, 160

Zaide, Gregorio F. 173
Zhongguo ren 3, 29
Zielenziger, Michael 159